Codes of Ethics for the Helping Professions

Third Edition

BROOKS/COLE
CENGAGE Learning™

Australia • Brazil • Japan • Korea • Mexico • Singapore • Spain • United Kingdom • United States

ISBN-13: 978-0-495-18717-2
ISBN-10: 0-495-18717-8

Brooks/Cole, Cengage Learning
10 Davis Drive
Belmont, CA 94002-3098
USA

For more information about our products,
contact us at:
academic.cengage.com

For permission to use material from this text or
product, submit a request online at
www.**cengage.com/permissions**
Any additional questions about permissions
can be submitted by email to
permissionrequest@cengage.com

Contents

American Association for Marriage and Family Therapy
Code of Ethics

Preamble

The Board of Directors of the American Association for Marriage and Family Therapy (AAMFT) hereby promulgates, pursuant to Article 2, Section 2.013 of the Association's Bylaws, the Revised AAMFT Code of Ethics, effective July 1, 2001.

The AAMFT strives to honor the public trust in marriage and family therapists by setting standards for ethical practice as described in this Code. The ethical standards define professional expectations and are enforced by the AAMFT Ethics Committee. The absence of an explicit reference to a specific behavior or situation in the Code does not mean that the behavior is ethical or unethical. The standards are not exhaustive. Marriage and family therapists who are uncertain about the ethics of a particular course of action are encouraged to seek counsel from consultants, attorneys, supervisors, colleagues, or other appropriate authorities.

Both law and ethics govern the practice of marriage and family therapy. When making decisions regarding professional behavior, marriage and family therapists must consider the AAMFT Code of Ethics and applicable laws and regulations. If the AAMFT Code of Ethics prescribes a standard higher than that required by law, marriage and family therapists must meet the higher standard of the AAMFT Code of Ethics. Marriage and family therapists comply with the mandates of law, but make known their commitment to the AAMFT Code of Ethics and take steps to resolve the conflict in a responsible manner. The AAMFT supports legal mandates for reporting of alleged unethical conduct.

The AAMFT Code of Ethics is binding on Members of AAMFT in all membership categories, AAMFT-Approved Supervisors, and applicants for membership and the Approved Supervisor designation (hereafter, AAMFT Member). AAMFT members have an obligation to be familiar with the AAMFT Code of Ethics and its application to their professional services. Lack of awareness or misunderstanding of an ethical standard is not a defense to a charge of unethical conduct.

The process for filing, investigating, and resolving complaints of unethical conduct is described in the current Procedures for Handling Ethical Matters of the AAMFT Ethics Committee. Persons accused are considered innocent by the Ethics Committee until proven guilty, except as otherwise provided, and are entitled to due process. If an AAMFT Member resigns in anticipation of, or during the course of, an ethics investigation, the Ethics Committee will complete its investigation. Any publication of action taken by the Association will include the fact that the Member attempted to resign during the investigation.

Contents

1. Responsibilty to clients
2. Confidentiality
3. Professional competence and integrity
4. Responsibility to students and supervisees
5. Responsibility to research participants
6. Responsibility to the profession
7. Financial arrangements
8. Advertising

Principle I: Responsibility to Clients

Marriage and family therapists advance the welfare of families and individuals. They respect the rights of those persons seeking their assistance, and make reasonable efforts to ensure that their services are used appropriately.

1.1. Marriage and family therapists provide professional assistance to persons without discrimination on the basis of race, age, ethnicity, socioeconomic status, disability, gender, health status, religion, national origin, or sexual orientation.

1.2 Marriage and family therapists obtain appropriate informed consent to therapy or related procedures as early as feasible in the therapeutic relationship, and use language that is reasonably understandable to clients. The content of informed consent may vary depending upon the client and treatment plan; however, informed consent generally necessitates that the client: (a) has the capacity to consent; (b) has been adequately informed of significant information concerning treatment processes and procedures; (c) has been adequately informed of potential risks and benefits of treatments for which generally recognized standards do not yet exist; (d) has freely and without undue influence expressed consent; and (e) has provided consent that is appropriately documented. When persons, due to age or mental status, are legally incapable of giving informed consent, marriage and family therapists obtain informed permission from a legally authorized person, if such substitute consent is legally permissible.

1.3 Marriage and family therapists are aware of their influential positions with respect to clients, and they avoid exploiting the trust and dependency of such persons. Therapists, therefore, make every effort to avoid conditions and multiple relationships with clients that could impair professional judgment or increase the risk of exploitation. Such relationships include, but are not limited to, business or close personal relationships with a client or the client's immediate family. When the risk of impairment or exploitation exists due to conditions or multiple roles, therapists take appropriate precautions.

1.4 Sexual intimacy with clients is prohibited.

1.5 Sexual intimacy with former clients is likely to be harmful and is therefore prohibited for two years following the termination of therapy or last professional contact. In an effort to avoid exploiting the trust and dependency of clients, marriage and family therapists should not engage in sexual intimacy with former clients after the two years following termination or last professional contact. Should therapists engage in sexual intimacy with former clients following two years after termination or last professional contact, the burden shifts to the therapist to demonstrate that there has been no exploitation or injury to the former client or to the client's immediate family.

1.6 Marriage and family therapists comply with applicable laws regarding the reporting of alleged unethical conduct.

1.7 Marriage and family therapists do not use their professional relationships with clients to further their own interests.

1.8 Marriage and family therapists respect the rights of clients to make decisions and help them to understand the consequences of these decisions. Therapists clearly advise the clients that they have the responsibility to make decisions regarding relationships such as cohabitation, marriage, divorce, separation, reconciliation, custody, and visitation.

1.9 Marriage and family therapists continue therapeutic relationships only so long as it is reasonably clear that clients are benefiting from the relationship.

1.10 Marriage and family therapists assist persons in obtaining other therapeutic services if the therapist is unable or unwilling, for appropriate reasons, to provide professional help.

1.11 Marriage and family therapists do not abandon or neglect clients in treatment without making reasonable arrangements for the continuation of such treatment.

1.12 Marriage and family therapists obtain written informed consent from clients before videotaping, audio recording, or permitting third-party observation.

1.13 Marriage and family therapists, upon agreeing to provide services to a person or entity at the request of a third party, clarify, to the extent feasible and at the outset of the service, the nature of the relationship with each party and the limits of confidentiality.

Principle II: Confidentiality

Marriage and family therapists have unique confidentiality concerns because the client in a therapeutic relationship may be more than one person. Therapists respect and guard the confidences of each individual client.

2.1 Marriage and family therapists disclose to clients and other interested parties, as early as feasible in their professional contacts, the nature of confidentiality and possible limitations of the clients' right to confidentiality. Therapists review with clients the circumstances where confidential information may be requested and where disclosure of confidential information may be legally required. Circumstances may necessitate repeated disclosures.

2.2 Marriage and family therapists do not disclose client confidences except by written authorization or waiver, or where mandated or permitted by law. Verbal authorization will not be sufficient except in emergency situations, unless prohibited by law. When providing couple, family or group treatment, the therapist does not disclose information outside the treatment context without a written authorization from each individual competent to execute a waiver. In the context of couple, family or group treatment, the therapist may not reveal any individual's confidences to others in the client unit without the prior written permission of that individual.

2.3 Marriage and family therapists use client and/or clinical materials in teaching, writing, consulting, research, and public presentations only if a written waiver has been obtained in accordance with Subprinciple 2.2, or when appropriate steps have been taken to protect client identity and confidentiality.

2.4 Marriage and family therapists store, safeguard, and dispose of client records in ways that maintain confidentiality and in accord with applicable laws and professional standards.

2.5 Subsequent to the therapist moving from the area, closing the practice, or upon the death of the therapist, a marriage and family therapist arranges for the storage, transfer, or disposal of client records in ways that maintain confidentiality and safeguard the welfare of clients.

2.6 Marriage and family therapists, when consulting with colleagues or referral sources, do not share confidential information that could reasonably lead to the identification of a client, research participant, supervisee, or other person with whom they have a confidential relationship unless they have obtained the prior written consent of the client, research participant, supervisee, or other person with whom they have a confidential relationship. Information may be shared only to the extent necessary to achieve the purposes of the consultation.

Principle III: Professional Competence and Integrity

Marriage and family therapists maintain high standards of professional competence and integrity.

3.1 Marriage and family therapists pursue knowledge of new developments and maintain competence in marriage and family therapy through education, training, or supervised experience.

3.2 Marriage and family therapists maintain adequate knowledge of and adhere to applicable laws, ethics, and professional standards.

3.3 Marriage and family therapists seek appropriate professional assistance for their personal problems or conflicts that may impair work performance or clinical judgment.

3.4 Marriage and family therapists do not provide services that create a conflict of interest that may impair work performance or clinical judgment.

3.5 Marriage and family therapists, as presenters, teachers, supervisors, consultants and researchers, are dedicated to high standards of scholarship, present accurate information, and disclose potential conflicts of interest.

3.6 Marriage and family therapists maintain accurate and adequate clinical and financial records.

3.7 While developing new skills in specialty areas, marriage and family therapists take steps to ensure the competence of their work and to protect clients from possible harm. Marriage and family therapists practice in specialty areas new to them only after appropriate education, training, or supervised experience.

3.8 Marriage and family therapists do not engage in sexual or other forms of harassment of clients, students, trainees, supervisees, employees, colleagues, or research subjects.

3.9 Marriage and family therapists do not engage in the exploitation of clients, students, trainees, supervisees, employees, colleagues, or research subjects.

3.10 Marriage and family therapists do not give to or receive from clients (a) gifts of substantial value or (b) gifts that impair the integrity or efficacy of the therapeutic relationship.

3.11 Marriage and family therapists do not diagnose, treat, or advise on problems outside the recognized boundaries of their competencies.

3.12 Marriage and family therapists make efforts to prevent the distortion or misuse of their clinical and research findings.

3.13 Marriage and family therapists, because of their ability to influence and alter the lives of others, exercise special care when making public their professional recommendations and opinions through testimony or other public statements.

3.14 To avoid a conflict of interests, marriage and family therapists who treat minors or adults involved in custody or visitation actions may not also perform forensic evaluations for custody, residence, or visitation of the minor. The marriage and family therapist who treats the minor may provide the court or mental health professional performing the evaluation with information about the minor from the marriage and family therapist's perspective as a treating marriage and family therapist, so long as the marriage and family therapist does not violate confidentiality.

3.15 Marriage and family therapists are in violation of this Code and subject to termination of membership or other appropriate action if they: (a) are convicted of any felony; (b) are convicted of a misdemeanor related to their qualifications or functions; (c) engage in conduct which could lead to conviction of a felony, or a misdemeanor related to their qualifications or functions; (d) are expelled from or disciplined by other professional organizations; (e) have their licenses or certificates suspended or revoked or are otherwise disciplined by regulatory bodies; (f) continue to practice marriage and family therapy while no longer competent to do so because they are impaired by physical or mental causes or the abuse of alcohol or other substances; or (g) fail to cooperate with the Association at any point from the inception of an ethical complaint through the completion of all proceedings regarding that complaint.

Principle IV: Responsibility to Students and Supervisees

Marriage and family therapists do not exploit the trust and dependency of students and supervisees.

4.1 Marriage and family therapists are aware of their influential positions with respect to students and supervisees, and they avoid exploiting the trust and dependency of such persons. Therapists, therefore, make every effort to avoid conditions and multiple relationships that could impair professional objectivity or increase the risk of exploitation. When the risk of impairment or exploitation exists due to conditions or multiple roles, therapists take appropriate precautions.

4.2 Marriage and family therapists do not provide therapy to current students or supervisees.

4.3 Marriage and family therapists do not engage in sexual intimacy with students or supervisees during the evaluative or training relationship between the therapist and student or supervisee. Should a supervisor engage in sexual activity with a former supervisee, the burden of proof shifts to the supervisor to demonstrate that there has been no exploitation or injury to the supervisee.

4.4 Marriage and family therapists do not permit students or supervisees to perform or to hold themselves out as competent to perform professional services beyond their training, level of experience, and competence.

4.5 Marriage and family therapists take reasonable measures to ensure that services provided by supervisees are professional.

4.6 Marriage and family therapists avoid accepting as supervisees or students those individuals with whom a prior or existing relationship could compromise the therapist's objectivity. When such situations cannot be avoided, therapists take appropriate precautions to maintain objectivity. Examples of such relationships include, but are not limited to, those individuals with whom the therapist has a current or prior sexual, close personal, immediate familial, or therapeutic relationship.

4.7 Marriage and family therapists do not disclose supervisee confidences except by written authorization or waiver, or when mandated or permitted by law. In educational or training settings where there are multiple supervisors, disclosures are permitted only to other professional colleagues, administrators, or employers who share responsibility for training of the supervisee. Verbal authorization will not be sufficient except in emergency situations, unless prohibited by law.

Principle V: Responsibility to Research Participants

Investigators respect the dignity and protect the welfare of research participants, and are aware of applicable laws and regulations and professional standards governing the conduct of research.

5. 1 Investigators are responsible for making careful examinations of ethical acceptability in planning studies. To the extent that services to research participants may be compromised by participation in research, investigators seek the ethical advice of qualified professionals not directly involved in the investigation and observe safeguards to protect the rights of research participants.

5. 2 Investigators requesting participant involvement in research inform participants of the aspects of the research that might reasonably be expected to influence willingness to participate. Investigators are especially sensitive to the possibility of diminished consent when participants are also receiving clinical services, or have impairments which limit understanding and/or communication, or when participants are children.

5.3 Investigators respect each participant's freedom to decline participation in or to withdraw from a research study at any time. This obligation requires special thought and consideration when investigators or other members of the research team are in positions of authority or influence over participants. Marriage and family therapists, therefore, make every effort to avoid multiple relationships with research participants that could impair professional judgment or increase the risk of exploitation.

5.4 Information obtained about a research participant during the course of an investigation is confidential unless there is a waiver previously obtained in writing. When the possibility exists that others, including family members, may obtain access to such information, this possibility, together with the plan for protecting confidentiality, is explained as part of the procedure for obtaining informed consent.

Principle VI: Responsibility to the Profession

Marriage and family therapists respect the rights and responsibilities of professional colleagues and participate in activities that advance the goals of the profession.

6.1 Marriage and family therapists remain accountable to the standards of the profession when acting as members or employees of organizations. If the mandates of an organization with which a marriage and family therapist is affiliated, through employment, contract or otherwise, conflict with the AAMFT Code of Ethics, marriage and family therapists make known to the organization their commitment to the AAMFT Code of Ethics and attempt to resolve the conflict in a way that allows the fullest adherence to the Code of Ethics.

6.2 Marriage and family therapists assign publication credit to those who have contributed to a publication in proportion to their contributions and in accordance with customary professional publication practices.

6.3 Marriage and family therapists do not accept or require authorship credit for a publication based on research from a student's program, unless the therapist made a substantial contribution beyond being a faculty advisor or research committee member. Coauthorship on a student thesis, dissertation, or project should be determined in accordance with principles of fairness and justice.

6.4 Marriage and family therapists who are the authors of books or other materials that are published or distributed do not plagiarize or fail to cite persons to whom credit for original ideas or work is due.

6.5 Marriage and family therapists who are the authors of books or other materials published or distributed by an organization take reasonable precautions to ensure that the organization promotes and advertises the materials accurately and factually.

6.6 Marriage and family therapists participate in activities that contribute to a better community and society, including devoting a portion of their professional activity to services for which there is little or no financial return.

6.7 Marriage and family therapists are concerned with developing laws and regulations pertaining to marriage and family therapy that serve the public interest, and with altering such laws and regulations that are not in the public interest.

6.8 Marriage and family therapists encourage public participation in the design and delivery of professional services and in the regulation of practitioners.

Principle VII: Financial Arrangements

Marriage and family therapists make financial arrangements with clients, third-party payors, and supervisees that are reasonably understandable and conform to accepted professional practices.

7.1 Marriage and family therapists do not offer or accept kickbacks, rebates, bonuses, or other remuneration for referrals; fee-for-service arrangements are not prohibited.

7.2 Prior to entering into the therapeutic or supervisory relationship, marriage and family therapists clearly disclose and explain to clients and supervisees: (a) all financial arrangements and fees related to professional services, including charges for canceled or missed appointments; (b) the use of collection agencies or legal measures for nonpayment; and (c) the procedure for obtaining payment from the client, to the extent allowed by law, if payment is denied by the third-party payor. Once services have begun, therapists provide reasonable notice of any changes in fees or other charges.

7.3 Marriage and family therapists give reasonable notice to clients with unpaid balances of their intent to seek collection by agency or legal recourse. When such action is taken, therapists will not disclose clinical information.

7.4 Marriage and family therapists represent facts truthfully to clients, third-party payors, and supervisees regarding services rendered.

7.5 Marriage and family therapists ordinarily refrain from accepting goods and services from clients in return for services rendered. Bartering for professional services may be conducted only if: (a) the supervisee or client requests it, (b) the relationship is not exploitative, (c) the professional relationship is not distorted, and (d) a clear written contract is established.

7.6 Marriage and family therapists may not withhold records under their immediate control that are requested and needed for a client's treatment solely because payment has not been received for past services, except as otherwise provided by law.

Principle VIII: Advertising

Marriage and family therapists engage in appropriate informational activities, including those that enable the public, referral sources, or others to choose professional services on an informed basis.

8.1 Marriage and family therapists accurately represent their competencies, education, training, and experience relevant to their practice of marriage and family therapy.

8.2 Marriage and family therapists ensure that advertisements and publications in any media (such as directories, announcements, business cards, newspapers, radio, television, Internet, and facsimiles) convey information that is necessary for the public to make an appropriate selection of professional services. Information could include: (a) office information, such as name, address, telephone number, credit card acceptability, fees, languages spoken, and office hours; (b) qualifying clinical degree (see subprinciple 8.5); (c) other earned degrees (see subprinciple 8.5) and state or provincial licensures and/or certifications; (d) AAMFT clinical member status; and (e) description of practice.

8.3 Marriage and family therapists do not use names that could mislead the public concerning the identity, responsibility, source, and status of those practicing under that name, and do not hold themselves out as being partners or associates of a firm if they are not.

8.4 Marriage and family therapists do not use any professional identification (such as a business card, office sign, letterhead, Internet, or telephone or association directory listing) if it includes a statement or claim that is false, fraudulent, misleading, or deceptive.

8.5 In representing their educational qualifications, marriage and family therapists list and claim as evidence only those earned degrees: (a) from institutions accredited by regional accreditation sources recognized by the United States Department of Education, (b) from institutions recognized by states or provinces that license or certify marriage and family therapists, or (c) from equivalent foreign institutions.

8.6 Marriage and family therapists correct, wherever possible, false, misleading, or inaccurate information and representations made by others concerning the therapist's qualifications, services, or products.

8.7 Marriage and family therapists make certain that the qualifications of their employees or supervisees are represented in a manner that is not false, misleading, or deceptive.

8.8 Marriage and family therapists do not represent themselves as providing specialized services unless they have the appropriate education, training, or supervised experience.

This Code is published by:
American Association for Marriage and Family Therapy
1133 15th Street, NW Suite 300
Washington, DC 20005-2710
(202) 452-0109
(202) 223-2329 FAX
www.aamft.org

American Counseling Association
Code of Ethics

Mission

The mission of the American Counseling Association is to enhance the quality of life in society by promoting the development of professional counselors, advancing the counseling profession, and using the profession and practice of counseling to promote respect for human dignity and diversity.

ACA Code of Ethics Purpose

1. The *ACA Code of Ethics* serves five main purposes:
2. The *Code* enables the association to clarify to current and future members, and to those served by members, the nature of the ethical responsibilities held in common by its members.
3. The *Code* helps support the mission of the association.
4. The *Code* establishes principles that define ethical behavior and best practices of association members.
5. The *Code* serves as an ethical guide designed to assist members in constructing a professional course of action that best serves those utilizing counseling services and best promotes the values of the counseling profession.
6. The *Code* serves as the basis for processing of ethical complaints and inquiries initiated against members of the association.

The ACA Code of Ethics contains eight main sections that address the following areas:

Section A: The Counseling Relationship
Section B: Confidentiality, Privileged Communication, and Privacy
Section C: Professional Responsibility
Section D: Relationships With Other Professionals
Section E: Evaluation, Assessment, and Interpretation
Section F: Supervision, Training, and Teaching
Section G: Research and Publication
Section H: Resolving Ethical Issues

Each section of the ACA Code of Ethics begins with an Introduction. The introductions to each section discuss what counselors should aspire to with regard to ethical behavior and responsibility. The Introduction helps set the tone for that particular section and provides a starting point that invites reflection on the ethical mandates contained in each part of the ACA Code of Ethics.

When counselors are faced with ethical dilemmas that are difficult to resolve, they are expected to engage in a carefully considered ethical decision-making process. Reasonable differences of opinion can and do exist among counselors with respect to the ways in which values, ethical principles, and ethical standards would be applied when they conflict. While there is no specific ethical decision-making model that is most effective, counselors are expected to be familiar with a credible model of decision making that can bear public scrutiny and its application. Through a chosen ethical decision-making process and evaluation of the context of the situation, counselors are empowered to make decisions that help expand the capacity of people to grow and develop. A brief glossary is given to provide readers with a concise description of some of the terms used in the *ACA Code of Ethics*.

ACA Code of Ethics Preamble

The American Counseling Association is an educational, scientific, and professional organization whose members work in a variety of settings and serve in multiple capacities. ACA members are dedicated to the enhancement of human development throughout the life span. Association members recognize diversity and embrace a cross- cultural approach in support of the worth, dignity, potential, and uniqueness of people within their social and cultural contexts.

Professional values are an important way of living out an ethical commitment. Values inform principles. Inherently held values that guide our behaviors or exceed prescribed behaviors are deeply ingrained in the counselor and developed out of personal dedication, rather than the mandatory requirement of an external organization.

Section A: The Counseling Relationship

Introduction

Counselors encourage client growth and development in ways that foster the interest and welfare of clients and promote formation of healthy relationships. Counselors actively attempt to understand the diverse cultural backgrounds of the clients they serve. Counselors also explore their own cultural identities and how these affect their values and beliefs about the counseling process. Counselors are encouraged to contribute to society by devoting a portion of their professional activity to services for which there is little or no financial return (pro bono publico).

A.1. Welfare of Those Served by Counselors

A.1.a. Primary Responsibility
The primary responsibility of counselors is to respect the dignity and to promote the welfare of clients.

A.1.b. Records
Counselors maintain records necessary for rendering professional services to their clients and as required by laws, regulations, or agency or institution procedures. Counselors include sufficient and timely documentation in their client records to facilitate the delivery and continuity of needed services. Counselors take reasonable steps to ensure that documentation in records accurately reflects client progress and services provided. If errors are made in client records, counselors take steps to properly note the correction of such errors according to agency or institutional policies. *(See A.12.g.7., B.6., B.6.g., G.2.j.)*

A.1.c. Counseling Plans
Counselors and their clients work jointly in devising integrated counseling plans that offer reasonable promise of success and are consistent with abilities and circumstances of clients. Counselors and clients regularly review counseling plans to assess their continued viability and effectiveness, respecting the freedom of choice of clients. *(See A.2.a., A.2.d., A.12.g.)*

A.1.d. Support Network Involvement
Counselors recognize that support networks hold various meanings in the lives of clients and consider enlisting the support, understanding, and involvement of others (e.g., religious/spiritual/community leaders, family members, friends) as positive resources, when appropriate, with client consent.

A.1.e. Employment Needs
Counselors work with their clients considering employment in jobs that are consistent with the overall abilities, vocational limitations, physical restrictions, general temperament, interest and aptitude patterns, social skills, education, general qualifications, and other relevant characteristics and needs of clients. When appropriate, counselors appropriately trained in career development will assist in the placement of clients in positions that are consistent with the interest, culture, and the welfare of clients, employers, and/or the public.

A.2. Informed Consent in the Counseling Relationship

(See A.12.g., B.5., B.6.b., E.3., E.13.b., F.1.c., G.2.a.)

A.2.a. Informed Consent
Clients have the freedom to choose whether to enter into or remain in a counseling relationship and need adequate information about the counseling process and the counselor. Counselors have an obligation to review in writing and verbally with clients the rights and responsibilities of both the counselor and the client. Informed consent is an ongoing part of the counseling process, and counselors appropriately document discussions of informed consent throughout the counseling relationship.

A.2.b. Types of Information Needed

Counselors explicitly explain to clients the nature of all services provided. They inform clients about issues such as, but not limited to, the following: the purposes, goals, techniques, procedures, limitations, potential risks, and benefits of services; the counselor's qualifications, credentials, and relevant experience; continuation of services upon the incapacitation or death of a counselor; and other pertinent information. Counselors take steps to ensure that clients understand the implications of diagnosis, the intended use of tests and reports, fees, and billing arrangements. Clients have the right to confidentiality and to be provided with an explanation of its limitations (including how supervisors and/or treatment team professionals are involved); to obtain clear information about their records; to participate in the ongoing counseling plans; and to refuse any services or modality change and to be advised of the consequences of such refusal.

A.2.c. Developmental and Cultural Sensitivity

Counselors communicate information in ways that are both developmentally and culturally appropriate. Counselors use clear and understandable language when discussing issues related to informed consent. When clients have difficulty understanding the language used by counselors, they provide necessary services (e.g., arranging for a qualified interpreter or translator) to ensure comprehension by clients. In collaboration with clients, counselors consider cultural implications of informed consent procedures and, where possible, counselors adjust their practices accordingly.

A.2.d. Inability to Give Consent

When counseling minors or persons unable to give voluntary consent, counselors seek the assent of clients to services, and include them in decision making as appropriate. Counselors recognize the need to balance the ethical rights of clients to make choices, their capacity to give consent or assent to receive services, and parental or familial legal rights and responsibilities to protect these clients and make decisions on their behalf.

A.3. Clients Served by Others

When counselors learn that their clients are in a professional relationship with another mental health professional, they request release from clients to inform the other professionals and strive to establish positive and collaborative professional relationships.

A.4. Avoiding Harm and Imposing Values

A.4.a. Avoiding Harm

Counselors act to avoid harming their clients, trainees, and research participants and to minimize or to remedy unavoidable or unanticipated harm.

A.4.b. Personal Values

Counselors are aware of their own values, attitudes, beliefs, and behaviors and avoid imposing values that are inconsistent with counseling goals. Counselors respect the diversity of clients, trainees, and research participants.

A.5. Roles and Relationships With Clients

(See F.3., F.10., G.3.)

A.5.a. Current Clients

Sexual or romantic counselor–client interactions or relationships with current clients, their romantic partners, or their family members are prohibited.

A.5.b. Former Clients

Sexual or romantic counselor–client interactions or relationships with former clients, their romantic partners, or their family members are prohibited for a period of 5 years following the last professional contact. Counselors, before engaging in sexual or romantic interactions or relationships with clients, their romantic partners, or client family members after 5 years following the last professional contact, demonstrate forethought and document (in written form) whether the interactions or relationship can be viewed as exploitive in some way and/or whether there is still potential to harm the former client; in cases of potential exploitation and/or harm, the counselor avoids entering such an interaction or relationship.

A.5.c. Nonprofessional Interactions or Relationships (Other Than Sexual or Romantic Interactions or Relationships)

Counselor–client nonprofessional relationships with clients, former clients, their romantic partners, or their family members should be avoided, except when the interaction is potentially beneficial to the client. *(See A.5.d.)*

A.5.d. Potentially Beneficial Interactions

When a counselor–client nonprofessional interaction with a client or former client may be potentially beneficial to the client or former client, the counselor must document in case records, prior to the interaction (when feasible), the rationale for such an interaction, the potential benefit, and anticipated consequences for the client or former client and other individuals significantly involved with the client or former client. Such interactions should be initiated with appropriate client consent. Where unintentional harm occurs to the client or former client, or to an individual significantly involved with the client or former client, due to the nonprofessional interaction, the counselor must show evidence of an attempt to remedy such harm. Examples of potentially beneficial interactions include, but are not limited to, attending a formal ceremony (e.g., a wedding/commitment ceremony or graduation); purchasing a service or product provided by a client or former client (excepting unrestricted bartering); hospital visits to an ill family member; mutual membership in a professional association, organization, or community. *(See A.5.c.)*

A.5.e. Role Changes in the Professional Relationship

When a counselor changes a role from the original or most recent contracted relationship, he or she obtains informed consent from the client and explains the right of the client to refuse services related to the change. Examples of role changes include

1. changing from individual to relationship or family counseling, or vice versa;
2. changing from a nonforensic evaluative role to a therapeutic role, or vice versa;
3. changing from a counselor to a researcher role (i.e., enlisting clients as research participants), or vice versa; and
4. changing from a counselor to a mediator role, or vice versa.

Clients must be fully informed of any anticipated consequences (e.g., financial, legal, personal, or therapeutic) of counselor role changes.

A.6. Roles and Relationships at Individual, Group, Institutional, and Societal Levels

A.6.a. Advocacy

When appropriate, counselors advocate at individual, group, institutional, and societal levels to examine potential barriers and obstacles that inhibit access and/or the growth and development of clients.

A.6.b. Confidentiality and Advocacy

Counselors obtain client consent prior to engaging in advocacy efforts on behalf of an identifiable client to improve the provision of services and to work toward removal of systemic barriers or obstacles that inhibit client access, growth, and development.

A.7. Multiple Clients

When a counselor agrees to provide counseling services to two or more persons who have a relationship, the counselor clarifies at the outset which person or persons are clients and the nature of the relationships the counselor will have with each involved person. If it becomes apparent that the counselor may be called upon to perform potentially conflicting roles, the counselor will clarify, adjust, or withdraw from roles appropriately. *(See A.8.a., B.4.)*

A.8. Group Work

(See B.4.a.)

A.8.a. Screening

Counselors screen prospective group counseling/therapy participants. To the extent possible, counselors select members whose needs and goals are compatible with goals of the group, who will not impede the group process, and whose well-being will not be jeopardized by the group experience.

A.8.b. Protecting Clients

In a group setting, counselors take reasonable precautions to protect clients from physical, emotional, or psychological trauma.

A.9. End-of-Life Care for Terminally Ill Clients

A.9.a. Quality of Care

Counselors strive to take measures that enable clients

1. to obtain high quality end-of-life care for their physical, emotional, social, and spiritual needs;
2. to exercise the highest degree of self-determination possible;
3. to be given every opportunity possible to engage in informed decision making regarding their end-of-life care; and
4. to receive complete and adequate assessment regarding their ability to make competent, rational decisions on their own behalf from a mental health professional who is experienced in end-of-life care practice.

A.9.b. Counselor Competence, Choice, and Referral

Recognizing the personal, moral, and competence issues related to 6 ACA Code of Ethics end-of-life decisions, counselors may choose to work or not work with terminally ill clients who wish to explore their end-of-life options. Counselors provide appropriate referral information to ensure that clients receive the necessary help.

A.9.c. Confidentiality

Counselors who provide services to terminally ill individuals who are considering hastening their own deaths have the option of breaking or not breaking confidentiality, depending on applicable laws and the specific circumstances of the situation and after seeking consultation or supervision from appropriate professional and legal parties. *(See B.5.c., B.7.c.)*

A.10. Fees and Bartering

A.10.a. Accepting Fees From Agency Clients

Counselors refuse a private fee or other remuneration for rendering services to persons who are entitled to such services through the counselor's employing agency or institution. The policies of a particular agency may make explicit provisions for agency clients to receive counseling services from members of its staff in private practice. In such instances, the clients must be informed of other options open to them should they seek private counseling services.

A.10.b. Establishing Fees

In establishing fees for professional counseling services, counselors consider the financial status of clients and locality. In the event that the established fee structure is inappropriate for a client, counselors assist clients in attempting to find comparable services of acceptable cost.

A.10.c. Nonpayment of Fees

If counselors intend to use collection agencies or take legal measures to collect fees from clients who do not pay for services as agreed upon, they first inform clients of intended actions and offer clients the opportunity to make payment.

A.10.d. Bartering

Counselors may barter only if the relationship is not exploitive or harmful and does not place the counselor in an unfair advantage, if the client requests it, and if such arrangements are an accepted practice among professionals in the community. Counselors consider the cultural implications of bartering and discuss relevant concerns with clients and document such agreements in a clear written contract.

A.10.e. Receiving Gifts

Counselors understand the challenges of accepting gifts from clients and recognize that in some cultures, small gifts are a token of respect and showing gratitude. When determining whether or not to accept a gift from clients, counselors take into account the therapeutic relationship, the monetary value of the gift, a client's motivation for giving the gift, and the counselor's motivation for wanting or declining the gift.

A.11. Termination and Referral

A.11.a. Abandonment Prohibited

Counselors do not abandon or neglect clients in counseling. Counselors assist in making appropriate arrangements for the continuation of treatment, when necessary, during interruptions such as vacations, illness, and following termination.

A.11.b. Inability to Assist Clients

If counselors determine an inability to be of professional assistance to clients, they avoid entering or continuing counseling relationships. Counselors are knowledgeable about culturally and clinically appropriate referral resources and suggest these alternatives. If clients decline the suggested referrals, counselors should discontinue the relationship.

A.11.c. Appropriate Termination

Counselors terminate a counseling relationship when it becomes reasonably apparent that the client no longer needs assistance, is not likely to benefit, or is being harmed by continued counseling. Counselors may terminate counseling when in jeopardy of harm by the client, or another person with whom the client has a relationship, or when clients do not pay fees as agreed upon. Counselors provide pretermination counseling and recommend other service providers when necessary.

A.11.d. Appropriate Transfer of Services

When counselors transfer or refer clients to other practitioners, they ensure that appropriate clinical and administrative processes are completed and open communication is maintained with both clients and practitioners.

A.12. Technology Applications

A.12.a. Benefits and Limitations

Counselors inform clients of the benefits and limitations of using information technology applications in the counseling process and in business/ billing procedures. Such technologies include but are not limited to computer hardware and software, telephones, the World Wide Web, the Internet, online assessment instruments and other communication devices.

A.12.b. Technology-Assisted
Services

When providing technology-assisted distance counseling services, counselors determine that clients are intellectually, emotionally, and physically capable of using the application and that the application is appropriate for the needs of clients.

A.12.c. Inappropriate Services

When technology-assisted distance counseling services are deemed inappropriate by the counselor or client, counselors consider delivering services face to face.

A.12.d. Access

Counselors provide reasonable access to computer applications when providing technology-assisted distance counseling services.

A.12.e. Laws and Statutes

Counselors ensure that the use of technology does not violate the laws of any local, state, national, or international entity and observe all relevant statutes.

A.12.f. Assistance

Counselors seek business, legal, and technical assistance when using technology applications, particularly when the use of such applications crosses state or national boundaries.

A.12.g. Technology and Informed Consent

As part of the process of establishing informed consent, counselors do the following:

1. Address issues related to the difficulty of maintaining the confidentiality of electronically transmitted communications.
2. Inform clients of all colleagues, supervisors, and employees, such as Informational Technology (IT) administrators, who might have authorized or unauthorized access to electronic transmissions.
3. Urge clients to be aware of all authorized or unauthorized users 7 ACA Code of Ethics including family members and fellow employees who have access to any technology clients may use in the counseling process.
4. Inform clients of pertinent legal rights and limitations governing the practice of a profession over state lines or international boundaries.
5. Use encrypted Web sites and e-mail communications to help ensure confidentiality when possible.
6. When the use of encryption is not possible, counselors notify clients of this fact and limit electronic transmissions to general communications that are not client specific.
7. Inform clients if and for how long archival storage of transaction records are maintained.
8. Discuss the possibility of technology failure and alternate methods of service delivery.

9. Inform clients of emergency procedures, such as calling 911 or a local crisis hotline, when the counselor is not available.
10. Discuss time zone differences, local customs, and cultural or language differences that might impact service delivery.
11. Inform clients when technology assisted distance counseling services are not covered by insurance. *(See A.2.)*

A.12.h. Sites on the World Wide Web
Counselors maintaining sites on the World Wide Web (the Internet) do the following:
1. Regularly check that electronic links are working and professionally appropriate.
2. Establish ways clients can contact the counselor in case of technology failure.
3. Provide electronic links to relevant state licensure and professional certification boards to protect consumer rights and facilitate addressing ethical concerns.
4. Establish a method for verifying client identity.
5. Obtain the written consent of the legal guardian or other authorized legal representative prior to rendering services in the event the client is a minor child, an adult who is legally incompetent, or an adult incapable of giving informed consent.
6. Strive to provide a site that is accessible to persons with disabilities.
7. Strive to provide translation capabilities for clients who have a different primary language while also addressing the imperfect nature of such translations.
8. Assist clients in determining the validity and reliability of information found on the World Wide Web and other technology applications.

Section B: Confidentiality, Privileged Communication, and Privacy

Introduction
Counselors recognize that trust is a cornerstone of the counseling relationship. Counselors aspire to earn the trust of clients by creating an ongoing partnership, establishing and upholding appropriate boundaries, and maintaining confidentiality. Counselors communicate the parameters of confidentiality in a culturally competent manner.

B.1. Respecting Client Rights

B.1.a. Multicultural/Diversity Considerations
Counselors maintain awareness and sensitivity regarding cultural meanings of confidentiality and privacy. Counselors respect differing views toward disclosure of information. Counselors hold ongoing discussions with clients as to how, when, and with whom information is to be shared.

B.1.b. Respect for Privacy
Counselors respect client rights to privacy. Counselors solicit private information from clients only when it is beneficial to the counseling process.

B.1.c. Respect for Confidentiality
Counselors do not share confidential information without client consent or without sound legal or ethical justification.

B.1.d. Explanation of Limitations
At initiation and throughout the counseling process, counselors inform clients of the limitations of confidentiality and seek to identify foreseeable situations in which confidentiality must be breached. *(See A.2.b.)*

B.2. Exceptions
B.2.a. Danger and Legal Requirements
The general requirement that counselors keep information confidential does not apply when disclosure is required to protect clients or identified others from serious and foreseeable harm or when legal requirements demand that confidential information must be revealed. Counselors consult with other professionals when in doubt as to the validity of an exception. Additional considerations apply when addressing end-of-life issues.
(See A.9.c.)

B.2.b. Contagious, Life-Threatening Diseases

When clients disclose that they have a disease commonly known to be both communicable and life threatening, counselors may be justified in disclosing information to identifiable third parties, if they are known to be at demonstrable and high risk of contracting the disease. Prior to making a disclosure, counselors confirm that there is such a diagnosis and assess the intent of clients to inform the third parties about their disease or to engage in any behaviors that may be harmful to an identifiable third party.

B.2.c. Court-Ordered Disclosure

When subpoenaed to release confidential or privileged information without a client's permission, counselors obtain written, informed consent from the client or take steps to prohibit the disclosure or have it limited as narrowly as possible due to potential harm to the client or counseling relationship.

B.2.d. Minimal Disclosure

To the extent possible, clients are informed before confidential information is disclosed and are involved in the disclosure decision-making process. When circumstances require the disclosure of confidential information, only essential information is revealed.

B.3. Information Shared With Others

B.3.a. Subordinates

Counselors make every effort to ensure that privacy and confidentiality of clients are maintained by subordinates, including employees, supervisees, students, clerical assistants, and volunteers. *(See F.1.c.)*

B.3.b. Treatment Teams

When client treatment involves a continued review or participation by a treatment team, the client will be informed of the team's existence and composition, information being shared, and the purposes of sharing such information.

B.3.c. Confidential Settings

Counselors discuss confidential information only in settings in which they can reasonably ensure client privacy.

B.3.d. Third-Party Payers

Counselors disclose information to third-party payers only when clients have authorized such disclosure.

B.3.e. Transmitting Confidential Information

Counselors take precautions to ensure the confidentiality of information transmitted through the use of computers, electronic mail, facsimile machines, telephones, voicemail, answering machines, and other electronic or computer technology. *(See A.12.g.)*

B.3.f. Deceased Clients

Counselors protect the confidentiality of deceased clients, consistent with legal requirements and agency or setting policies.

B.4. Groups and Families

B.4.a. Group Work

In group work, counselors clearly explain the importance and parameters of confidentiality for the specific group being entered.

B.4.b. Couples and Family Counseling

In couples and family counseling, counselors clearly define who is considered "the client" and discuss expectations and limitations of confidentiality. Counselors seek agreement and document in writing such agreement among all involved parties having capacity to give consent concerning each individual's right to confidentiality and any obligation to preserve the confidentiality of information known.

B.5. Clients Lacking Capacity to Give Informed Consent

B.5.a. Responsibility to Clients

When counseling minor clients or adult clients who lack the capacity to give voluntary, informed consent, counselors protect the confidentiality of information received in the counseling relationship as specified by federal and state laws, written policies, and applicable ethical standards.

B.5.b. Responsibility to Parents and Legal Guardians

Counselors inform parents and legal guardians about the role of counselors and the confidential nature of the counseling relationship. Counselors are sensitive to the cultural diversity of families and respect the inherent rights and responsibilities of parents/guardians over the welfare of their children/charges according to law. Counselors work to establish, as appropriate, collaborative relationships with parents/guardians to best serve clients.

B.5.c. Release of Confidential Information

When counseling minor clients or adult clients who lack the capacity to give voluntary consent to release confidential information, counselors seek permission from an appropriate third party to disclose information. In such instances, counselors inform clients consistent with their level of understanding and take culturally appropriate measures to safeguard client confidentiality.

B.6. Records

B.6.a. Confidentiality of Records

Counselors ensure that records are kept in a secure location and that only authorized persons have access to records.

B.6.b. Permission to Record

Counselors obtain permission from clients prior to recording sessions through electronic or other means.

B.6.c. Permission to Observe

Counselors obtain permission from clients prior to observing counseling sessions, reviewing session transcripts, or viewing recordings of sessions with supervisors, faculty, peers, or others within the training environment.

B.6.d. Client Access

Counselors provide reasonable access to records and copies of records when requested by competent clients. Counselors limit the access of clients to their records, or portions of their records, only when there is compelling evidence that such access would cause harm to the client. Counselors document the request of clients and the rationale for withholding some or all of the record in the files of clients. In situations involving multiple clients, counselors provide individual clients with only those parts of records that related directly to them and do not include confidential information related to any other client.

B.6.e. Assistance With Records

When clients request access to their records, counselors provide assistance and consultation in interpreting counseling records.

B.6.f. Disclosure or Transfer

Unless exceptions to confidentiality exist, counselors obtain written permission from clients to disclose or transfer records to legitimate third parties. Steps are taken to ensure that receivers of counseling records are sensitive to their confidential nature.
(See A.3., E.4.)

B.6.g. Storage and Disposal After Termination

Counselors store records following termination of services to ensure reasonable future access, maintain records in accordance with state and federal statutes governing records, and dispose of client records and other sensitive materials in a manner that protects client confidentiality. When records are of an artistic nature, counselors obtain client (or guardian) consent with regards to handling of such records or documents.
(See A.1.b.)

B.6.h. Reasonable Precautions

Counselors take reasonable precautions to protect client confidentiality in the event of the counselor's termination of practice, incapacity, or death. *(See C.2.h.)*

B.7. Research and Training

B.7.a. Institutional Approval

When institutional approval is required, counselors provide accurate information about their research proposals and obtain approval prior to conducting their research. They conduct research in accordance with the approved research protocol.

B.7.b. Adherence to Guidelines

Counselors are responsible for understanding and adhering to state, federal, agency, or institutional policies or applicable guidelines regarding confidentiality in their research practices.

B.7.c. Confidentiality of Information Obtained in Research

Violations of participant privacy and confidentiality are risks of participation in research involving human participants. Investigators maintain all research records in a secure manner. 9 ACA Code of Ethics They explain to participants the risks of violations of privacy and confidentiality and disclose to participants any limits of confidentiality that reasonably can be expected. Regardless of the degree to which confidentiality will be maintained, investigators must disclose to participants any limits of confidentiality that reasonably can be expected. *(See G.2.e.)*

B.7.d. Disclosure of Research Information
Counselors do not disclose confidential information that reasonably could lead to the identification of a research participant unless they have obtained the prior consent of the person. Use of data derived from counseling relationships for purposes of training, research, or publication is confined to content that is disguised to ensure the anonymity of the individuals involved.
(See G.2.a., G.2.d.)

B.7.e. Agreement for Identification
Identification of clients, students, or supervisees in a presentation or publication is permissible only when they have reviewed the material and agreed to its presentation or publication.
(See G.4.d.)

B.8. Consultation

B.8.a. Agreements
When acting as consultants, counselors seek agreements among all parties involved concerning each individual's rights to confidentiality, the obligation of each individual to preserve confidential information, and the limits of confidentiality of information shared by others.

B.8.b. Respect for Privacy
Information obtained in a consulting relationship is discussed for professional purposes only with persons directly involved with the case. Written and oral reports present only data germane to the purposes of the consultation, and every effort is made to protect client identity and to avoid undue invasion of privacy.

B.8.c. Disclosure of Confidential Information
When consulting with colleagues, counselors do not disclose confidential information that reasonably could lead to the identification of a client or other person or organization with whom they have a confidential relationship unless they have obtained the prior consent of the person or organization or the disclosure cannot be avoided. They disclose information only to the extent necessary to achieve the purposes of the consultation. *(See D.2.d.)*

Section C: Professional Responsibility

Introduction
Counselors aspire to open, honest, and accurate communication in dealing with the public and other professionals. They practice in a nondiscriminatory manner within the boundaries of professional and personal competence and have a responsibility to abide by the *ACA Code of Ethics*. Counselors actively participate in local, state, and national associations that foster the development and improvement of counseling. Counselors advocate to promote change at the individual, group, institutional, and societal levels that improve the quality of life for individuals and groups and remove potential barriers to the provision or access of appropriate services being offered. Counselors have a responsibility to the public to engage in counseling practices that are based on rigorous research methodologies. In addition, counselors engage in self-care activities to maintain and promote their emotional, physical, mental, and spiritual well-being to best meet their professional responsibilities.

C.1. Knowledge of Standards

Counselors have a responsibility to read, understand, and follow the *ACA Code of Ethics* and adhere to applicable laws and regulations.

C.2. Professional Competence

C.2.a. Boundaries of Competence
Counselors practice only within the boundaries of their competence, based on their education, training, supervised experience, state and national professional credentials, and appropriate professional experience. Counselors gain knowledge, personal awareness, sensitivity, and skills pertinent to working with a diverse client population. *(See A.9.b., C.4.e., E.2., F.2., F.11.b.)*

C.2.b. New Specialty Areas of Practice
Counselors practice in specialty areas new to them only after appropriate education, training, and supervised experience. While developing skills in new specialty areas, counselors take steps to ensure the competence of their work and to protect others from possible harm. *(See F.6.f.)*

C.2.c. Qualified for Employment
Counselors accept employment only for positions for which they are qualified by education, training, supervised experience, state and national professional credentials, and appropriate professional experience. Counselors hire for professional counseling positions only individuals who are qualified and competent for those positions.

C.2.d. Monitor Effectiveness
Counselors continually monitor their effectiveness as professionals and take steps to improve when necessary. Counselors in private practice take reasonable steps to seek peer supervision as needed to evaluate their efficacy as counselors.

C.2.e. Consultation on Ethical Obligations
Counselors take reasonable steps to consult with other counselors or related professionals when they have questions regarding their ethical obligations or professional practice.

C.2.f. Continuing Education
Counselors recognize the need for continuing education to acquire and maintain a reasonable level of awareness of current scientific and professional information in their fields of activity. They take steps to maintain competence in the skills they use, are open to new procedures, and keep current with the diverse populations and specific populations with whom they work.

C.2.g. Impairment
Counselors are alert to the signs of impairment from their own physical, mental, or emotional problems and refrain from offering or providing professional services when such impairment is likely to harm a client or others. They seek assistance for problems that reach the level of professional impairment, and, if necessary, they limit, suspend, or terminate their professional responsibilities until such time it is determined that they may safely resume their work. Counselors assist colleagues or supervisors in recognizing their own professional impairment and provide consultation and assistance when warranted with colleagues or supervisors showing signs of impairment and intervene as appropriate to prevent imminent harm to clients.
(See A.11.b., F.8.b.)

C.2.h. Counselor Incapacitation or Termination of Practice
When counselors leave a practice, they follow a prepared plan for transfer of clients and files. Counselors prepare and disseminate to an identified colleague or "records custodian" a plan for the transfer of clients and files in the case of their incapacitation, death, or termination of practice.

C.3. Advertising and Soliciting Clients

C.3.a. Accurate Advertising
When advertising or otherwise representing their services to the public, counselors identify their credentials in an accurate manner that is not false, misleading, deceptive, or fraudulent.

C.3.b. Testimonials
Counselors who use testimonials do not solicit them from current clients nor former clients nor any other persons who may be vulnerable to undue influence.

C.3.c. Statements by Others
Counselors make reasonable efforts to ensure that statements made by others about them or the profession of counseling are accurate.

C.3.d. Recruiting Through Employment
Counselors do not use their places of employment or institutional affiliation to recruit or gain clients, supervisees, or consultees for their private practices.

C.3.e. Products and Training Advertisements

Counselors who develop products related to their profession or conduct workshops or training events ensure that the advertisements concerning these products or events are accurate and disclose adequate information for consumers to make informed choices. *(See C.6.d.)*

C.3.f. Promoting to Those Served

Counselors do not use counseling, teaching, training, or supervisory relationships to promote their products or training events in a manner that is deceptive or would exert undue influence on individuals who may be vulnerable. However, counselor educators may adopt textbooks they have authored for instructional purposes.

C.4. Professional Qualifications

C.4.a. Accurate Representation

Counselors claim or imply only professional qualifications actually completed and correct any known misrepresentations of their qualifications by others. Counselors truthfully represent the qualifications of their professional colleagues. Counselors clearly distinguish between paid and volunteer work experience and accurately describe their continuing education and specialized training.
(See C.2.a.)

C.4.b. Credentials

Counselors claim only licenses or certifications that are current and in good standing.

C.4.c. Educational Degrees

Counselors clearly differentiate between earned and honorary degrees.

C.4.d. Implying Doctoral-Level Competence

Counselors clearly state their highest earned degree in counseling or closely related field. Counselors do not imply doctoral-level competence when only possessing a master's degree in counseling or a related field by referring to themselves as "Dr." in a counseling context when their doctorate is not in counseling or related field.

C.4.e. Program Accreditation Status

Counselors clearly state the accreditation status of their degree programs at the time the degree was earned.

C.4.f. Professional Membership

Counselors clearly differentiate between current, active memberships and former memberships in associations. Members of the American Counseling Association must clearly differentiate between professional membership, which implies the possession of at least a master's degree in counseling, and regular membership, which is open to individuals whose interests and activities are consistent with those of ACA but are not qualified for professional membership.

C.5. Nondiscrimination

Counselors do not condone or engage in discrimination based on age, culture, disability, ethnicity, race, religion/ spirituality, gender, gender identity, sexual orientation, marital status/ partnership, language preference, socioeconomic status, or any basis proscribed by law. Counselors do not discriminate against clients, students, employees, supervisees, or research participants in a manner that has a negative impact on these persons.

C.6.Public Responsibility

C.6.a. Sexual Harassment

Counselors do not engage in or condone sexual harassment. Sexual harassment is defined as sexual solicitation, physical advances, or verbal or nonverbal conduct that is sexual in nature, that occurs in connection with professional activities or roles, and that either

1. is unwelcome, is offensive, or creates a hostile workplace or learning environment, and counselors know or are told this; or

2. is sufficiently severe or intense to be perceived as harassment to a reasonable person in the context in which the behavior occurred. Sexual harassment can consist of a single intense or severe act or multiple persistent or pervasive acts.

C.6.b. Reports to Third Parties
Counselors are accurate, honest, and objective in reporting their professional activities and judgments to appropriate third parties, including courts, health insurance companies, those who are the recipients of evaluation reports, and others. *(See B.3., E.4.)*

C.6.c. Media Presentations
When counselors provide advice or comment by means of public lectures, demonstrations, radio or television programs, prerecorded tapes, technology-based applications, printed articles, mailed material, or other media, they take reasonable precautions to ensure that
1. the statements are based on appropriate professional counseling literature and practice,
2. the statements are otherwise consistent with the *ACA Code of Ethics,* and
3. the recipients of the information are not encouraged to infer that a professional counseling relationship has been established.

C.6.d. Exploitation of Others
Counselors do not exploit others in their professional relationships. *(See C.3.e.)*

C.6.e. Scientific Bases for Treatment Modalities
Counselors use techniques/ procedures/ modalities that are grounded in theory and/or have an empirical or scientific foundation. Counselors who do not must define the techniques/ procedures as "unproven" or "developing" and explain the potential risks and ethical considerations of using such techniques/procedures and take steps to protect clients from possible harm. *(See A.4.a., E.5.c., E.5.d.)*

C.7. Responsibility to Other Professionals

C.7.a. Personal Public Statements
When making personal statements in a public context, counselors clarify that they are speaking from their personal perspectives and that they are not speaking on behalf of all counselors or the profession.

Section D: Relationships With Other Professionals

Introduction
Professional counselors recognize that the quality of their interactions with colleagues can influence the quality of services provided to clients. They work to become knowledgeable about colleagues within and outside the field of counseling. Counselors develop positive working relationships and systems of communication with colleagues to enhance services to clients.

D.1. Relationships With Colleagues, Employers, and Employees

D.1.a. Different Approaches
Counselors are respectful of approaches to counseling services that differ from their own. Counselors are respectful of traditions and practices of other professional groups with which they work.

D.1.b. Forming Relationships
Counselors work to develop and strengthen interdisciplinary relations with colleagues from other disciplines to best serve clients.

D.1.c. Interdisciplinary Teamwork
Counselors who are members of interdisciplinary teams delivering multifaceted services to clients, keep the focus on how to best serve the clients. They participate in and contribute to decisions that affect the well-being of clients by drawing on the perspectives, values, and experiences of the counseling profession and those of colleagues from other disciplines. *(See A.1.a.)*

D.1.d. Confidentiality
When counselors are required by law, institutional policy, or extraordinary circumstances to serve in more than one role in judicial or administrative proceedings, they clarify role expectations and the parameters of confidentiality with their colleagues. *(See B.1.c., B.1.d., B.2.c., B.2.d., B.3.b.)*

D.1.e. Establishing Professional and Ethical Obligations

Counselors who are members of interdisciplinary teams clarify professional and ethical obligations of the team as a whole and of its individual members. When a team decision raises ethical concerns, counselors first attempt to resolve the concern within the team. If they cannot reach resolution among team members, counselors pursue other avenues to address their concerns consistent with client well-being.

D.1.f. Personnel Selection and Assignment

Counselors select competent staff and assign responsibilities compatible with their skills and experiences.

D.1.g. Employer Policies

The acceptance of employment in an agency or institution implies that counselors are in agreement with its general policies and principles. Counselors strive to reach agreement with employers as to acceptable standards of conduct that allow for changes in institutional policy conducive to the growth and development of clients.

D.1.h. Negative Conditions

Counselors alert their employers of inappropriate policies and practices. They attempt to effect changes in such policies or procedures through constructive action within the organization. When such policies are potentially disruptive or damaging to clients or may limit the effectiveness of services provided and change cannot be effected, counselors take appropriate further action. Such action may include referral to appropriate certification, accreditation, or state licensure organizations, or voluntary termination of employment.

D.1.i. Protection From Punitive Action

Counselors take care not to harass or dismiss an employee who has acted in a responsible and ethical manner to expose inappropriate employer policies or practices.

D.2. Consultation

D.2.a. Consultant Competency

Counselors take reasonable steps to ensure that they have the appropriate resources and competencies when providing consultation services. Counselors provide appropriate referral resources when requested or needed. *(See C.2.a.)*

D.2.b. Understanding Consultees

When providing consultation, counselors attempt to develop with their consultees a clear understanding of problem definition, goals for change, and predicted consequences of interventions selected.

D.2.c. Consultant Goals

The consulting relationship is one in which consultee adaptability and growth toward self-direction are consistently encouraged and cultivated.

D.2.d. Informed Consent in Consultation

When providing consultation, counselors have an obligation to review, in writing and verbally, the rights and responsibilities of both counselors and consultees. Counselors use clear and understandable language to inform all parties involved about the purpose of the services to be provided, relevant costs, potential risks and benefits, and the limits of confidentiality.

Working in conjunction with the consultee, counselors attempt to develop a clear definition of the problem, goals for change, and predicted consequences of interventions that are culturally responsive and appropriate to the needs of consultees. *(See A.2.a., A.2.b.)*

Section E: Evaluation, Assessment, and Interpretation

Introduction

Counselors use assessment instruments as one component of the counseling process, taking into account the client personal and cultural context. Counselors promote the well-being of individual clients or groups of clients by developing and using appropriate educational, psychological, and career assessment instruments.

E.1. General

E.1.a. Assessment

The primary purpose of educational, psychological, and career assessment is to provide measurements that are valid and reliable in either comparative or absolute terms. These include, but are not limited to, measurements of ability, personality, interest, intelligence, achievement, and performance. Counselors recognize the need to interpret the statements in this section as applying to both quantitative and qualitative assessments.

E.1.b. Client Welfare

Counselors do not misuse assessment results and interpretations, and they take reasonable steps to prevent others from misusing the information these techniques provide. They respect the client's right to know the results, the interpretations made, and the bases for counselors' conclusions and recommendations.

E.2. Competence to Use and Interpret Assessment Instruments

E.2.a. Limits of Competence

Counselors utilize only those testing and assessment services for which they have been trained and are competent. Counselors using technology assisted test interpretations are trained in the construct being measured and the specific instrument being used prior to using its technology based application. Counselors take reasonable measures to ensure the proper use of psychological and career assessment techniques by persons under their supervision.
(See A.12.)

E.2.b. Appropriate Use

Counselors are responsible for the appropriate application, scoring, interpretation, and use of assessment instruments relevant to the needs of the client, whether they score and interpret such assessments themselves or use technology or other services.

E.2.c. Decisions Based on Results

Counselors responsible for decisions involving individuals or policies that are based on assessment results have a thorough understanding of educational, psychological, and career measurement, including validation criteria, assessment research, and guidelines for assessment development and use.

E.3. Informed Consent in Assessment

E.3.a. Explanation to Clients

Prior to assessment, counselors explain the nature and purposes of assessment and the specific use of results by potential recipients. The explanation will be given in the language of the client (or other legally authorized person on behalf of the client), unless an explicit exception has been agreed upon in advance. Counselors consider the client's personal or cultural context, the level of the client's understanding of the results, and the impact of the results on the client. *(See A.2., A.12.g., F.1.c.)*

E.3.b. Recipients of Results

Counselors consider the examinee's welfare, explicit understandings, and prior agreements in determining who receives the assessment results. Counselors include accurate and appropriate interpretations with any release of individual or group assessment results. *(See B.2.c., B.5.)*

E.4. Release of Data to Qualified Professionals

Counselors release assessment data in which the client is identified only with the consent of the client or the client's legal representative. Such data are released only to persons recognized by counselors as qualified to interpret the data. *(See B.1., B.3., B.6.b.)*

E.5. Diagnosis of Mental Disorders

E.5.a. Proper Diagnosis

Counselors take special care to provide proper diagnosis of mental disorders. Assessment techniques (including personal interview) used to determine client care (e.g., locus of treatment, type of treatment, or recommended follow-up) are carefully selected and appropriately used.

E.5.b. Cultural Sensitivity
Counselors recognize that culture affects the manner in which clients' problems are defined. Clients' socioeconomic and cultural experiences are considered when diagnosing mental disorders. *(See A.2.c.)*
E.5.c. Historical and Social Prejudices in the Diagnosis of Pathology
Counselors recognize historical and social prejudices in the misdiagnosis and pathologizing of certain individuals and groups and the role of mental health professionals in perpetuating these prejudices through diagnosis and treatment.
E.5.d. Refraining From Diagnosis
Counselors may refrain from making and/or reporting a diagnosis if they believe it would cause harm to the client or others.

E.6. Instrument Selection E.6.a. Appropriateness of Instruments

Counselors carefully consider the validity, reliability, psychometric limitations, and appropriateness of instruments when selecting assessments.
E.6.b. Referral Information
If a client is referred to a third party for assessment, the counselor provides specific referral questions and sufficient objective data about the client to ensure that appropriate assessment instruments are utilized. *(See A.9.b., B.3.)*
E.6.c. Culturally Diverse Populations
Counselors are cautious when selecting assessments for culturally diverse populations to avoid the use of instruments that lack appropriate psychometric properties for the client population. *(See A.2.c., E.5.b.)*

E.7. Conditions of Assessment Administration

(See A.12.b., A.12.d.)
E.7.a. Administration Conditions
Counselors administer assessments under the same conditions that were established in their standardization. When assessments are not administered under standard conditions, as may be necessary to accommodate clients with disabilities, or when unusual behavior or irregularities occur during the administration, those conditions are noted in interpretation, and the results may be designated as invalid or of questionable validity.
E.7.b. Technological Administration
Counselors ensure that administration programs function properly and provide clients with accurate results when technological or other electronic methods are used for assessment administration.
E.7.c. Unsupervised Assessments
Unless the assessment instrument is designed, intended, and validated for self-administration and/or scoring, 13 ACA Code of Ethics counselors do not permit inadequately supervised use.
E.7.d. Disclosure of Favorable Conditions
Prior to administration of assessments, conditions that produce most favorable assessment results are made known to the examinee.

E.8. Multicultural Issues/Diversity in Assessment

Counselors use with caution assessment techniques that were normed on populations other than that of the client. Counselors recognize the effects of age, color, culture, disability, ethnic group, gender, race, language preference, religion, spirituality, sexual orientation, and socioeconomic status on test administration and interpretation, and place test results in proper perspective with other relevant factors. *(See A.2.c., E.5.b.)*

E.9. Scoring and Interpretation of Assessments

E.9.a. Reporting
In reporting assessment results, counselors indicate reservations that exist regarding validity or reliability due to circumstances of the assessment or the inappropriateness of the norms for the person tested.

E.9.b. Research Instruments

Counselors exercise caution when interpreting the results of research instruments not having sufficient technical data to support respondent results. The specific purposes for the use of such instruments are stated explicitly to the examinee.

E.9.c. Assessment Services

Counselors who provide assessment scoring and interpretation services to support the assessment process confirm the validity of such interpretations. They accurately describe the purpose, norms, validity, reliability, and applications of the procedures and any special qualifications applicable to their use. The public offering of an automated test interpretations service is considered a professional-to-professional consultation. The formal responsibility of the consultant is to the consultee, but the ultimate and overriding responsibility is to the client.
(See D.2.)

E.10. Assessment Security

Counselors maintain the integrity and security of tests and other assessment techniques consistent with legal and contractual obligations. Counselors do not appropriate, reproduce, or modify published assessments or parts thereof without acknowledgment and permission from the publisher.

E.11. Obsolete Assessments and Outdated Results

Counselors do not use data or results from assessments that are obsolete or outdated for the current purpose. Counselors make every effort to prevent the misuse of obsolete measures and assessment data by others.

E.12. Assessment Construction

Counselors use established scientific procedures, relevant standards, and current professional knowledge for assessment design in the development, publication, and utilization of educational and psychological assessment techniques.

E.13. Forensic Evaluation: Evaluation for Legal Proceedings

E.13.a. Primary Obligations

When providing forensic evaluations, the primary obligation of counselors is to produce objective findings that can be substantiated based on information and techniques appropriate to the evaluation, which may include examination of the individual and/ or review of records. Counselors are entitled to form professional opinions based on their professional knowledge and expertise that can be supported by the data gathered in evaluations. Counselors will define the limits of their reports or testimony, especially when an examination of the individual has not been conducted.

E.13.b. Consent for Evaluation

Individuals being evaluated are informed in writing that the relationship is for the purposes of an evaluation and is not counseling in nature, and entities or individuals who will receive the evaluation report are identified. Written consent to be evaluated is obtained from those being evaluated unless a court orders evaluations to be conducted without the written consent of individuals being evaluated. When children or vulnerable adults are being evaluated, informed written consent is obtained from a parent or guardian.

E.13.c. Client Evaluation Prohibited

Counselors do not evaluate individuals for forensic purposes they currently counsel or individuals they have counseled in the past. Counselors do not accept as counseling clients individuals they are evaluating or individuals they have evaluated in the past for forensic purposes.

E.13.d. Avoid Potentially Harmful Relationships

Counselors who provide forensic evaluations avoid potentially harmful professional or personal relationships with family members, romantic partners, and close friends of individuals they are evaluating or have evaluated in the past.

Section F: Supervision, Training, and Teaching

Introduction

Counselors aspire to foster meaningful and respectful professional relationships and to maintain appropriate boundaries with supervisees and students. Counselors have theoretical and pedagogical foundations for their work and aim to be fair, accurate, and honest in their assessments of counselors-in-training.

F.1. Counselor Supervision and Client Welfare

F.1.a. Client Welfare

A primary obligation of counseling supervisors is to monitor the services provided by other counselors or counselors-in-training. Counseling supervisors monitor client welfare and supervisee clinical performance and professional development. To fulfill these obligations, supervisors meet regularly with supervisees to review case notes, samples of clinical work, or live observations. Supervisees have a responsibility to understand and follow the *ACA Code of Ethics*.

F.1.b. Counselor Credentials

Counseling supervisors work to ensure that clients are aware of the qualifications of the supervisees who render services to the clients. *(See A.2.b.)*

F.1.c. Informed Consent and Client Rights

Supervisors make supervisees aware of client rights including the protection of client privacy and confidentiality in the counseling relationship. Supervisees provide clients with professional disclosure information and inform them of how the supervision process influences the limits of confidentiality. Supervisees make clients aware of who will have access to records of the counseling relationship and how these records will be used. *(See A.2.b., B.1.d.)*

F.2. Counselor Supervision Competence

F.2.a. Supervisor Preparation

Prior to offering clinical supervision services, counselors are trained in supervision methods and techniques. Counselors who offer clinical supervision services regularly pursue continuing education activities including both counseling and supervision topics and skills. *(See C.2.a., C.2.f.)*

F.2.b. Multicultural Issues/Diversity in Supervision

Counseling supervisors are aware of and address the role of multiculturalism/diversity in the supervisory relationship.

F.3. Supervisory Relationships

F.3.a. Relationship Boundaries With Supervisees

Counseling supervisors clearly define and maintain ethical professional, personal, and social relationships with their supervisees. Counseling supervisors avoid nonprofessional relationships with current supervisees. If supervisors must assume other professional roles (e.g., clinical and administrative supervisor, instructor) with supervisees, they work to minimize potential conflicts and explain to supervisees the expectations and responsibilities associated with each role. They do not engage in any form of nonprofessional interaction that may compromise the supervisory relationship.

F.3.b. Sexual Relationships

Sexual or romantic interactions or relationships with current supervisees are prohibited.

F.3.c. Sexual Harassment

Counseling supervisors do not condone or subject supervisees to sexual harassment. *(See C.6.a.)*

F.3.d. Close Relatives and Friends

Counseling supervisors avoid accepting close relatives, romantic partners, or friends as supervisees.

F.3.e. Potentially Beneficial Relationships

Counseling supervisors are aware of the power differential in their relationships with supervisees. If they believe nonprofessional relationships with a supervisee may be potentially beneficial to the supervisee, they take precautions similar to those taken by counselors when working with clients. Examples of potentially beneficial interactions or relationships include attending a formal ceremony; hospital visits; providing support during a stressful event; or mutual membership in a professional association, organization, or community. Counseling supervisors engage in open discussions with supervisees when they consider entering into relationships with them outside of their roles as clinical and/or administrative supervisors. Before engaging in nonprofessional relationships, supervisors discuss with supervisees and document the rationale for such interactions, potential benefits or drawbacks, and anticipated consequences for the supervisee. Supervisors clarify the specific nature and limitations of the additional role(s) they will have with the supervisee.

F.4. Supervisor Responsibilities

F.4.a. Informed Consent for Supervision
Supervisors are responsible for incorporating into their supervision the principles of informed consent and participation. Supervisors inform supervisees of the policies and procedures to which they are to adhere and the mechanisms for due process appeal of individual supervisory actions.

F.4.b. Emergencies and Absences
Supervisors establish and communicate to supervisees procedures for contacting them or, in their absence, alternative on-call supervisors to assist in handling crises.

F.4.c. Standards for Supervisees
Supervisors make their supervisees aware of professional and ethical standards and legal responsibilities. Supervisors of postdegree counselors encourage these counselors to adhere to professional standards of practice. (See C.1.)

F.4.d. Termination of the Supervisory Relationship
Supervisors or supervisees have the right to terminate the supervisory relationship with adequate notice. Reasons for withdrawal are provided to the other party. When cultural, clinical, or professional issues are crucial to the viability of the supervisory relationship, both parties make efforts to resolve differences. When termination is warranted, supervisors make appropriate referrals to possible alternative supervisors.

F.5. Counseling Supervision Evaluation, Remediation, and Endorsement

F.5.a. Evaluation
Supervisors document and provide supervisees with ongoing performance appraisal and evaluation feedback and schedule periodic formal evaluative sessions throughout the supervisory relationship.

F.5.b. Limitations
Through ongoing evaluation and appraisal, supervisors are aware of the limitations of supervisees that might impede performance. Supervisors assist supervisees in securing remedial assistance when needed. They recommend dismissal from training programs, applied counseling settings, or state or voluntary professional credentialing processes when those supervisees are unable to provide competent professional services. Supervisors seek consultation and document their decisions to dismiss or refer supervisees for assistance. They ensure that supervisees are aware of options available to them to address such decisions. (See C.2.g.)

F.5.c. Counseling for Supervisees
If supervisees request counseling, supervisors provide them with acceptable referrals. Counselors do not provide counseling services to supervisees. Supervisors address interpersonal competencies in terms of the impact of these issues on clients, the supervisory relationship, and professional functioning. (See F.3.a.)

F.5.d. Endorsement
Supervisors endorse supervisees for certification, licensure, employment, or completion of an academic or training program only when they believe supervisees are qualified for the endorsement. Regardless of qualifications, supervisors do not endorse supervisees whom they believe to be impaired in any way that would interfere with the performance of the duties associated with the endorsement.

15 ACA Code of Ethics

F.6. Responsibilities of Counselor Educators

F.6.a. Counselor Educators
Counselor educators who are responsible for developing, implementing, and supervising educational programs are skilled as teachers and practitioners. They are knowledgeable regarding the ethical, legal, and regulatory aspects of the profession, are skilled in applying that knowledge, and make students and

supervisees aware of their responsibilities. Counselor educators conduct counselor education and training programs in an ethical manner and serve as role models for professional behavior. *(See C.1., C.2.a., C.2.c.)*

F.6.b. Infusing Multicultural Issues/Diversity
Counselor educators infuse material related to multicultluralism/diversity into all courses and workshops for the development of professional counselors.

F.6.c. Integration of Study and Practice
Counselor educators establish education and training programs that integrate academic study and supervised practice.

F.6.d. Teaching Ethics
Counselor educators make students and supervisees aware of the ethical responsibilities and standards of the profession and the ethical responsibilities of students to the profession. Counselor educators infuse ethical considerations throughout the curriculum. *(See C.1.)*

F.6.e. Peer Relationships
Counselor educators make every effort to ensure that the rights of peers are not compromised when students or supervisees lead counseling groups or provide clinical supervision. Counselor educators take steps to ensure that students and supervisees understand they have the same ethical obligations as counselor educators, trainers, and supervisors.

F.6.f. Innovative Theories and Techniques
When counselor educators teach counseling techniques/procedures that are innovative, without an empirical foundation, or without a well-grounded theoretical foundation, they define the counseling techniques/procedures as "unproven" or "developing" and explain to students the potential risks and ethical considerations of using such techniques/procedures.

F.6.g. Field Placements
Counselor educators develop clear policies within their training programs regarding field placement and other clinical experiences. Counselor educators provide clearly stated roles and responsibilities for the student or supervisee, the site supervisor, and the program supervisor. They confirm that site supervisors are qualified to provide supervision and inform site supervisors of their professional and ethical responsibilities in this role.

F.6.h. Professional Disclosure
Before initiating counseling services, counselors-in-training disclose their status as students and explain how this status affects the limits of confidentiality. Counselor educators ensure that the clients at field placements are aware of the services rendered and the qualifications of the students and supervisees rendering those services. Students and supervisees obtain client permission before they use any information concerning the counseling relationship in the training process. *(See A.2.b.)*

F.7. Student Welfare

F.7.a. Orientation
Counselor educators recognize that orientation is a developmental process that continues throughout the educational and clinical training of students. Counseling faculty provide prospective students with information about the counselor education program's expectations:
1. the type and level of skill and knowledge acquisition required for successful completion of the training;
2. program training goals, objectives, and mission, and subject matter to be covered;
3. bases for evaluation;
4. training components that encourage self-growth or self-disclosure as part of the training process;
5. the type of supervision settings and requirements of the sites for required clinical field experiences;
6. student and supervisee evaluation and dismissal policies and procedures; and
7. up-to-date employment prospects for graduates.

F.7.b. Self-Growth Experiences
Counselor education programs delineate requirements for self-disclosure or self-growth experiences in their admission and program materials. Counselor educators use professional judgment when designing training experiences they conduct that require student and supervisee selfgrowth or self-disclosure. Students and supervisees are made aware of the ramifications their self-disclosure may have when

counselors whose primary role as teacher, trainer, or supervisor requires acting on ethical obligations to the profession. Evaluative components of experiential training experiences explicitly delineate predetermined academic standards that are separate and do not depend on the student's level of selfdisclosure. Counselor educators may require trainees to seek professional help to address any personal concerns that may be affecting their competency.

F.8. Student Responsibilities

F.8.a. Standards for Students

Counselors-in-training have a responsibility to understand and follow the *ACA Code of Ethics* and adhere to applicable laws, regulatory policies, and rules and policies governing professional staff behavior at the agency or placement setting. Students have the same obligation to clients as those required of professional counselors.
(See C.1., H.1.)

F.8.b. Impairment

Counselors-in-training refrain from offering or providing counseling services when their physical, mental, or emotional problems are likely to harm a client or others. They are alert to the signs of impairment, seek assistance for problems, and notify their program supervisors when they are aware that they are unable to effectively provide services. In addition, they seek appropriate professional services for themselves to remediate the problems that are interfering with their ability to provide services to others. *(See A.1., C.2.d., C.2.g.)*

F.9. Evaluation and Remediation of Students F.9.a. Evaluation

Counselors clearly state to students, prior to and throughout the training program, the levels of competency expected, appraisal methods, and timing of evaluations for both didactic and clinical competencies. Counselor educators provide students 16 ACA Code of Ethics with ongoing performance appraisal and evaluation feedback throughout the training program.

F.9.b. Limitations

Counselor educators, throughout ongoing evaluation and appraisal, are aware of and address the inability of some students to achieve counseling competencies that might impede performance. Counselor educators
1. assist students in securing remedial assistance when needed,
2. seek professional consultation and document their decision to dismiss or refer students for assistance, and
3. ensure that students have recourse in a timely manner to address decisions to require them to seek assistance or to dismiss them and provide students with due process according to institutional policies and procedures.
(See C.2.g.)

F.9.c. Counseling for Students

If students request counseling or if counseling services are required as part of a remediation process, counselor educators provide acceptable referrals.

F. 10. Roles and Relationships Between Counselor Educators and Students

F.10.a. Sexual or Romantic Relationships

Sexual or romantic interactions or relationships with current students are prohibited.

F.10.b. Sexual Harassment

Counselor educators do not condone or subject students to sexual harassment. *(See C.6.a.)*

F.10.c. Relationships With Former Students

Counselor educators are aware of the power differential in the relationship between faculty and students. Faculty members foster open discussions with former students when considering engaging in a social, sexual, or other intimate relationship. Faculty members discuss with the former student how their former relationship may affect the change in relationship.

F.10.d. Nonprofessional Relationships

Counselor educators avoid nonprofessional or ongoing professional relationships with students in which there is a risk of potential harm to the student or that may compromise the training experience or grades assigned. In addition, counselor educators do not accept any form of professional services, fees, commissions, reimbursement, or remuneration from a site for student or supervisee placement.

F.10.e. Counseling Services
Counselor educators do not serve as counselors to current students unless this is a brief role associated with a training experience.

F.10.f. Potentially Beneficial Relationships
Counselor educators are aware of the power differential in the relationship between faculty and students. If they believe a nonprofessional relationship with a student may be potentially beneficial to the student, they take precautions similar to those taken by counselors when working with clients. Examples of potentially beneficial interactions or relationships include, but are not limited to, attending a formal ceremony; hospital visits; providing support during a stressful event; or mutual membership in a professional association, organization, or community. Counselor educators engage in open discussions with students when they consider entering into relationships with students outside of their roles as teachers and supervisors. They discuss with students the rationale for such interactions, the potential benefits and drawbacks, and the anticipated consequences for the student. Educators clarify the specific nature and limitations of the additional role(s) they will have with the student prior to engaging in a nonprofessional relationship. Nonprofessional relationships with students should be time-limited and initiated with student consent.

F.11. Multicultural/Diversity Competence in Counselor Education and Training Programs

F.11.a. Faculty Diversity
Counselor educators are committed to recruiting and retaining a diverse faculty.

F.11.b. Student Diversity
Counselor educators actively attempt to recruit and retain a diverse student body. Counselor educators demonstrate commitment to multicultural/diversity competence by recognizing and valuing diverse cultures and types of abilities students bring to the training experience. Counselor educators provide appropriate accommodations that enhance and support diverse student well-being and academic performance.

F.11.c. Multicultural/Diversity Competence
Counselor educators actively infuse multicultural/diversity competency in their training and supervision practices. They actively train students to gain awareness, knowledge, and skills in the competencies of multicultural practice. Counselor educators include case examples, role-plays, discussion questions, and other classroom activities that promote and represent various cultural perspectives.

Section G: Research and Publication

Introduction
Counselors who conduct research are encouraged to contribute to the knowledge base of the profession and promote a clearer understanding of the conditions that lead to a healthy and more just society. Counselors support efforts of researchers by participating fully and willingly whenever possible. Counselors minimize bias and respect diversity in designing and implementing research programs.

G.1. Research Responsibilities

G.1.a. Use of Human Research Participants
Counselors plan, design, conduct, and report research in a manner that is consistent with pertinent ethical principles, federal and state laws, host institutional regulations, and scientific standards governing research with human research participants.

G.1.b. Deviation From Standard Practice
Counselors seek consultation and observe stringent safeguards to protect the rights of research participants when a research problem suggests a deviation from standard or acceptable practices.

G.1.c. Independent Researchers
When independent researchers do not have access to an Institutional Review Board (IRB), they should consult with researchers who are familiar with IRB procedures to provide appropriate safeguards.

G.1.d. Precautions to Avoid Injury

Counselors who conduct research with human participants are responsible for the welfare of participants throughout the research process and should take reasonable precautions to avoid causing injurious psychological, emotional, physical, or social effects to participants.

G.1.e. Principal Researcher Responsibility

The ultimate responsibility for ethical research practice lies with the principal researcher. All others involved in the research activities share ethical obligations and responsibility for their own actions.

G.1.f. Minimal Interference

Counselors take reasonable precautions to avoid causing disruptions in the lives of research participants that could be caused by their involvement in research.

G.1.g. Multicultural/Diversity Considerations in Research

When appropriate to research goals, counselors are sensitive to incorporating research procedures that take into account cultural considerations. They seek consultation when appropriate.

G.2. Rights of Research Participants

(See A.2, A.7.)

G.2.a. Informed Consent in Research

Individuals have the right to consent to become research participants. In seeking consent, counselors use language that

1. accurately explains the purpose and procedures to be followed,
2. identifies any procedures that are experimental or relatively untried,
3. describes any attendant discomforts and risks,
4. describes any benefits or changes in individuals or organizations that might be reasonably expected,
5. discloses appropriate alternative procedures that would be advantageous for participants,
6. offers to answer any inquiries concerning the procedures,
7. describes any limitations on confidentiality,
8. describes the format and potential target audiences for the dissemination of research findings, and
9. instructs participants that they are free to withdraw their consent and to discontinue participation in the project at any time without penalty.

G.2.b. Deception

Counselors do not conduct research involving deception unless alternative procedures are not feasible and the prospective value of the research justifies the deception. If such deception has the potential to cause physical or emotional harm to research participants, the research is not conducted, regardless of prospective value. When the methodological requirements of a study necessitate concealment or deception, the investigator explains the reasons for this action as soon as possible during the debriefing.

G.2.c. Student/Supervisee
Participation

Researchers who involve students or supervisees in research make clear to them that the decision regarding whether or not to participate in research activities does not affect one's academic standing or supervisory relationship. Students or supervisees who choose not to participate in educational research are provided with an appropriate alternative to fulfill their academic or clinical requirements.

G.2.d. Client Participation

Counselors conducting research involving clients make clear in the informed consent process that clients are free to choose whether or not to participate in research activities. Counselors take necessary precautions to protect clients from adverse consequences of declining or withdrawing from participation.

G.2.e. Confidentiality of Information

Information obtained about research participants during the course of an investigation is confidential. When the possibility exists that others may obtain access to such information, ethical research practice requires that the possibility, together with the plans for protecting confidentiality, be explained to participants as a part of the procedure for obtaining informed consent.

G.2.f. Persons Not Capable of Giving Informed Consent

When a person is not capable of giving informed consent, counselors provide an appropriate explanation to, obtain agreement for participation from, and obtain the appropriate consent of a legally authorized person.

G.2.g. Commitments to Participants

Counselors take reasonable measures to honor all commitments to research participants.
(See A.2.c.)

G.2.h. Explanations After Data Collection

After data are collected, counselors provide participants with full clarification of the nature of the study to remove any misconceptions participants might have regarding the research. Where scientific or human values justify delaying or withholding information, counselors take reasonable measures to avoid causing harm.

G.2.i. Informing Sponsors Counselors inform sponsors, institutions, and publication channels regarding research procedures and outcomes. Counselors ensure that appropriate bodies and authorities are given pertinent information and acknowledgement.

G.2.j. Disposal of Research Documents and Records

Within a reasonable period of time following the completion of a research project or study, counselors take steps to destroy records or documents (audio, video, digital, and written) containing confidential data or information that identifies research participants. When records are of an artistic nature, researchers obtain participant consent with regard to handling of such records or documents. *(See B.4.a, B.4.g.)*

G.3. Relationships With Research Participants When Research Involves Intensive or Extended Interactions)

G.3.a. Nonprofessional Relationships

Nonprofessional relationships with research participants should be avoided.

G.3.b. Relationships With Research Participants

Sexual or romantic counselor–research participant interactions or relationships with current research participants are prohibited.

G.3.c. Sexual Harassment and Research Participants

Researchers do not condone or subject research participants to sexual harassment.

18 ACA Code of Ethics

G.3.d. Potentially Beneficial Interactions

When a nonprofessional interaction between the researcher and the research participant may be potentially beneficial, the researcher must document, prior to the interaction (when feasible), the rationale for such an interaction, the potential benefit, and anticipated consequences for the research participant. Such interactions should be initiated with appropriate consent of the research participant. Where unintentional harm occurs to the research participant due to the nonprofessional interaction, the researcher must show evidence of an attempt to remedy such harm.

G.4. Reporting Results

G.4.a. Accurate Results

Counselors plan, conduct, and report research accurately. They provide thorough discussions of the limitations of their data and alternative hypotheses. Counselors do not engage in misleading or fraudulent research, distort data, misrepresent data, or deliberately bias their results. They explicitly mention all variables and conditions known to the investigator that may have affected the outcome of a study or the interpretation of data. They describe the extent to which results are applicable for diverse populations.

G.4.b. Obligation to Report Unfavorable Results

Counselors report the results of any research of professional value. Results that reflect unfavorably on institutions, programs, services, prevailing opinions, or vested interests are not withheld.

G.4.c. Reporting Errors

If counselors discover significant errors in their published research, they take reasonable steps to correct such errors in a correction erratum, or through other appropriate publication means.

G.4.d. Identity of Participants

Counselors who supply data, aid in the research of another person, report research results, or make original data available take due care to disguise the identity of respective participants in the absence of specific authorization from the participants to do otherwise. In situations where participants self-identify their involvement in research studies, researchers take active steps to ensure that data is adapted/changed to protect the identity and welfare of all parties and that discussion of results does not cause harm to participants.

G.4.e. Replication Studies
Counselors are obligated to make available sufficient original research data to qualified professionals who may wish to replicate the study.

G.5. Publication

G.5.a. Recognizing Contributions
When conducting and reporting research, counselors are familiar with and give recognition to previous work on the topic, observe copyright laws, and give full credit to those to whom credit is due.

G.5.b. Plagiarism
Counselors do not plagiarize, that is, they do not present another person's work as their own work.

G.5.c. Review/Republication of Data or Ideas
Counselors fully acknowledge and make editorial reviewers aware of prior publication of ideas or data where such ideas or data are submitted for review or publication.

G.5.d. Contributors
Counselors give credit through joint authorship, acknowledgment, footnote statements, or other appropriate means to those who have contributed significantly to research or concept development in accordance with such contributions. The principal contributor is listed first and minor technical or professional contributions are acknowledged in notes or introductory statements.

G.5.e. Agreement of Contributors
Counselors who conduct joint research with colleagues or students/ supervisees establish agreements in advance regarding allocation of tasks, publication credit, and types of acknowledgement that will be received.

G.5.f. Student Research
For articles that are substantially based on students course papers, projects, dissertations or theses, and on which students have been the primary contributors, they are listed as principal authors.

G.5.g. Duplicate Submission
Counselors submit manuscripts for consideration to only one journal at a time. Manuscripts that are published in whole or in substantial part in another journal or published work are not submitted for publication without acknowledgment and permission from the previous publication.

G.5.h. Professional Review
Counselors who review material submitted for publication, research, or other scholarly purposes respect the confidentiality and proprietary rights of those who submitted it. Counselors use care to make publication decisions based on valid and defensible standards. Counselors review article submissions in a timely manner and based on their scope and competency in research methodologies. Counselors who serve as reviewers at the request of editors or publishers make every effort to only review materials that are within their scope of competency and use care to avoid personal biases.

Section H : Resolving Ethical Issues

Introduction
Counselors behave in a legal, ethical, and moral manner in the conduct of their professional work. They are aware that client protection and trust in the profession depend on a high level of professional conduct. They hold other counselors to the same standards and are willing to take appropriate action to ensure that these standards are upheld. Counselors strive to resolve ethical dilemmas with direct and open communication among all parties involved and seek consultation with colleagues and supervisors when necessary. Counselors incorporate ethical practice into their daily professional work. They engage in ongoing professional development regarding current topics in ethical and legal issues in counseling.

H.1. Standards and the Law

(See F.9.a.)

H.1.a. Knowledge

Counselors understand the *ACA Code of Ethics* and other applicable ethics codes from other professional organizations or from certification and licensure bodies of which they are members. Lack of knowledge or misunderstanding of an ethical responsibility is not a 19 ACA Code of Ethics defense against a charge of unethical conduct.

H.1.b. Conflicts Between Ethics and Laws

If ethical responsibilities conflict with law, regulations, or other governing legal authority, counselors make known their commitment to the *ACA Code of Ethics* and take steps to resolve the conflict. If the conflict cannot be resolved by such means, counselors may adhere to the requirements of law, regulations, or other governing legal authority.

H.2. Suspected Violations

H.2.a. Ethical Behavior Expected

Counselors expect colleagues to adhere to the *ACA Code of Ethics*. When counselors possess knowledge that raises doubts as to whether another counselor is acting in an ethical manner, they take appropriate action. *(See H.2.b., H.2.c.)*

H.2.b. Informal Resolution

When counselors have reason to believe that another counselor is violating or has violated an ethical standard, they attempt first to resolve the issue informally with the other counselor if feasible, provided such action does not violate confidentiality rights that may be involved.

H.2.c. Reporting Ethical Violations

If an apparent violation has substantially harmed, or is likely to substantially harm a person or organization and is not appropriate for informal resolution or is not resolved properly, counselors take further action appropriate to the situation. Such action might include referral to state or national committees on professional ethics, voluntary national certification bodies, state licensing boards, or to the appropriate institutional authorities. This standard does not apply when an intervention would violate confidentiality rights or when counselors have been retained to review the work of another counselor whose professional conduct is in question.

H.2.d. Consultation

When uncertain as to whether a particular situation or course of action may be in violation of the *ACA Code of Ethics,* counselors consult with other counselors who are knowledgeable about ethics and the *ACA Code of Ethics,* with colleagues, or with appropriate authorities

H.2.e. Organizational Conflicts

If the demands of an organization with which counselors are affiliated pose a conflict with the *ACA Code of Ethics,* counselors specify the nature of such conflicts and express to their supervisors or other responsible officials their commitment to the *ACA Code of Ethics.* When possible, counselors work toward change within the organization to allow full adherence to the *ACA Code of Ethics.* In doing so, they address any confidentiality issues.

H.2.f. Unwarranted Complaints

Counselors do not initiate, participate in, or encourage the filing of ethics complaints that are made with reckless disregard or willful ignorance of facts that would disprove the allegation.

H.2.g. Unfair Discrimination Against Complainants and Respondents

Counselors do not deny persons employment, advancement, admission to academic or other programs, tenure, or promotion based solely upon their having made or their being the subject of an ethics complaint. This does not preclude taking action based upon the outcome of such proceedings or considering other appropriate information.

H.3. Cooperation With Ethics Committees

Counselors assist in the process of enforcing the *ACA Code of Ethics*. Counselors cooperate with investigations, proceedings, and requirements of the ACA Ethics Committee or ethics committees of other duly constituted associations or boards having jurisdiction over those charged with a violation. Counselors are familiar with the *ACA Policy and Procedures for Processing Complains of Ethical Violations* and use it as a reference for assisting in the enforcement of the *ACA Code of Ethics.*

Glossary of Terms

Advocacy – promotion of the well-being of individuals and groups, and the counseling profession within systems and organizations. Advocacy seeks to remove barriers and obstacles that inhibit access, growth, and development.

Assent – to demonstrate agreement, when a person is otherwise not capable or competent to give formal consent (e.g., informed consent) to a counseling service or plan.

Client – an individual seeking or referred to the professional services of a counselor for help with problem resolution or decision making.

Counselor – a professional (or a student who is a counselorin- training) engaged in a counseling practice or other counseling-related services. Counselors fulfill many roles and responsibilities such as counselor educators, researchers, supervisors, practitioners, and consultants.

Counselor Educator – a professional counselor engaged primarily in developing, implementing, and supervising the educational preparation of counselors-in-training.

Counselor Supervisor – a professional counselor who engages in a formal relationship with a practicing counselor or counselor-in-training for the purpose of overseeing that individual's counseling work or clinical skill development.

Culture – membership in a socially constructed way of living, which incorporates collective values, beliefs, norms, boundaries, and lifestyles that are cocreated with others who share similar worldviews comprising biological, psychosocial, historical, psychological, and other factors.

Diversity – the similarities and differences that occur within and across cultures, and the intersection of cultural and social identities.

Documents – any written, digital, audio, visual, or artistic recording of the work within the counseling relationship between counselor and client.

Examinee – a recipient of any professional counseling service that includes educational, psychological, and career appraisal utilizing qualitative or quantitative techniques.

Forensic Evaluation – any formal assessment conducted for court or other legal proceedings.

Multicultural/Diversity Competence – a capacity whereby counselors possess cultural and diversity awareness and knowledge about self and others, and how this awareness and knowledge is applied effectively in practice with clients and client groups.

Multicultural/Diversity Counseling – counseling that recognizes diversity and embraces approaches that support the worth, dignity, potential, and uniqueness of individuals within their historical, cultural, economic, political, and psychosocial contexts.

Student – an individual engaged in formal educational preparation as a counselor-in-training.

Supervisee – a professional counselor or counselor-in-training whose counseling work or clinical skill development is being overseen in a formal supervisory relationship by a qualified trained professional.

Supervisor – counselors who are trained to oversee the professional clinical work of counselors and counselors-in-training.

Teaching – all activities engaged in as part of a formal educational program designed to lead to a graduate degree in counseling.

Training – the instruction and practice of skills related to the counseling profession. Training contributes to the ongoing proficiency of students and professional counselors.

American Mental Health Counselors Association
Code of Ethics

Preamble

Mental health counselors believe in the dignity and worth of the individual. They are committed to increasing knowledge of human behavior and understanding of themselves and others. While pursuing these endeavors, they make every reasonable effort to protect the welfare of those who seek their services, or of any subject that may be the object of study. They use their skills only for purposes consistent with these values and do not knowingly permit their misuse by others. While demanding for themselves freedom of inquiry and community, mental health counselors accept the responsibility this freedom confers: competence, objectivity in the application of skills, and concern for the best interest of clients, colleagues, and society in general. In the pursuit of these ideals, mental health counselors subscribe to the following principles:

> Principle 1: Welfare of the Consumer
> Principle 2: Clients' Rights
> Principle 3: Confidentiality
> Principle 4: Utilization of Assessment Techniques
> Principle 5: Pursuit of Research Activities
> Principle 6: Consulting
> Principle 7: Competence
> Principle 8: Professional Relationships
> Principle 9: Supervisee, Student and Employee Relationships
> Principle 10: Moral and Legal Standards
> Principle 11: Professional Responsibility
> Principle 12: Private Practice
> Principle 13: Public Statements
> Principle 14: Internet On-Line Counseling
> Principle 15: Resolution of Ethical Problems

Clinical Issues
Principle 1: Welfare of the Consumer

A) Primary Responsibility

1. The primary responsibility of the mental health counselor is to respect the dignity and integrity of the client. Client growth and development are encouraged in ways that foster the client's interest and promote welfare.
2. Mental health counselors are aware of their influential position with respect to their clients, and avoid exploiting the trust and fostering dependency of their clients.
3. Mental health counselors fully inform consumers as to the purpose and nature of any evaluation, treatment, education or training procedure and they fully acknowledge that the consumer has the freedom of choice with regard to participation.

B) Counseling Plans

Mental health counselors and their clients work jointly in devising integrated, individual counseling plans that offer reasonable promise of success and are consistent with the abilities and circumstances of the client. Counselors and clients regularly review counseling plans to ensure their continued viability and effectiveness, respecting the client's freedom of choice.

C) Freedom of Choice

Mental health counselors offer clients the freedom to choose whether to enter into a counseling relationship and determine which professionals will provide the counseling. Restrictions that limit clients' choices are fully explained.

D) Clients Served by Others

1. If a client is receiving services from another mental health professional or counselor, the mental health counselor secures consent from the client, informs that professional of the arrangement, and develops a clear agreement to avoid confusion and conflicts for the client.

2. Mental health counselors are aware of the intimacy and responsibilities inherent in the counseling relationship. They maintain respect for the client and avoid actions that seek to meet their personal needs at the expense of the client. Mental health counselors are aware of their own values, attitudes, beliefs and behaviors, and how these apply in a diverse society. They avoid imposing their values on the consumer.

E) Diversity

1. Mental health counselors do not condone or engage in any discrimination based on age, color, culture, disability, ethnic group, gender, race, religion, sexual orientation, marital status or socioeconomic status.
2. Mental health counselors will actively attempt to understand the diverse cultural backgrounds of the clients with whom they work. This includes learning how the counselor's own cultural/ethical/racial/religious identity impacts his or her own values and beliefs about the counseling process. When there is a conflict between the client's goals, identity and/or values and those of the mental health counselor, a referral to an appropriate colleague must be arranged.

F) Dual Relationships

Mental health counselors are aware of their influential position with respect to their clients and avoid exploiting the trust and fostering dependency of the client.

1. Mental health counselors make every effort to avoid dual relationships with clients that could impair professional judgement or increase the risk of harm. Examples of such relationships may include, but are not limited to: familial, social, financial, business, or close personal relationships with the clients.
2. Mental health counselors do not accept as clients individuals with whom they are involved in an administrative, supervisory, and evaluative nature. When acting as supervisors, trainers, or employers, mental health counselors accord recipients informed choice, confidentiality and protection from physical and mental harm.

3. When a dual relationship cannot be avoided, counselors take appropriate professional precautions such as informed consent, consultation, supervision and documentation to ensure that judgement is not impaired and no exploitation has occurred.

G) Sexual Relationships

Sexual relationships with clients are strictly prohibited. Mental health counselors do not counsel persons with whom they have had a previous sexual relationship.

H) Former Clients

Counselors do not engage in sexual intimacies with former clients within a minimum of two years after terminating the counseling relationship. The mental health counselor has the responsibility to examine and document thoroughly that such relations did not have an exploitative nature based on factors such as duration of counseling, amount of time since counseling, termination circumstances, the client's personal history and mental status, adverse impact on the client, and actions by the counselor suggesting a plan to initiate a sexual relationship with the client after termination.

I) Multiple Clients

When mental health counselors agree to provide counseling services to two or more persons who have a relationship (such as husband and wife, or parents and children), counselors clarify at the outset which person or persons are clients, and the nature of the relationship they will have with each involved person. If it becomes apparent that counselors may be called upon to perform potentially conflicting roles, they clarify, adjust, or withdraw from roles appropriately.

J) Informed Consent

Mental health counselors are responsible for making their services readily accessible to clients in a manner that facilitates the clients' abilities to make an informed choice when selecting a provider. This responsibility includes a clear description of what the client can expect in the way of tests, reports, billing, therapeutic regime and schedules, and the use of the mental health counselor's statement of professional disclosure. In the event that a client is a minor or possesses disabilities that would prohibit informed consent, the mental health counselor acts in the client's best interest.

K) Conflict of Interest

Mental health counselors are aware of possible conflicts of interests that may involve the organization in which they are employed and their client. When conflicts occur, mental health counselors clarify the nature of the conflict and inform all parties of the nature and direction of their loyalties and responsibilities, and keep all parties informed of their commitments.

L) Fees and Bartering

1. Mental health counselors clearly explain to clients, prior to entering the counseling relationship, all financial arrangements related to professional services, including the use of collection agencies or legal measures for nonpayment.
2. In establishing fees for professional counseling services, mental health counselors consider the financial status of their clients and locality. In the event that the payment of the mental health counselor's usual fees would create undue hardship for the client, assistance is provided in attempting to find comparable services at an acceptable cost.
3. Mental health counselors ordinarily refrain from accepting goods or services from clients in return for counseling service because such arrangements create inherent potential for conflicts, exploitation and distortion of the professional relationship. Participation in bartering is only used when there is no exploitation, if the client requests it, if a clear written contract is established, and if such an arrangement is an accepted practice among professionals in the community.

M) Pro Bono Service

Mental health counselors contribute to society by devoting a portion of their professional activity to services for which there is little or no financial return.

N) Consulting

Mental health counselors may choose to consult with any other professionally competent person about a client. In choosing a consultant, the mental health counselor should avoid placing the consultant in a conflict of interest situation that would preclude the consultant from being a proper party to the mental health counselor's effort to help the client.

O) Group Work

1. Mental health counselors screen prospective group counseling/therapy participants. Every effort is made to select members whose needs and goals are compatible with goals of the group, who will not impede the group process, and whose well being will not be jeopardized by the group experience.
2. In the group setting, mental health counselors take reasonable precautions to protect clients from physical and psychological harm or trauma.
3. When the client is engaged in short term group treatment/training programs, i.e. marathons and other encounter type or growth groups, the members ensure that there is professional assistance available during and following the group experience.

P) Termination and Referral

Mental health counselors do not abandon or neglect their clients in counseling. Assistance is given in making appropriate arrangements for the continuation of treatment, when necessary, during interruptions such as vacation and following termination.

Q) Inability to assist clients

If the mental health counselor determines that their services are not beneficial to the client, they avoid entering or terminate immediately a counseling relationship. Mental health counselors are knowledgeable about referral sources and appropriate referrals are made. If clients decline the suggested referral, mental health counselors discontinue the relationship.

R) Appropriate Termination

Mental health counselors terminate a counseling relationship, securing a client's agreement when possible, when it is reasonably clear that the client is no longer benefiting, when services are no longer required, when counseling no longer serves the needs and interests of the client, when clients do not pay fees charged, or when agency or institution limits do not allow provision of further counseling services.

Principle 2: Clients' Rights

The following apply to all consumers of mental health services, including both in- and out-patients and all state, county, local, and private care mental health facilities, as well as clients of mental health practitioners in private practice.

The client has the right:

A) To be treated with dignity, consideration and respect at all times;

B) To expect quality service provided by concerned, trained, professional and competent staff;

C) To expect complete confidentiality within the limits of the law, and to be informed about the legal exceptions to confidentiality; and to expect that no information will be released without the client's knowledge and written consent;

D) To a clear working contract in which business items, such as time of sessions, payment plans/fees, absences, access, emergency procedures, and third-party reimbursement procedures are discussed;

E) To a clear statement of the purposes, goals, techniques, rules of procedure and limitations, as well as the potential dangers of the services to be performed, and all other information related to or likely to affect the ongoing mental health counseling relationship;

F) To appropriate information regarding the mental health counselor's education, training, skills, license and practice limitations and to request and receive referrals to other clinicians when appropriate;

G) To full, knowledgeable, and responsible participation in the ongoing treatment plan to the maximum extent feasible;

H) To obtain information about their case record and to have this information explained clearly and directly;

I) To request information and/or consultation regarding the conduct and progress of their therapy;

J) To refuse any recommended services and to be advised of the consequences of this action;

K) To a safe environment free of emotional, physical and sexual abuse;

L) To a client grievance procedure, including requests for consultation and/or mediation; and to file a complaint with the mental health counselor's supervisor, and/or the appropriate credentialing body; and

M) To a clearly defined ending process, and to discontinue therapy at any time.

Principle 3: Confidentiality

Mental health counselors have a primary obligation to safeguard information about individuals obtained in the course of practice, teaching, or research. Personal information is communicated to others only with the person's written consent or in those circumstances where there is clear and imminent danger to the client, to others or to society. Disclosure of counseling information is restricted to what is necessary, relevant and verifiable.

A) At the outset of any counseling relationship, mental health counselors make their clients aware of their rights in regard to the confidential nature of the counseling relationship. They fully disclose the limits of, or exceptions to, confidentiality, and/or the existence of privileged communication, if any.

B) All materials in the official record shall be shared with the client, who shall have the right to decide what information may be shared with anyone beyond the immediate provider of service and be informed of the implications of the materials to be shared.

C) Confidentiality belongs to the clients. They may direct the mental health counselor, in writing, to release information to others. The release of information without the consent of the client may only take place under the most extreme circumstances. The protection of life, as in the case of suicidal or homicidal clients, exceeds the requirements of confidentiality. The protection of a child, an elderly person, or a person not competent to care for themselves from physical or sexual abuse or neglect requires that a report be made to a legally constituted authority. The mental health counselor complies with all state and federal statutes concerning mandated reporting of suicidality, homicidality, child abuse, incompetent person abuse and elder abuse. The protection of the public or another individual from a contagious condition known to be fatal also requires action that may include reporting the willful infection of another with the condition.

The mental health counselor (or staff member) does not release information by request unless accompanied by a specific release of information or a valid court order. Mental health counselors will comply with the order of a court to release information but they will inform the client of the receipt of such an order. A subpoena is insufficient to release information. In such a case, the counselor must inform his client of the situation and, if the client refuses release, coordinate between the client's attorney and the requesting attorney so as to protect client confidentiality and one's own legal welfare.

In the case of all of the above exceptions to confidentiality, the mental health counselor will release only such information as is necessary to accomplish the action required by the exception.

D) The anonymity of clients served in public and other agencies is preserved, if at all possible, by withholding names and personal identifying data. If external conditions require reporting such information, the client shall be so informed.

E) Information received in confidence by one agency or person shall not be forwarded to another person or agency without the client's written permission.

F) Service providers have the responsibility to ensure the accuracy and to indicate the validity of data shared with their parties.

G) Case reports presented in classes, professional meetings, or publications shall be so disguised that no identification is possible unless the client or responsible authority has read the report and agreed in writing to its presentation or publication.

H) Counseling reports and records are maintained under conditions of security, and provisions are made for their destruction when they have outlived their usefulness. Mental health counselors ensure that all persons in his or her employ, volunteers, and community aides maintain privacy and confidentiality.

I) Mental health counselors who ask that an individual reveal personal information in the course of interviewing, testing or evaluation, or who allow such information to be divulged, do so only after making certain that the person or authorized representative is fully aware of the purposes of the interview, testing or evaluation, and of the ways in which the information will be used.

J) Sessions with clients may be taped or otherwise recorded only with their written permission or the written permission of a responsible guardian. Even with a guardian's written consent, one should not record a session against the expressed wishes of a client. Such tapes shall be destroyed when they have outlived their usefulness.

K) Where a child or adolescent is the primary client, or the client is not competent to give consent, the interests of the minor or the incompetent client shall be paramount. Where appropriate, a parent(s) or guardian(s) may be included in the counseling process. The mental health counselor must still take measures to safeguard the client's confidentiality.

L) In work with families, the rights of each family member should be safeguarded. The provider of service also has the responsibility to discuss the contents of the record with the parent and/or child, as appropriate, and to keep separate those parts, which should remain the property of each family member.

M) In work with groups, the rights of each group member should be safeguarded. The provider of service also has the responsibility to discuss the need for each member to respect the confidentiality of each other member of the group. He must also remind the group of the limits on and risk to confidentiality inherent in the group process.

N) When using a computer to store confidential information, mental health counselors take measures to control access to such information. When such information has outlived its usefulness, it should be deleted from the system.

Principle 4: Utilization of Assessment Techniques

A) Test Selection

1. In choosing a particular test, mental health counselors should ascertain that there is sufficient evidence in the test manual of its applicability in measuring a certain trait or construct. The manual should fully describe the development of the test, the rationale, and data pertaining to item selection and test construction. The manual should explicitly state the purposes and applications for which the test is intended, and provide reliability and validity data about the test. The manual should furthermore identify the qualifications necessary to properly administer and interpret the test.

2. In selecting a particular combination of tests, mental health counselors need to be able to justify the logic of those choices.

3. Mental health counselors should employ only those tests for which they judge themselves competent by training, education, or experience. In familiarizing themselves with new tests, counselors thoroughly read the manual and seek workshops, supervision, or other forms of training.

4. Mental health counselors avoid using outdated or obsolete tests, and strive to remain current regarding test publication and revision.

5. Tests selected for individual testing must be appropriate for that individual in that appropriate norms exist for variables such as age, gender, and race. The test form must fit the client. If the

test must be used in the absence of available information regarding the above subsamples, the limitations of generalizability should be duly noted.

B) Test Administration

1. Mental health counselors should faithfully follow instructions for administration of a test in order to ensure standardization. Failure to consistently follow test instructions will result in test error and incorrect estimates of the trait or behavior being measured.
2. Tests should only be employed in appropriate professional settings or as recommended by instructors or supervisors for training purposes. It is best to avoid giving tests to relatives, close friends or business associates, in that doing so constructs a dual professional/personal relationship, which is to be avoided.
3. Mental health counselors should provide the test taker with appropriate information regarding the reason for assessment, the approximate length of time required, and to whom the report will be distributed. Issues of confidentiality must be addressed, and the client must be given the opportunity to ask questions of the examiner prior to beginning the procedure.
4. Care should be taken to provide an appropriate assessment environment in regard to temperature, privacy, comfort, and freedom from distractions.
5. Information should be solicited regarding any possible handicaps, such as problems with visual or auditory acuity, limitations of hand/eye coordination, illness, or other factors. If the disabilities cannot be accommodated effectively, the test may need to be postponed or the limitations of applicability of the test results noted in the test report.
6. Professionals who supervise others should ensure that their trainees have sufficient knowledge and experience before utilizing the tests for clinical purposes.
7. Mental health counselors must be able to document appropriate education, training, and experience in areas of assessment they perform.

C) Test Interpretation

1. Interpretation of test or test battery results should be based on multiple sources of convergent data and an understanding of the tests' foundations and limits.
2. Mental health counselors must be careful not to make conclusions unless empirical evidence is present to justify the statement. If such evidence is lacking, one should not make diagnostic or prognostic formulations.
3. Interpretation of test results should take into account the many qualitative influences on test-taking behavior, such as health, energy, motivation, and the like. Description and analysis of alternative explanations should be provided with the interpretations.
4. One should not make firm conclusions in the absence of published information that establishes a satisfactory degree of test validity, particularly predictive validity.
5. Multicultural factors must be considered in test interpretation and diagnosis, and formulation of prognosis and treatment recommendations.
6. Mental health counselors should avoid biased or incorrect interpretation by assuring that the test norms reference the population taking the test.
7. Mental health counselors are responsible for evaluating the quality of computer software interpretations of test data. Mental health counselors should obtain information regarding validity of computerized test interpretation before utilizing such an approach.
8. Supervisors should ensure that their supervisees have had adequate training in interpretation before entrusting them to evaluate tests in a semi-autonomous fashion.

9. Any individual or organization offering test scoring or interpretation services must be able to demonstrate that their programs are based on sufficient and appropriate research to establish the validity of the programs and procedures used in arriving at interpretations. The public offering of an automated test interpretation service will be considered a professional-to-professional consultation. The formal responsibility of the consultant is to the consultee, but his or her ultimate and overriding responsibility is to the client.
10. Mental health counselors who have the responsibility for making decisions about clients or policies based on test results should have a thorough understanding of counseling theory, assessment techniques, and test research.
11. Mental health counselors do not represent computerized test interpretations as their own and

clearly designate such computerized results.

D) Test Reporting
1. Mental health counselors should write reports in a clear fashion, avoiding excessive jargon or clinical terms that are likely to confuse the lay reader.
2. Mental health counselors should strive to provide test results in as positive and nonjudgmental manner as possible.
3. Mindful that one's report reflects on the reputation of oneself and one's profession, reports are carefully proofread so as to be free of spelling, style, and grammatical errors as much as is possible.
4. Clients should be clearly informed about who will be allowed to review the report and, in the absence of a valid court order, must sign appropriate releases of information permitting such release. Mental health counselors must not release the report or findings in the absence of the aforementioned releases or order.
5. Mental health counselors are responsible for ensuring the confidentiality and security of test reports, test data, and test materials.
6. Mental health counselors must offer the client the opportunity to receive feedback about the test results, interpretations, and the range of error for such data.
7. Transmissions of test data or test reports by fax or e-mail must be accomplished in a secure manner, with guarantees that the receiving device is capable of providing a confidential transmission only to the party who has been permitted to receive the document.

8. Mental health counselors should train his or her staff to respect the confidentiality of test reports in the context of typing, filing, or mailing them.
9. Mental health counselors (or staff members) do not release a psychological evaluation by request unless accompanied by a specific release of information or a valid court order. A subpoena is insufficient to release a report. In such a case, the counselor must inform his/her client of the situation and, if the client refuses release, coordinate between the client's attorney and the requesting attorney so as to protect client confidentiality and one's own legal welfare.

Principle 5: Pursuit of Research Activities

Mental health counselors who conduct research must do so with regard to ethical principles. The decision to undertake research should rest upon a considered judgment by the individual counselor about how best to contribute to counseling and to human welfare. Mental health counselors carry out their investigations with respect for the people who participate and with concern for their dignity and welfare.
1. The ethical researcher seeks advice from other professionals if any plan of research suggests a deviation from any ethical principle of research with human subjects. Such deviation must still protect the dignity and welfare of the client and places on the researcher a special burden to act in the subject's interest.
2. The ethical researcher is open and honest in the relationship with research participants.
   a) The ethical researcher informs the participant of all features of the research that might be expected to influence willingness to participate and explains to the participant all other aspects about which the participant inquires.

   b) Where scientific or human values justify delaying or withholding information, the investigator acquires a special responsibility to assure that there are no damaging consequences for the participants.
   c) Following the collection of the data, the ethical researcher must provide the participant with a full clarification of the nature of the study to remove any misconceptions that may have arisen.
   d) As soon as possible, the participant is to be informed of the reasons for concealment or deception that are part of the methodological requirements of a study.
   e) Such misinformation must be minimized and full disclosure must be made at the conclusion of all research studies.
   f) The ethical researcher understands that failure to make full disclosure to a research participant gives added emphasis to the researcher's abiding responsibility to protect the welfare and dignity

of the participant.

3. The ethical researcher protects participants from physical and mental discomfort, harm and danger. If the risks of such consequences exist, the investigator is required to inform the participant of that fact, secure consent before proceeding, and take all possible measures to minimize the distress.

4. The ethical researcher instructs research participants that they are free to withdraw their consent and from participation at any time.

5. The ethical researcher understands that information obtained about research participants during the course of an investigation is confidential. When the possibility exists that others may obtain access to such information, the participant must be made aware of the possibility and the plans for protecting confidentiality as a part of the procedure for obtaining informed consent.

6. The ethical researcher gives sponsoring agencies, host institutions, and publication channels the same respect and opportunity for informed consent that they accord to individual research participants.

7. The ethical researcher is aware of his or her obligation to future research workers and ensures that host institutions are given feedback information and proper acknowledgement.

Principle 6: Consulting

A) Mental health counselors acting as consultants must have a high degree of self-awareness of their own values, knowledge, skills and needs in entering a helping relationship that involves human and/or organizational change. The focus of the consulting relationship should be on the issues to be resolved and not on the personal characteristics of those presenting the consulting issues.

B) Mental health counselors should develop an understanding of the problem presented by the client and should secure an agreement with the consultation client, specifying the terms and nature of the consulting relationship.

C) Mental health counselors must be reasonably certain that they and their clients have the competencies and resources necessary to follow the consultation plan.

D) Mental health counselors should encourage adaptability and growth toward self-direction. Mental health counselors should avoid becoming a decision-maker or substitute for the client.

E) When announcing consultant availability for services, mental health counselors conscientiously adhere to professional standards.

F) Mental health counselors keep all proprietary information confidential.

G) Mental health counselors avoid conflicts of interest in selecting consultation clients.

Professional Issues
Principle 7: Competence

The maintenance of high standards of professional competence is a responsibility shared by all mental health counselors in the best interests of the public and the profession. Mental health counselors recognize the boundaries of their particular competencies and the limitations of their expertise. Mental health counselors only provide those services and use only those techniques for which they are qualified by education, techniques or experience. Mental health counselors maintain knowledge of relevant scientific and professional information related to the services they render, and they recognize the need for on-going education.

A) Mental health counselors accurately represent their competence, education, training and experience.

B) As teaching professionals, mental health counselors perform their duties based on careful preparation in order that their instruction is accurate, up to date and educational.

C) Mental health counselors recognize the need for continued education and training in the area of cultural diversity and competency. Mental health counselors are open to new procedures and sensitive to the diversity of varying populations and changes in expectations and values over time.

D) Mental health counselors and practitioners recognize that their effectiveness depends in part upon their ability to maintain sound and healthy interpersonal relationships. They are aware that any unhealthy activity would compromise sound professional judgement and competency. In the event that personal problems arise and are affecting professional services, they will seek competent professional assistance to determine whether they should limit, suspend or terminate services to their clients.

E) Mental health counselors have a responsibility both to the individual who is served and to the institution within which the service is performed to maintain high standards of professional conduct. Mental health counselors strive to maintain the highest level of professional services offered to the agency, organization or institution in providing the highest caliber of professional services. The acceptance of employment in an institution implies that the mental health counselor is in substantial agreement with the general policies and principles of the institution. If, despite concerted efforts, the member cannot reach an agreement with the employer as to acceptable standards of conduct that allows for changes in institutional policy conducive to the positive growth and development of counselors, then terminating the affiliation should be seriously considered.

G) Ethical behavior among professional associates, mental health counselors and non-mental health counselors is expected at all times. When information is possessed that raises serious doubts as to the ethical behavior of professional colleagues, whether association members or not, the mental health counselor is obligated to take action to attempt to rectify such a condition. Such action shall utilize the institution's channels first and then utilize procedures established by the state licensure board.

H) Mental health counselors are aware of the intimacy of the counseling relationship, maintain a healthy respect for the integrity of the client, and avoid engaging in activities that seek to meet the mental health counselor's personal needs at the expense of the client. Through awareness of the negative impact of both racial and sexual stereotyping and discrimination, the member strives to ensure the individual rights and personal dignity of the client in the counseling relationship.

Principle 8: Professional Relationships

Mental health counselors act with due regard for the needs and feelings of their colleagues in counseling and other professions. Mental health counselors respect the prerogatives and obligations of the institutions or organizations with which they associate.

A) Mental health counselors understand how related professions complement their work and make full use of other professional, technical, and administrative resources that best serve the interests of consumers. The absence of formal relationships with other professional workers does not relieve mental health counselors from the responsibility of securing for their clients the best possible professional services; indeed, this circumstance presents a challenge to the professional competence of mental health counselors, requiring special sensitivity to problems outside their areas of training, and foresight, diligence, and tact in obtaining the professional assistance needed by clients.

B) Mental health counselors know and take into account the traditions and practices of other professional groups with which they work and cooperate fully with members of such groups when research, services and other functions are shared, or in working for the benefit of public welfare.

C) Mental health counselors treat professional colleagues with the same dignity and respect afforded to clients. Professional discourse should be free of personal attacks.

D) Mental health counselors strive to provide positive conditions for those they employ and to spell out clearly the conditions of such employment. They encourage their employees to engage in activities that facilitate their further professional development.

E) Mental health counselors respect the viability, reputation, and proprietary rights of organizations that they serve. Mental health counselors show due regard for the interest of their present or perspective employers. In those instances where they are critical of policies, they attempt to effect change by constructive action within the organization.

F) In pursuit of research, mental health counselors are to give sponsoring agencies, host institutions, and publication channels the same respect and opportunity for giving informed consent that they accord to individual research participants. They are aware of their obligation to future research workers and insure that host institutions are given feedback information and proper acknowledgement.

G) Credit is assigned to those who have contributed to a publication, in proportion to their contribution.

H) Mental health counselors do not accept or offer referral fees from other professionals.

I) When mental health counselors violate ethical standards, mental health counselors who know firsthand of such activities should, if possible, attempt to rectify the situation. Failing an informal solution, mental

44

health counselors should bring such unethical activities to the attention of the appropriate state licensure board committee on ethics and professional conduct. Only after all professional alternatives have been utilized will mental health counselors begin legal action for resolution.

Principle 9: Supervisee, Student and Employee Relationships

Mental health counselors have an ethical concern for the integrity and welfare of supervisees, students, and employees. They maintain these relationships on a professional and confidential basis. They recognize the influential position they have with regard to both current and former supervisees, students and employees. They avoid exploiting their trust and dependency.

A) Mental health counselors do not engage in ongoing counseling relationships with current supervisees, students and employees.

B) All forms of sexual behavior with supervisees, students and employees are unethical. Further, mental health counselors do not engage in sexual or other harassment of supervisees, students, employees or colleagues.

C) Mental health counselor supervisors advise their supervisees, students and employees against offering or engaging in or holding themselves out as competent to engage in professional services beyond their training, level of experience and competence.

D) Mental health counselors make every effort to avoid dual relationships with supervisees, students and employees that could impair their judgment or increase the risk of personal or financial exploitation. When a dual relationship can not be avoided, mental health counselors take appropriate professional precautions to make sure that judgment is not impaired. Examples of such dual relationships include, but are not limited to, a supervisee who receives supervision as a benefit of employment, or a student in a small college where the only available counselor on campus is an instructor.

E) Mental health counselors do not disclose supervisee confidences except:
1. To prevent clear and eminent danger to a person or persons.
2. As mandated by law.
    a) As in mandated child or senior abuse reporting.
    b) Where the counselor is a defendant in a civil, criminal or disciplinary action.
    c) In educational or training settings where only other professionals who will share responsibility for the training of the supervisee are present.
    d) Where there is a waiver of confidentiality obtained in writing prior to such a release of information.

F) Supervisees must make their clients aware in their informed consent statement that they are under supervision and they must provide their clients with the name and credentials of their supervisor.

G) Mental health counselors require their supervisees, students and employees to adhere to the Code of Ethics. Students and supervisees have the same obligations to clients as those required of mental health counselors.

Principle 10: Moral and Legal Standards

Mental health counselors recognize that they have a moral, legal and ethical responsibility to the community and to the general public. Mental health counselors should be aware of the prevailing community standards and the impact of professional standards on the community.

A) To protect students, mental health counselors/teachers will be aware of diverse backgrounds of students and will see that material is treated objectively and fairly to reflect the multicultural community in which they live.

B) Providers of counseling services conform to the statutes relating to such services as established by their state and its regulating professional board(s).

C) As employees, mental health counselors refuse to participate in an employer's practices that are inconsistent with the moral and legal standards established by federal or state legislation regarding the treatment of employees. In particular and for example, mental health counselors will not condone practices that result in illegal or otherwise unjustified discrimination on the basis of race, sex, religion or national origin in hiring, promotion or training.

D) In providing counseling services to clients, mental health counselors avoid any action that will violate or diminish the legal and civil rights of clients or of others that may be effected by the action.

E) Sexual conduct, not limited to sexual intercourse, between mental health counselors and clients is specifically in violation of this Code of Ethics. This does not, however, prohibit the use of explicit instructional aids including films and videotapes. Such use is within excepted practices of trained and competent sex therapists.

Principle 11: Professional Responsibility

In their commitment to the understanding of human behavior, mental health counselors value objectivity and integrity, and in providing services they maintain the highest standards. They accept responsibility for the consequences of their work and make every effort to ensure that their services are used appropriately.

A) Mental health counselors accept ultimate responsibility for selecting appropriate areas for investigation and the methods relevant to minimize the possibility that their finding will be misleading. They provide thorough discussion of the limitations of their data and alternative hypotheses, especially where their work touches on social policy or might be misconstrued to the detriment of specific age, sex, ethnic, socioeconomic, or other social categories. In publishing reports of their work, they never discard observations that may modify the interpretation of results. Mental health counselors take credit only for the work they have actually done. In pursuing research, mental health counselors ascertain that their efforts will not lead to changes in individuals or organizations unless such changes are part of the agreement at the time of obtaining informed consent. Mental health counselors clarify in advance the expectations for sharing and utilizing research data. They avoid dual relationships that may limit objectivity, whether theoretical, political, or monetary, so that interference with data, subjects, and milieu is kept to a minimum.

B) As employees of an institution or agency, mental health counselors have the responsibility to remain alert to institutional pressures that may distort reports of counseling findings or use them in ways counter to the promotion of human welfare.

C) When serving as members of governmental or other organizational bodies, mental health counselors remain accountable as individuals to the Code of Ethics of the American Mental Health Counselors Association.

D) As teachers, mental health counselors recognize their primary obligation to help others acquire knowledge and skill. They maintain high standards of scholarship and objectivity by presenting counseling information fully and accurately, and by giving appropriate recognition to alternative viewpoints.

E) As practitioners, mental health counselors know that they bear a heavy social responsibility because their recommendations and professional actions may alter the lives of others. They therefore remained fully cognizant of their impact and alert to personal, social, organizational, financial or political situations or pressures that might lead to the misuse of their influence.

F) Mental health counselors provide reasonable and timely feedback to employees, trainees, supervisors, students, clients, and others whose work they may evaluate.

Principle 12: Private Practice

A) A mental health counselor should assist, where permitted by legislation or judicial decision, the profession in fulfilling its duty to make counseling services available in private settings.

B) In advertising services as a private practitioner, mental health counselors should advertise the services in such a manner so as to accurately inform the public as to services, expertise, profession, and techniques of counseling in a professional manner. Mental health counselors who assume an executive leadership role in the organization shall not permit their name to be used in professional notices during periods when not actively engaged in the private practice of counseling. Mental health counselors advertise the following: highest relevant degree, type and level of certification or license, and type and/or description of services or other relevant information. Such information should not contain false, inaccurate, misleading, partial, out of context, descriptive material or statements.

C) Mental health counselors may join in partnership/corporation with other mental health counselors and/or other professionals provided that each mental health counselor of the partnership or corporation makes clear his/her separate specialties, buying name in compliance with the regulations of the locality.

D) Mental health counselors have an obligation to withdraw from an employment relationship or a counseling relationship if it is believed that employment will result in violation of the Code of Ethics, if their mental capacity or physical condition renders it difficult to carry out an effective professional relationship, or if the mental health counselor is discharged by the client because the counseling relationship is no longer productive for the client.

E) Mental health counselors should adhere and support the regulations for private practice in the locality where the services are offered.

F) Mental health counselors refrain from attempts to utilize one's institutional affiliation to recruit clients for one's private practice. Mental health counselors are to refrain from offering their services in the private sector when they are employed by an institution in which this is prohibited by stated policy that reflects conditions of employment.

Principle 13: Public Statements

Mental health counselors in their professional roles may be expected or required to make public statements providing counseling information or professional opinions; or supply information about the availability of counseling products and services. In making such statements, mental health counselors take into full account the limits and uncertainties of present counseling knowledge and techniques. They represent, as accurately and objectively as possible, their professional qualifications, expertise, affiliations, and functions, as well as those of the institutions or organizations with which the statements may be associated. All public statements, announcements of services, and promotional activities should serve the purpose of providing sufficient information to aid the consumer public in making informed judgements and choices on matters that concern it. When announcing professional counseling services, mental health counselors may describe or explain those services offered but may not evaluate as to their quality or uniqueness and do not allow for testimonials by implication. All public statements should be otherwise consistent with this Code of Ethics.

Principle 14: Internet On-Line Counseling

Mental health counselors engaged in delivery of services that involves the telephone, teleconferencing and the Internet in which these areas are generally recognized, standards for preparatory training do not yet exist. Mental health counselors take responsible steps to ensure the competence of their work and protect patients, clients, students, research participants and others from harm.

A) Confidentiality

Mental health counselors ensure that clients are provided sufficient information to adequately address and explain the limitations of computer technology in the counseling process in general and the difficulties of ensuring complete client confidentiality of information transmitted through electronic communications over the Internet through on-line counseling. Professional counselors inform clients of the limitations of confidentiality and identify foreseeable situations in which confidentiality must be breached in light of the law in both the state in which the client is located and the state in which the professional counselor is licensed. Mental health counselors shall become aware of the means for reporting and protecting suicidal clients in their locale. Mental health counselors shall become aware of the means for reporting homicidal clients in the client's jurisdiction.

B) Mental Health Counselor Identification

Mental health counselors provide a readily visible notice advising clients of the identities of all professional counselor(s) who will have access to the information transmitted by the client. Mental health counselors provide background information on all professional communications, including education, licensing and certification, and practice information.

C) Client Identification

Professional counselors identify clients, verify identities of clients, and obtain alternative methods of contacting clients in emergency situations.

D) Client Waiver

Mental health counselors require clients to execute client waiver agreements stating that the client acknowledges the limitations inherent in ensuring client confidentiality of information transmitted through on-line counseling and acknowledge the limitations that are inherent in a counseling process that is not provided face-to-face. Limited training in the area of on-line counseling must be explained and the client's informed consent must be secured.

E) Electronic Transfer of Client Information

Mental health counselors electronically transfer client confidential information to authorized third-party recipients only when both the professional counselor and the authorized recipient have "secure" transfer and acceptance communication capabilities;the recipient is able to effectively protect the confidentiality of the client's confidential information to be transferred; and the informed written consent of the client, acknowledging the limits of confidentiality, has been obtained.

F) Establishing the On-Line Counseling Relationship

1. **Appropriateness of On-line Counseling**

   Mental health counselors develop an appropriate in-take procedure for potential clients to determine whether on-line counseling is appropriate for the needs of the client. Mental health counselors warn potential clients that on-line counseling services may not be appropriate in certain situations and, to the extent possible, inform the client of specific limitations, potential risks, and/or potential benefits relevant to the client's anticipated use of on-line counseling services. Mental health counselors ensure that clients are intellectually, emotionally, and physically capable of using on-line counseling services, and of understanding the potential risks and/or limitations of such services.

2. **Counseling Plans**

   Mental health counselors develop individual on-line counseling plans that are consistent with both the client's individual circumstances and the limitations of on-line counseling. Mental health counselors who determine that on-line counseling is inappropriate for the client should avoid entering into or immediately terminate the on-line counseling relationship and encourage the client to continue the counseling relationship through a traditional alternative method of counseling.

3. **Boundaries of Competence**

   Mental health counselors provide on-line counseling services only in practice areas within their expertise. Mental health counselors do not provide services to clients in states where doing so would violate local licensure laws or regulations.

G) Legal Considerations

Mental health counselors confirm that the provision of on-line services are not prohibited by or otherwise violate any applicable state or local statutes, rules, regulations or ordinances, codes of professional membership organizations and certifying boards, and/or codes of state licensing boards.

Principle 15 Resolution of Ethical Problems

Neither the American Mental Health Counselors Association, its Board of Directors, nor its National Committee on Ethics investigate or adjudicate ethical complaints. In the event a member has his or her license suspended or revoked by an appropriate state licensure board, the AMHCA Board of Directors may then act in accordance with AMHCA's National By-Laws to suspend or revoke his or her membership.

Any member so suspended may apply for reinstatement upon the reinstatement of his or her licensure.

Code of Ethics, American Mental Health Counselors Association (AMHCA, 2000).
Reprinted with permission.

American Psychological Association
Ethical Principles of Psychologists and Code of Conduct

Contents

Introduction and Applicability

The American Psychological Association's (APA's) Ethical Principles of Psychologists and Code of Conduct (hereinafter referred to as the Ethics Code) consists of an Introduction, a Preamble, five General Principles (A – E), and specific Ethical Standards. The Introduction discusses the intent, organization, procedural considerations, and scope of application of the Ethics Code. The Preamble and General Principles are aspirational goals to guide psychologists toward the highest ideals of psychology. Although the Preamble and General Principles are not themselves enforceable rules, they should be considered by psychologists in arriving at an ethical course of action. The Ethical Standards set forth enforceable rules for conduct as psychologists. Most of the Ethical Standards are written broadly, in order to apply to psychologists in varied roles, although the application of an Ethical Standard may vary depending on the context. The Ethical Standards are not exhaustive. The fact that a given conduct is not specifically addressed by an Ethical Standard does not mean that it is necessarily either ethical or unethical.

This Ethics Code applies only to psychologists' activities that are part of their scientific, educational, or professional roles as psychologists. Areas covered include but are not limited to the clinical, counseling, and school practice of psychology; research; teaching; supervision of trainees; public service; policy development; social intervention; development of assessment instruments; conducting assessments; educational counseling; organizational consulting; forensic activities; program design and evaluation; and administration. This Ethics Code applies to these activities across a variety of contexts, such as in person, postal, telephone, internet, and other electronic transmissions. These activities shall be distinguished from the purely private conduct of psychologists, which is not within the purview of the Ethics Code.

Membership in the APA commits members and student affiliates to comply with the standards of the APA Ethics Code and to the rules and procedures used to enforce them. Lack of awareness or misunderstanding of an Ethical Standard is not itself a defense to a charge of unethical conduct.

The procedures for filing, investigating, and resolving complaints of unethical conduct are described in the current Rules and Procedures of the APA Ethics Committee. APA may impose sanctions on its members for violations of the standards of the Ethics Code, including termination of APA membership, and may notify other bodies and individuals of its actions. Actions that violate the standards of the Ethics Code may also lead to the imposition of sanctions on psychologists or students whether or not they are APA members by bodies other than APA, including state psychological associations, other professional groups, psychology boards, other state or federal agencies, and payors for health services. In addition, APA may take action against a member after his or her conviction of a felony, expulsion or suspension from an affiliated state psychological association, or suspension or loss of licensure. When the sanction to be imposed by APA is less than expulsion, the 2001 Rules and Procedures do not guarantee an opportunity for an in-person hearing, but generally provide that complaints will be resolved only on the basis of a submitted record.

The Ethics Code is intended to provide guidance for psychologists and standards of professional conduct that can be applied by the APA and by other bodies that choose to adopt them. The Ethics Code is not intended to be a basis of civil liability. Whether a psychologist has violated the Ethics Code standards does not by itself determine whether the psychologist is legally liable in a court action, whether a contract is enforceable, or whether other legal consequences occur.

The modifiers used in some of the standards of this Ethics Code (e.g., *reasonably, appropriate, potentially*) are included in the standards when they would (1) allow professional judgment on the part of psychologists, (2) eliminate injustice or inequality that would occur without the modifier, (3) ensure applicability across the broad range of activities conducted by psychologists, or (4) guard against a set of rigid rules that might be quickly outdated. As used in this Ethics Code, the term *reasonable* means the prevailing professional judgment of psychologists engaged in similar activities in similar circumstances, given the knowledge the psychologist had or should have had at the time.

In the process of making decisions regarding their professional behavior, psychologists must consider this Ethics Code in addition to applicable laws and psychology board regulations. In applying the Ethics Code to their professional work, psychologists may consider other materials and guidelines that have been adopted or endorsed by scientific and professional psychological organizations and the dictates of their own conscience, as well as consult with others within the field. If this Ethics Code establishes a higher standard of conduct than is required by law, psychologists must meet the higher ethical standard. If psychologists' ethical responsibilities conflict with law, regulations, or other governing legal authority, psychologists make known their commitment to this Ethics Code and take steps to resolve the conflict in a responsible manner. If the conflict is unresolvable via such means, psychologists may adhere to the requirements of the law, regulations, or other governing authority in keeping with basic principles of human rights.

Preamble

Psychologists are committed to increasing scientific and professional knowledge of behavior and people's understanding of themselves and others and to the use of such knowledge to improve the condition of individuals, organizations, and society. Psychologists respect and protect civil and human rights and the central importance of freedom of inquiry and expression in research, teaching, and publication. They strive to help the public in developing informed judgments and choices concerning human behavior. In doing so, they perform many roles, such as researcher, educator, diagnostician, therapist, supervisor, consultant, administrator, social interventionist, and expert witness. This Ethics Code provides a common set of principles and standards upon which psychologists build their professional and scientific work.

This Ethics Code is intended to provide specific standards to cover most situations encountered by psychologists. It has as its goals the welfare and protection of the individuals and groups with whom psychologists work and the education of members, students, and the public regarding ethical standards of the discipline.

The development of a dynamic set of ethical standards for psychologists' work-related conduct requires a personal commitment and lifelong effort to act ethically; to encourage ethical behavior by students, supervisees, employees, and colleagues; and to consult with others concerning ethical problems.

General Principles

This section consists of General Principles. General Principles, as opposed to Ethical Standards, are aspirational in nature. Their intent is to guide and inspire psychologists toward the very highest ethical ideals of the profession. General Principles, in contrast to Ethical Standards, do not represent obligations and should not form the basis for imposing sanctions. Relying upon General Principles for either of these reasons distorts both their meaning and purpose.

Principle A: Beneficence and Nonmaleficence

Psychologists strive to benefit those with whom they work and take care to do no harm. In their professional actions, psychologists seek to safeguard the welfare and rights of those with whom they interact professionally and other affected persons, and the welfare of animal subjects of research. When conflicts occur among psychologists' obligations or concerns, they attempt to resolve these conflicts in a responsible fashion that avoids or minimizes harm. Because psychologists' scientific and professional judgments and actions may affect the lives of others, they are alert to and guard against personal, financial, social, organizational, or political factors that might lead to misuse of their influence. Psychologists strive to be aware of the possible effect of their own physical and mental health on their ability to help those with whom they work.

Principle B: Fidelity and Responsibility

Psychologists establish relationships of trust with those with whom they work. They are aware of their professional and scientific responsibilities to society and to the specific communities in which they work. Psychologists uphold professional standards of conduct, clarify their professional roles and obligations, accept appropriate responsibility for their behavior, and seek to manage conflicts of interest that could lead to exploitation or harm. Psychologists consult with, refer to, or cooperate with other professionals and institutions to the extent needed to serve the best interests of those with whom they work. They are concerned about the ethical compliance of their colleagues' scientific and professional conduct. Psychologists strive to contribute a portion of their professional time for little or no compensation or personal advantage.

Principle C: Integrity

Psychologists seek to promote accuracy, honesty, and truthfulness in the science, teaching, and practice of psychology. In these activities psychologists do not steal, cheat, or engage in fraud, subterfuge, or intentional misrepresentation of fact. Psychologists strive to keep their promises and to avoid unwise or unclear commitments. In situations in which deception may be ethically justifiable to maximize benefits and minimize harm, psychologists have a serious obligation to consider the need for, the possible consequences of, and their responsibility to correct any resulting mistrust or other harmful effects that arise from the use of such techniques.

Principle D: Justice

Psychologists recognize that fairness and justice entitle all persons to access to and benefit from the contributions of psychology and to equal quality in the processes, procedures, and services being conducted by psychologists. Psychologists exercise reasonable judgment and take precautions to ensure that their potential biases, the boundaries of their competence, and the limitations of their expertise do not lead to or condone unjust practices.

Principle E: Respect for People's Rights and Dignity

Psychologists respect the dignity and worth of all people, and the rights of individuals to privacy, confidentiality, and self-determination. Psychologists are aware that special safeguards may be necessary to protect the rights and welfare of persons or communities whose vulnerabilities impair autonomous decision making. Psychologists are aware of and respect cultural, individual, and role differences, including those based on age, gender, gender identity, race, ethnicity, culture, national origin, religion, sexual orientation, disability, language, and socioeconomic status and consider these factors when working with members of such groups. Psychologists try to eliminate the effect on their work of biases based on those factors, and they do not knowingly participate in or condone activities of others based upon such prejudices.

Ethical Standards

1. Resolving Ethical Issues

1.01 Misuse of Psychologists' Work
If psychologists learn of misuse or misrepresentation of their work, they take reasonable steps to correct or minimize the misuse or misrepresentation.

1.02 Conflicts Between Ethics and Law, Regulations, or Other Governing Legal Authority
If psychologists' ethical responsibilities conflict with law, regulations, or other governing legal authority, psychologists make known their commitment to the Ethics Code and take steps to resolve the conflict. If the conflict is unresolvable via such means, psychologists may adhere to the requirements of the law, regulations, or other governing legal authority.

1.03 Conflicts Between Ethics and Organizational Demands
If the demands of an organization with which psychologists are affiliated or for whom they are working conflict with this Ethics Code, psychologists clarify the nature of the conflict, make known their commitment to the Ethics Code, and to the extent feasible, resolve the conflict in a way that permits adherence to the Ethics Code.

1.04 Informal Resolution of Ethical Violations

When psychologists believe that there may have been an ethical violation by another psychologist, they attempt to resolve the issue by bringing it to the attention of that individual, if an informal resolution appears appropriate and the intervention does not violate any confidentiality rights that may be involved. (See also Standards 1.02, Conflicts Between Ethics and Law, Regulations, or Other Governing Legal Authority, and 1.03, Conflicts Between Ethics and Organizational Demands.)

1.05 Reporting Ethical Violations

If an apparent ethical violation has substantially harmed or is likely to substantially harm a person or organization and is not appropriate for informal resolution under Standard 1.04, Informal Resolution of Ethical Violations, or is not resolved properly in that fashion, psychologists take further action appropriate to the situation. Such action might include referral to state or national committees on professional ethics, to state licensing boards, or to the appropriate institutional authorities. This standard does not apply when an intervention would violate confidentiality rights or when psychologists have been retained to review the work of another psychologist whose professional conduct is in question. (See also Standard 1.02, Conflicts Between Ethics and Law, Regulations, or Other Governing Legal Authority.)

1.06 Cooperating With Ethics Committees

Psychologists cooperate in ethics investigations, proceedings, and resulting requirements of the APA or any affiliated state psychological association to which they belong. In doing so, they address any confidentiality issues. Failure to cooperate is itself an ethics violation. However, making a request for deferment of adjudication of an ethics complaint pending the outcome of litigation does not alone constitute noncooperation.

1.07 Improper Complaints

Psychologists do not file or encourage the filing of ethics complaints that are made with reckless disregard for or willful ignorance of facts that would disprove the allegation.

1.08 Unfair Discrimination Against Complainants and Respondents

Psychologists do not deny persons employment, advancement, admissions to academic or other programs, tenure, or promotion, based solely upon their having made or their being the subject of an ethics complaint. This does not preclude taking action based upon the outcome of such proceedings or considering other appropriate information.

2. Competence

2.01 Boundaries of Competence

(a) Psychologists provide services, teach, and conduct research with populations and in areas only within the boundaries of their competence, based on their education, training, supervised experience, consultation, study, or professional experience.

(b) Where scientific or professional knowledge in the discipline of psychology establishes that an understanding of factors associated with age, gender, gender identity, race, ethnicity, culture, national origin, religion, sexual orientation, disability, language, or socioeconomic status is essential for effective implementation of their services or research, psychologists have or obtain the training, experience, consultation, or supervision necessary to ensure the competence of their services, or they make appropriate referrals, except as provided in Standard 2.02, Providing Services in Emergencies.

(c) Psychologists planning to provide services, teach, or conduct research involving populations, areas, techniques, or technologies new to them undertake relevant education, training, supervised experience, consultation, or study.

(d) When psychologists are asked to provide services to individuals for whom appropriate mental health services are not available and for which psychologists have not obtained the competence necessary, psychologists with closely related prior training or experience may provide such services in order to ensure that services are not denied if they make a reasonable effort to obtain the competence required by using relevant research, training, consultation, or study.

(e) In those emerging areas in which generally recognized standards for preparatory training do not yet exist, psychologists nevertheless take reasonable steps to ensure the competence of their work and to protect clients/patients, students, supervisees, research participants, organizational clients, and others from harm.

(f) When assuming forensic roles, psychologists are or become reasonably familiar with the judicial or administrative rules governing their roles.

2.02 Providing Services in Emergencies

In emergencies, when psychologists provide services to individuals for whom other mental health services are not available and for which psychologists have not obtained the necessary training, psychologists may provide such services in order to ensure that services are not denied. The services are discontinued as soon as the emergency has ended or appropriate services are available.

2.03 Maintaining Competence

Psychologists undertake ongoing efforts to develop and maintain their competence.

2.04 Bases for Scientific and Professional Judgments

Psychologists' work is based upon established scientific and professional knowledge of the discipline. (See also Standards 2.01e, Boundaries of Competence, and 10.01b, Informed Consent to Therapy.)

2.05 Delegation of Work to Others

Psychologists who delegate work to employees, supervisees, or research or teaching assistants or who use the services of others, such as interpreters, take reasonable steps to (1) avoid delegating such work to persons who have a multiple relationship with those being served that would likely lead to exploitation or loss of objectivity; (2) authorize only those responsibilities that such persons can be expected to perform competently on the basis of their education, training, or experience, either independently or with the level of supervision being provided; and (3) see that such persons perform these services competently. (See also Standards 2.02, Providing Services in Emergencies; 3.05, Multiple Relationships; 4.01, Maintaining Confidentiality; 9.01, Bases for Assessments; 9.02, Use of Assessments; 9.03, Informed Consent in Assessments; and 9.07, Assessment by Unqualified Persons.)

2.06 Personal Problems and Conflicts

(a) Psychologists refrain from initiating an activity when they know or should know that there is a substantial likelihood that their personal problems will prevent them from performing their work-related activities in a competent manner.

(b) When psychologists become aware of personal problems that may interfere with their performing work-related duties adequately, they take appropriate measures, such as obtaining professional consultation or assistance, and determine whether they should limit, suspend, or terminate their work-related duties. (See also Standard 10.10, Terminating Therapy.)

3. Human Relations

3.01 Unfair Discrimination

In their work-related activities, psychologists do not engage in unfair discrimination based on age, gender, gender identity, race, ethnicity, culture, national origin, religion, sexual orientation, disability, socioeconomic status, or any basis proscribed by law.

3.02 Sexual Harassment

Psychologists do not engage in sexual harassment. Sexual harassment is sexual solicitation, physical advances, or verbal or nonverbal conduct that is sexual in nature, that occurs in connection with the psychologist's activities or roles as a psychologist, and that either (1) is unwelcome, is offensive, or creates a hostile workplace or educational environment, and the psychologist knows or is told this or (2) is sufficiently severe or intense to be abusive to a reasonable person in the context. Sexual harassment can consist of a single intense or severe act or of multiple persistent or pervasive acts. (See also Standard 1.08, Unfair Discrimination Against Complainants and Respondents.)

3.03 Other Harassment
Psychologists do not knowingly engage in behavior that is harassing or demeaning to persons with whom they interact in their work based on factors such as those persons' age, gender, gender identity, race, ethnicity, culture, national origin, religion, sexual orientation, disability, language, or socioeconomic status.

3.04 Avoiding Harm
Psychologists take reasonable steps to avoid harming their clients/patients, students, supervisees, research participants, organizational clients, and others with whom they work, and to minimize harm where it is foreseeable and unavoidable.

3.05 Multiple Relationships
(a) A multiple relationship occurs when a psychologist is in a professional role with a person and (1) at the same time is in another role with the same person, (2) at the same time is in a relationship with a person closely associated with or related to the person with whom the psychologist has the professional relationship, or (3) promises to enter into another relationship in the future with the person or a person closely associated with or related to the person.

A psychologist refrains from entering into a multiple relationship if the multiple relationship could reasonably be expected to impair the psychologist's objectivity, competence, or effectiveness in performing his or her functions as a psychologist, or otherwise risks exploitation or harm to the person with whom the professional relationship exists.

Multiple relationships that would not reasonably be expected to cause impairment or risk exploitation or harm are not unethical.

(b) If a psychologist finds that, due to unforeseen factors, a potentially harmful multiple relationship has arisen, the psychologist takes reasonable steps to resolve it with due regard for the best interests of the affected person and maximal compliance with the Ethics Code.

(c) When psychologists are required by law, institutional policy, or extraordinary circumstances to serve in more than one role in judicial or administrative proceedings, at the outset they clarify role expectations and the extent of confidentiality and thereafter as changes occur. (See also Standards 3.04, Avoiding Harm, and 3.07, Third-Party Requests for Services.)

3.06 Conflict of Interest
Psychologists refrain from taking on a professional role when personal, scientific, professional, legal, financial, or other interests or relationships could reasonably be expected to (1) impair their objectivity, competence, or effectiveness in performing their functions as psychologists or (2) expose the person or organization with whom the professional relationship exists to harm or exploitation.

3.07 Third-Party Requests for Services
When psychologists agree to provide services to a person or entity at the request of a third party, psychologists attempt to clarify at the outset of the service the nature of the relationship with all individuals or organizations involved. This clarification includes the role of the psychologist (e.g., therapist, consultant, diagnostician, or expert witness), an identification of who is the client, the probable uses of the services provided or the information obtained, and the fact that there may be limits to confidentiality. (See also Standards 3.05, Multiple Relationships, and 4.02, Discussing the Limits of Confidentiality.)

3.08 Exploitative Relationships
Psychologists do not exploit persons over whom they have supervisory, evaluative, or other authority such as clients/patients, students, supervisees, research participants, and employees. (See also

Standards 3.05, Multiple Relationships; 6.04, Fees and Financial Arrangements; 6.05, Barter With Clients/Patients; 7.07, Sexual Relationships With Students and Supervisees; 10.05, Sexual Intimacies With Current Therapy Clients/Patients; 10.06, Sexual Intimacies With Relatives or Significant Others of Current Therapy Clients/Patients; 10.07, Therapy With Former Sexual Partners; and 10.08, Sexual Intimacies With Former Therapy Clients/Patients.)

3.09 Cooperation With Other Professionals
When indicated and professionally appropriate, psychologists cooperate with other professionals in order to serve their clients/patients effectively and appropriately. (See also Standard 4.05, Disclosures.)

3.10 Informed Consent
(a) When psychologists conduct research or provide assessment, therapy, counseling, or consulting services in person or via electronic transmission or other forms of communication, they obtain the informed consent of the individual or individuals using language that is reasonably understandable to that person or persons except when conducting such activities without consent is mandated by law or governmental regulation or as otherwise provided in this Ethics Code. (See also Standards 8.02, Informed Consent to Research; 9.03, Informed Consent in Assessments; and 10.01, Informed Consent to Therapy.)

(b) For persons who are legally incapable of giving informed consent, psychologists nevertheless (1) provide an appropriate explanation, (2) seek the individual's assent, (3) consider such persons' preferences and best interests, and (4) obtain appropriate permission from a legally authorized person, if such substitute consent is permitted or required by law. When consent by a legally authorized person is not permitted or required by law, psychologists take reasonable steps to protect the individual's rights and welfare.

(c) When psychological services are court ordered or otherwise mandated, psychologists inform the individual of the nature of the anticipated services, including whether the services are court ordered or mandated and any limits of confidentiality, before proceeding.

(d) Psychologists appropriately document written or oral consent, permission, and assent. (See also Standards 8.02, Informed Consent to Research; 9.03, Informed Consent in Assessments; and 10.01, Informed Consent to Therapy.)

3.11 Psychological Services Delivered To or Through Organizations
(a) Psychologists delivering services to or through organizations provide information beforehand to clients and when appropriate those directly affected by the services about (1) the nature and objectives of the services, (2) the intended recipients, (3) which of the individuals are clients, (4) the relationship the psychologist will have with each person and the organization, (5) the probable uses of services provided and information obtained, (6) who will have access to the information, and (7) limits of confidentiality. As soon as feasible, they provide information about the results and conclusions of such services to appropriate persons.

(b) If psychologists will be precluded by law or by organizational roles from providing such information to particular individuals or groups, they so inform those individuals or groups at the outset of the service.

3.12 Interruption of Psychological Services
Unless otherwise covered by contract, psychologists make reasonable efforts to plan for facilitating services in the event that psychological services are interrupted by factors such as the psychologist's illness, death, unavailability, relocation, or retirement or by the client's/patient's relocation or financial limitations. (See also Standard 6.02c, Maintenance, Dissemination, and Disposal of Confidential Records of Professional and Scientific Work.)

4. Privacy And Confidentiality

4.01 Maintaining Confidentiality
Psychologists have a primary obligation and take reasonable precautions to protect confidential information obtained through or stored in any medium, recognizing that the extent and limits of confidentiality may be regulated by law or established by institutional rules or professional or scientific relationship. (See also Standard 2.05, Delegation of Work to Others.)

4.02 Discussing the Limits of Confidentiality
(a) Psychologists discuss with persons (including, to the extent feasible, persons who are legally incapable of giving informed consent and their legal representatives) and organizations with whom they establish a scientific or professional relationship (1) the relevant limits of confidentiality and (2) the foreseeable uses of the information generated through their psychological activities. (See also Standard 3.10, Informed Consent.)

(b) Unless it is not feasible or is contraindicated, the discussion of confidentiality occurs at the outset of the relationship and thereafter as new circumstances may warrant.

(c) Psychologists who offer services, products, or information via electronic transmission inform clients/patients of the risks to privacy and limits of confidentiality.

4.03 Recording
Before recording the voices or images of individuals to whom they provide services, psychologists obtain permission from all such persons or their legal representatives. (See also Standards 8.03, Informed Consent for Recording Voices and Images in Research; 8.05, Dispensing With Informed Consent for Research; and 8.07, Deception in Research.)

4.04 Minimizing Intrusions on Privacy
(a) Psychologists include in written and oral reports and consultations, only information germane to the purpose for which the communication is made.

(b) Psychologists discuss confidential information obtained in their work only for appropriate scientific or professional purposes and only with persons clearly concerned with such matters.

4.05 Disclosures
(a) Psychologists may disclose confidential information with the appropriate consent of the organizational client, the individual client/patient, or another legally authorized person on behalf of the client/patient unless prohibited by law.

(b) Psychologists disclose confidential information without the consent of the individual only as mandated by law, or where permitted by law for a valid purpose such as to (1) provide needed professional services; (2) obtain appropriate professional consultations; (3) protect the client/patient, psychologist, or others from harm; or (4) obtain payment for services from a client/patient, in which instance disclosure is limited to the minimum that is necessary to achieve the purpose. (See also Standard 6.04e, Fees and Financial Arrangements.)

4.06 Consultations
When consulting with colleagues, (1) psychologists do not disclose confidential information that reasonably could lead to the identification of a client/patient, research participant, or other person or organization with whom they have a confidential relationship unless they have obtained the prior consent of the person or organization or the disclosure cannot be avoided, and (2) they disclose information only to the extent necessary to achieve the purposes of the consultation. (See also Standard 4.01, Maintaining Confidentiality.)

4.07 Use of Confidential Information for Didactic or Other Purposes
Psychologists do not disclose in their writings, lectures, or other public media, confidential, personally identifiable information concerning their clients/patients, students, research participants, organizational clients, or other recipients of their services that they obtained during the course of their work, unless (1) they take reasonable steps to disguise the person or organization, (2) the person or organization has consented in writing, or (3) there is legal authorization for doing so.

5. Advertising and Other Public Statements

5.01 Avoidance of False or Deceptive Statements
(a) Public statements include but are not limited to paid or unpaid advertising, product endorsements, grant applications, licensing applications, other credentialing applications, brochures, printed matter, directory listings, personal resumes or curricula vitae, or comments for use in media such as print or electronic transmission, statements in legal proceedings, lectures and public oral presentations, and published materials. Psychologists do not knowingly make public statements that are false, deceptive, or fraudulent concerning their research, practice, or other work activities or those of persons or organizations with which they are affiliated.

(b) Psychologists do not make false, deceptive, or fraudulent statements concerning (1) their training, experience, or competence; (2) their academic degrees; (3) their credentials; (4) their institutional or association affiliations; (5) their services; (6) the scientific or clinical basis for, or results or degree of success of, their services; (7) their fees; or (8) their publications or research findings.

(c) Psychologists claim degrees as credentials for their health services only if those degrees (1) were earned from a regionally accredited educational institution or (2) were the basis for psychology licensure by the state in which they practice.

5.02 Statements by Others
(a) Psychologists who engage others to create or place public statements that promote their professional practice, products, or activities retain professional responsibility for such statements.

(b) Psychologists do not compensate employees of press, radio, television, or other communication media in return for publicity in a news item. (See also Standard 1.01, Misuse of Psychologists' Work.)

(c) A paid advertisement relating to psychologists' activities must be identified or clearly recognizable as such.

5.03 Descriptions of Workshops and Non-Degree-Granting Educational Programs
To the degree to which they exercise control, psychologists responsible for announcements, catalogs, brochures, or advertisements describing workshops, seminars, or other non-degree-granting educational programs ensure that they accurately describe the audience for which the program is intended, the educational objectives, the presenters, and the fees involved.

5.04 Media Presentations
When psychologists provide public advice or comment via print, internet, or other electronic transmission, they take precautions to ensure that statements (1) are based on their professional knowledge, training, or experience in accord with appropriate psychological literature and practice; (2) are otherwise consistent with this Ethics Code; and (3) do not indicate that a professional relationship has been established with the recipient. (See also Standard 2.04, Bases for Scientific and Professional Judgments.)

5.05 Testimonials
Psychologists do not solicit testimonials from current therapy clients/patients or other persons who because of their particular circumstances are vulnerable to undue influence.

5.06 In-Person Solicitation
Psychologists do not engage, directly or through agents, in uninvited in-person solicitation of business from actual or potential therapy clients/patients or other persons who because of their particular

circumstances are vulnerable to undue influence. However, this prohibition does not preclude (1) attempting to implement appropriate collateral contacts for the purpose of benefiting an already engaged therapy client/patient or (2) providing disaster or community outreach services.

6. Record Keeping and Fees

6.01 Documentation of Professional and Scientific Work and Maintenance of Records
Psychologists create, and to the extent the records are under their control, maintain, disseminate, store, retain, and dispose of records and data relating to their professional and scientific work in order to (1) facilitate provision of services later by them or by other professionals, (2) allow for replication of research design and analyses, (3) meet institutional requirements, (4) ensure accuracy of billing and payments, and (5) ensure compliance with law. (See also Standard 4.01, Maintaining Confidentiality.)

6.02 Maintenance, Dissemination, and Disposal of Confidential Records of Professional and Scientific Work
(a) Psychologists maintain confidentiality in creating, storing, accessing, transferring, and disposing of records under their control, whether these are written, automated, or in any other medium. (See also Standards 4.01, Maintaining Confidentiality, and 6.01, Documentation of Professional and Scientific Work and Maintenance of Records.)

(b) If confidential information concerning recipients of psychological services is entered into databases or systems of records available to persons whose access has not been consented to by the recipient, psychologists use coding or other techniques to avoid the inclusion of personal identifiers.

(c) Psychologists make plans in advance to facilitate the appropriate transfer and to protect the confidentiality of records and data in the event of psychologists' withdrawal from positions or practice. (See also Standards 3.12, Interruption of Psychological Services, and 10.09, Interruption of Therapy.)

6.03 Withholding Records for Nonpayment
Psychologists may not withhold records under their control that are requested and needed for a client's/patient's emergency treatment solely because payment has not been received.

6.04 Fees and Financial Arrangements
(a) As early as is feasible in a professional or scientific relationship, psychologists and recipients of psychological services reach an agreement specifying compensation and billing arrangements.

(b) Psychologists' fee practices are consistent with law.

(c) Psychologists do not misrepresent their fees.

(d) If limitations to services can be anticipated because of limitations in financing, this is discussed with the recipient of services as early as is feasible. (See also Standards 10.09, Interruption of Therapy, and 10.10, Terminating Therapy.)

(e) If the recipient of services does not pay for services as agreed, and if psychologists intend to use collection agencies or legal measures to collect the fees, psychologists first inform the person that such measures will be taken and provide that person an opportunity to make prompt payment. (See also Standards 4.05, Disclosures; 6.03, Withholding Records for Nonpayment; and 10.01, Informed Consent to Therapy.)

6.05 Barter With Clients/Patients
Barter is the acceptance of goods, services, or other nonmonetary remuneration from clients/patients in return for psychological services. Psychologists may barter only if (1) it is not clinically contraindicated, and (2) the resulting arrangement is not exploitative. (See also Standards 3.05, Multiple Relationships, and 6.04, Fees and Financial Arrangements.)

6.06 Accuracy in Reports to Payors and Funding Sources

In their reports to payors for services or sources of research funding, psychologists take reasonable steps to ensure the accurate reporting of the nature of the service provided or research conducted, the fees, charges, or payments, and where applicable, the identity of the provider, the findings, and the diagnosis. (See also Standards 4.01, Maintaining Confidentiality; 4.04, Minimizing Intrusions on Privacy; and 4.05, Disclosures.)

6.07 Referrals and Fees

When psychologists pay, receive payment from, or divide fees with another professional, other than in an employer-employee relationship, the payment to each is based on the services provided (clinical, consultative, administrative, or other) and is not based on the referral itself. (See also Standard 3.09, Cooperation With Other Professionals.)

7. Education and Training

7.01 Design of Education and Training Programs

Psychologists responsible for education and training programs take reasonable steps to ensure that the programs are designed to provide the appropriate knowledge and proper experiences, and to meet the requirements for licensure, certification, or other goals for which claims are made by the program. (See also Standard 5.03, Descriptions of Workshops and Non-Degree-Granting Educational Programs.)

7.02 Descriptions of Education and Training Programs

Psychologists responsible for education and training programs take reasonable steps to ensure that there is a current and accurate description of the program content (including participation in required course- or program-related counseling, psychotherapy, experiential groups, consulting projects, or community service), training goals and objectives, stipends and benefits, and requirements that must be met for satisfactory completion of the program. This information must be made readily available to all interested parties.

7.03 Accuracy in Teaching

(a) Psychologists take reasonable steps to ensure that course syllabi are accurate regarding the subject matter to be covered, bases for evaluating progress, and the nature of course experiences. This standard does not preclude an instructor from modifying course content or requirements when the instructor considers it pedagogically necessary or desirable, so long as students are made aware of these modifications in a manner that enables them to fulfill course requirements. (See also Standard 5.01, Avoidance of False or Deceptive Statements.)

(b) When engaged in teaching or training, psychologists present psychological information accurately. (See also Standard 2.03, Maintaining Competence.)

7.04 Student Disclosure of Personal Information

Psychologists do not require students or supervisees to disclose personal information in course- or program-related activities, either orally or in writing, regarding sexual history, history of abuse and neglect, psychological treatment, and relationships with parents, peers, and spouses or significant others except if (1) the program or training facility has clearly identified this requirement in its admissions and program materials or (2) the information is necessary to evaluate or obtain assistance for students whose personal problems could reasonably be judged to be preventing them from performing their training- or professionally related activities in a competent manner or posing a threat to the students or others.

7.05 Mandatory Individual or Group Therapy

(a) When individual or group therapy is a program or course requirement, psychologists responsible for that program allow students in undergraduate and graduate programs the option of selecting such therapy from practitioners unaffiliated with the program. (See also Standard 7.02, Descriptions of Education and Training Programs.)

(b) Faculty who are or are likely to be responsible for evaluating students' academic performance do not themselves provide that therapy. (See also Standard 3.05, Multiple Relationships.)

7.06 Assessing Student and Supervisee Performance

(a) In academic and supervisory relationships, psychologists establish a timely and specific process for providing feedback to students and supervisees. Information regarding the process is provided to the student at the beginning of supervision.

(b) Psychologists evaluate students and supervisees on the basis of their actual performance on relevant and established program requirements.

7.07 Sexual Relationships With Students and Supervisees

Psychologists do not engage in sexual relationships with students or supervisees who are in their department, agency, or training center or over whom psychologists have or are likely to have evaluative authority. (See also Standard 3.05, Multiple Relationships.)

8. Research and Publication

8.01 Institutional Approval

When institutional approval is required, psychologists provide accurate information about their research proposals and obtain approval prior to conducting the research. They conduct the research in accordance with the approved research protocol.

8.02 Informed Consent to Research

(a) When obtaining informed consent as required in Standard 3.10, Informed Consent, psychologists inform participants about (1) the purpose of the research, expected duration, and procedures; (2) their right to decline to participate and to withdraw from the research once participation has begun; (3) the foreseeable consequences of declining or withdrawing; (4) reasonably foreseeable factors that may be expected to influence their willingness to participate such as potential risks, discomfort, or adverse effects; (5) any prospective research benefits; (6) limits of confidentiality; (7) incentives for participation; and (8) whom to contact for questions about the research and research participants' rights. They provide opportunity for the prospective participants to ask questions and receive answers. (See also Standards 8.03, Informed Consent for Recording Voices and Images in Research; 8.05, Dispensing With Informed Consent for Research; and 8.07, Deception in Research.)

(b) Psychologists conducting intervention research involving the use of experimental treatments clarify to participants at the outset of the research (1) the experimental nature of the treatment; (2) the services that will or will not be available to the control group(s) if appropriate; (3) the means by which assignment to treatment and control groups will be made; (4) available treatment alternatives if an individual does not wish to participate in the research or wishes to withdraw once a study has begun; and (5) compensation for or monetary costs of participating including, if appropriate, whether reimbursement from the participant or a third-party payor will be sought. (See also Standard 8.02a, Informed Consent to Research.)

8.03 Informed Consent for Recording Voices and Images in Research

Psychologists obtain informed consent from research participants prior to recording their voices or images for data collection unless (1) the research consists solely of naturalistic observations in public places, and it is not anticipated that the recording will be used in a manner that could cause personal identification or harm, or (2) the research design includes deception, and consent for the use of the recording is obtained during debriefing. (See also Standard 8.07, Deception in Research.)

8.04 Client/Patient, Student, and Subordinate Research Participants

(a) When psychologists conduct research with clients/patients, students, or subordinates as participants, psychologists take steps to protect the prospective participants from adverse consequences of declining or withdrawing from participation.

(b) When research participation is a course requirement or an opportunity for extra credit, the prospective participant is given the choice of equitable alternative activities.

8.05 Dispensing With Informed Consent for Research

Psychologists may dispense with informed consent only (1) where research would not reasonably be assumed to create distress or harm and involves (a) the study of normal educational practices, curricula, or classroom management methods conducted in educational settings; (b) only anonymous questionnaires, naturalistic observations, or archival research for which disclosure of responses would not place participants at risk of criminal or civil liability or damage their financial standing, employability, or reputation, and confidentiality is protected; or (c) the study of factors related to job or organization effectiveness conducted in organizational settings for which there is no risk to participants' employability, and confidentiality is protected or (2) where otherwise permitted by law or federal or institutional regulations.

8.06 Offering Inducements for Research Participation

(a) Psychologists make reasonable efforts to avoid offering excessive or inappropriate financial or other inducements for research participation when such inducements are likely to coerce participation.

(b) When offering professional services as an inducement for research participation, psychologists clarify the nature of the services, as well as the risks, obligations, and limitations. (See also Standard 6.05, Barter With Clients/Patients.)

8.07 Deception in Research

(a) Psychologists do not conduct a study involving deception unless they have determined that the use of deceptive techniques is justified by the study's significant prospective scientific, educational, or applied value and that effective nondeceptive alternative procedures are not feasible.

(b) Psychologists do not deceive prospective participants about research that is reasonably expected to cause physical pain or severe emotional distress.

(c) Psychologists explain any deception that is an integral feature of the design and conduct of an experiment to participants as early as is feasible, preferably at the conclusion of their participation, but no later than at the conclusion of the data collection, and permit participants to withdraw their data. (See also Standard 8.08, Debriefing.)

8.08 Debriefing

(a) Psychologists provide a prompt opportunity for participants to obtain appropriate information about the nature, results, and conclusions of the research, and they take reasonable steps to correct any misconceptions that participants may have of which the psychologists are aware.

(b) If scientific or humane values justify delaying or withholding this information, psychologists take reasonable measures to reduce the risk of harm.

(c) When psychologists become aware that research procedures have harmed a participant, they take reasonable steps to minimize the harm.

8.09 Humane Care and Use of Animals in Research

(a) Psychologists acquire, care for, use, and dispose of animals in compliance with current federal, state, and local laws and regulations, and with professional standards.

(b) Psychologists trained in research methods and experienced in the care of laboratory animals supervise all procedures involving animals and are responsible for ensuring appropriate consideration of their comfort, health, and humane treatment.

(c) Psychologists ensure that all individuals under their supervision who are using animals have received instruction in research methods and in the care, maintenance, and handling of the species being used, to the extent appropriate to their role. (See also Standard 2.05, Delegation of Work to Others.)

(d) Psychologists make reasonable efforts to minimize the discomfort, infection, illness, and pain of animal subjects.

(e) Psychologists use a procedure subjecting animals to pain, stress, or privation only when an alternative procedure is unavailable and the goal is justified by its prospective scientific, educational, or applied value.

(f) Psychologists perform surgical procedures under appropriate anesthesia and follow techniques to avoid infection and minimize pain during and after surgery.

(g) When it is appropriate that an animal's life be terminated, psychologists proceed rapidly, with an effort to minimize pain and in accordance with accepted procedures.

8.10 Reporting Research Results
(a) Psychologists do not fabricate data. (See also Standard 5.01a, Avoidance of False or Deceptive Statements.)

(b) If psychologists discover significant errors in their published data, they take reasonable steps to correct such errors in a correction, retraction, erratum, or other appropriate publication means.

8.11 Plagiarism
Psychologists do not present portions of another's work or data as their own, even if the other work or data source is cited occasionally.

8.12 Publication Credit
(a) Psychologists take responsibility and credit, including authorship credit, only for work they have actually performed or to which they have substantially contributed. (See also Standard 8.12b, Publication Credit.)

(b) Principal authorship and other publication credits accurately reflect the relative scientific or professional contributions of the individuals involved, regardless of their relative status. Mere possession of an institutional position, such as department chair, does not justify authorship credit. Minor contributions to the research or to the writing for publications are acknowledged appropriately, such as in footnotes or in an introductory statement.

(c) Except under exceptional circumstances, a student is listed as principal author on any multiple-authored article that is substantially based on the student's doctoral dissertation. Faculty advisors discuss publication credit with students as early as feasible and throughout the research and publication process as appropriate. (See also Standard 8.12b, Publication Credit.)

8.13 Duplicate Publication of Data
Psychologists do not publish, as original data, data that have been previously published. This does not preclude republishing data when they are accompanied by proper acknowledgment.

8.14 Sharing Research Data for Verification
(a) After research results are published, psychologists do not withhold the data on which their conclusions are based from other competent professionals who seek to verify the substantive claims through reanalysis and who intend to use such data only for that purpose, provided that the confidentiality of the participants can be protected and unless legal rights concerning proprietary data preclude their release. This does not preclude psychologists from requiring that such individuals or groups be responsible for costs associated with the provision of such information.

(b) Psychologists who request data from other psychologists to verify the substantive claims through reanalysis may use shared data only for the declared purpose. Requesting psychologists obtain prior written agreement for all other uses of the data.

8.15 Reviewers

Psychologists who review material submitted for presentation, publication, grant, or research proposal review respect the confidentiality of and the proprietary rights in such information of those who submitted it.

9. Assessment

9.01 Bases for Assessments

(a) Psychologists base the opinions contained in their recommendations, reports, and diagnostic or evaluative statements, including forensic testimony, on information and techniques sufficient to substantiate their findings. (See also Standard 2.04, Bases for Scientific and Professional Judgments.)

(b) Except as noted in 9.01c, psychologists provide opinions of the psychological characteristics of individuals only after they have conducted an examination of the individuals adequate to support their statements or conclusions. When, despite reasonable efforts, such an examination is not practical, psychologists document the efforts they made and the result of those efforts, clarify the probable impact of their limited information on the reliability and validity of their opinions, and appropriately limit the nature and extent of their conclusions or recommendations. (See also Standards 2.01, Boundaries of Competence, and 9.06, Interpreting Assessment Results.)

(c) When psychologists conduct a record review or provide consultation or supervision and an individual examination is not warranted or necessary for the opinion, psychologists explain this and the sources of information on which they based their conclusions and recommendations.

9.02 Use of Assessments

(a) Psychologists administer, adapt, score, interpret, or use assessment techniques, interviews, tests, or instruments in a manner and for purposes that are appropriate in light of the research on or evidence of the usefulness and proper application of the techniques.

(b) Psychologists use assessment instruments whose validity and reliability have been established for use with members of the population tested. When such validity or reliability has not been established, psychologists describe the strengths and limitations of test results and interpretation.

(c) Psychologists use assessment methods that are appropriate to an individual's language preference and competence, unless the use of an alternative language is relevant to the assessment issues.

9.03 Informed Consent in Assessments

(a) Psychologists obtain informed consent for assessments, evaluations, or diagnostic services, as described in Standard 3.10, Informed Consent, except when (1) testing is mandated by law or governmental regulations; (2) informed consent is implied because testing is conducted as a routine educational, institutional, or organizational activity (e.g., when participants voluntarily agree to assessment when applying for a job); or (3) one purpose of the testing is to evaluate decisional capacity. Informed consent includes an explanation of the nature and purpose of the assessment, fees, involvement of third parties, and limits of confidentiality and sufficient opportunity for the client/patient to ask questions and receive answers.

(b) Psychologists inform persons with questionable capacity to consent or for whom testing is mandated by law or governmental regulations about the nature and purpose of the proposed assessment services, using language that is reasonably understandable to the person being assessed.

(c) Psychologists using the services of an interpreter obtain informed consent from the client/patient to use that interpreter, ensure that confidentiality of test results and test security are maintained, and include in their recommendations, reports, and diagnostic or evaluative statements, including forensic testimony, discussion of any limitations on the data obtained. (See also Standards 2.05, Delegation of Work to Others; 4.01, Maintaining Confidentiality; 9.01, Bases for Assessments; 9.06, Interpreting Assessment Results; and 9.07, Assessment by Unqualified Persons.)

9.04 Release of Test Data

(a) The term *test data* refers to raw and scaled scores, client/patient responses to test questions or stimuli, and psychologists' notes and recordings concerning client/patient statements and behavior during an examination. Those portions of test materials that include client/patient responses are included in the definition of *test data*. Pursuant to a client/patient release, psychologists provide test data to the client/patient or other persons identified in the release. Psychologists may refrain from releasing test data to protect a client/patient or others from substantial harm or misuse or misrepresentation of the data or the test, recognizing that in many instances release of confidential information under these circumstances is regulated by law. (See also Standard 9.11, Maintaining Test Security.)

(b) In the absence of a client/patient release, psychologists provide test data only as required by law or court order.

9.05 Test Construction

Psychologists who develop tests and other assessment techniques use appropriate psychometric procedures and current scientific or professional knowledge for test design, standardization, validation, reduction or elimination of bias, and recommendations for use.

9.06 Interpreting Assessment Results

When interpreting assessment results, including automated interpretations, psychologists take into account the purpose of the assessment as well as the various test factors, test-taking abilities, and other characteristics of the person being assessed, such as situational, personal, linguistic, and cultural differences, that might affect psychologists' judgments or reduce the accuracy of their interpretations. They indicate any significant limitations of their interpretations. (See also Standards 2.01b and c, Boundaries of Competence, and 3.01, Unfair Discrimination.)

9.07 Assessment by Unqualified Persons

Psychologists do not promote the use of psychological assessment techniques by unqualified persons, except when such use is conducted for training purposes with appropriate supervision. (See also Standard 2.05, Delegation of Work to Others.)

9.08 Obsolete Tests and Outdated Test Results

(a) Psychologists do not base their assessment or intervention decisions or recommendations on data or test results that are outdated for the current purpose.

(b) Psychologists do not base such decisions or recommendations on tests and measures that are obsolete and not useful for the current purpose.

9.09 Test Scoring and Interpretation Services

(a) Psychologists who offer assessment or scoring services to other professionals accurately describe the purpose, norms, validity, reliability, and applications of the procedures and any special qualifications applicable to their use.

(b) Psychologists select scoring and interpretation services (including automated services) on the basis of evidence of the validity of the program and procedures as well as on other appropriate considerations. (See also Standard 2.01b and c, Boundaries of Competence.)

(c) Psychologists retain responsibility for the appropriate application, interpretation, and use of assessment instruments, whether they score and interpret such tests themselves or use automated or other services.

9.10 Explaining Assessment Results

Regardless of whether the scoring and interpretation are done by psychologists, by employees or assistants, or by automated or other outside services, psychologists take reasonable steps to ensure that explanations of results are given to the individual or designated representative unless the nature of the relationship precludes provision of an explanation of results (such as in some organizational consulting, preemployment or security screenings, and forensic evaluations), and this fact has been clearly explained to the person being assessed in advance.

9.11. Maintaining Test Security

The term *test materials* refers to manuals, instruments, protocols, and test questions or stimuli and does not include *test data* as defined in Standard 9.04, Release of Test Data. Psychologists make reasonable efforts to maintain the integrity and security of test materials and other assessment techniques consistent with law and contractual obligations, and in a manner that permits adherence to this Ethics Code.

10. Therapy

10.01 Informed Consent to Therapy

(a) When obtaining informed consent to therapy as required in Standard 3.10, Informed Consent, psychologists inform clients/patients as early as is feasible in the therapeutic relationship about the nature and anticipated course of therapy, fees, involvement of third parties, and limits of confidentiality and provide sufficient opportunity for the client/patient to ask questions and receive answers. (See also Standards 4.02, Discussing the Limits of Confidentiality, and 6.04, Fees and Financial Arrangements.)

(b) When obtaining informed consent for treatment for which generally recognized techniques and procedures have not been established, psychologists inform their clients/patients of the developing nature of the treatment, the potential risks involved, alternative treatments that may be available, and the voluntary nature of their participation. (See also Standards 2.01e, Boundaries of Competence, and 3.10, Informed Consent.)

(c) When the therapist is a trainee and the legal responsibility for the treatment provided resides with the supervisor, the client/patient, as part of the informed consent procedure, is informed that the therapist is in training and is being supervised and is given the name of the supervisor.

10.02 Therapy Involving Couples or Families

(a) When psychologists agree to provide services to several persons who have a relationship (such as spouses, significant others, or parents and children), they take reasonable steps to clarify at the outset (1) which of the individuals are clients/patients and (2) the relationship the psychologist will have with each person. This clarification includes the psychologist's role and the probable uses of the services provided or the information obtained. (See also Standard 4.02, Discussing the Limits of Confidentiality.)

(b) If it becomes apparent that psychologists may be called on to perform potentially conflicting roles (such as family therapist and then witness for one party in divorce proceedings), psychologists take reasonable steps to clarify and modify, or withdraw from, roles appropriately. (See also Standard 3.05c, Multiple Relationships.)

10.03 Group Therapy

When psychologists provide services to several persons in a group setting, they describe at the outset the roles and responsibilities of all parties and the limits of confidentiality.

10.04 Providing Therapy to Those Served by Others

In deciding whether to offer or provide services to those already receiving mental health services elsewhere, psychologists carefully consider the treatment issues and the potential client's/patient's welfare. Psychologists discuss these issues with the client/patient or another legally authorized person on behalf of the client/patient in order to minimize the risk of confusion and conflict, consult with the other service providers when appropriate, and proceed with caution and sensitivity to the therapeutic issues.

10.05 Sexual Intimacies With Current Therapy Clients/Patients

Psychologists do not engage in sexual intimacies with current therapy clients/patients.

10.06 Sexual Intimacies With Relatives or Significant Others of Current Therapy Clients/Patients

Psychologists do not engage in sexual intimacies with individuals they know to be close relatives, guardians, or significant others of current clients/patients. Psychologists do not terminate therapy to circumvent this standard.

10.07 Therapy With Former Sexual Partners

Psychologists do not accept as therapy clients/patients persons with whom they have engaged in sexual intimacies.

10.08 Sexual Intimacies With Former Therapy Clients/Patients

(a) Psychologists do not engage in sexual intimacies with former clients/patients for at least two years after cessation or termination of therapy.

(b) Psychologists do not engage in sexual intimacies with former clients/patients even after a two-year interval except in the most unusual circumstances. Psychologists who engage in such activity after the two years following cessation or termination of therapy and of having no sexual contact with the former client/patient bear the burden of demonstrating that there has been no exploitation, in light of all relevant factors, including (1) the amount of time that has passed since therapy terminated; (2) the nature, duration, and intensity of the therapy; (3) the circumstances of termination; (4) the client's/patient's personal history; (5) the client's/patient's current mental status; (6) the likelihood of adverse impact on the client/patient; and (7) any statements or actions made by the therapist during the course of therapy suggesting or inviting the possibility of a posttermination sexual or romantic relationship with the client/patient. (See also Standard 3.05, Multiple Relationships.)

10.09 Interruption of Therapy

When entering into employment or contractual relationships, psychologists make reasonable efforts to provide for orderly and appropriate resolution of responsibility for client/patient care in the event that the employment or contractual relationship ends, with paramount consideration given to the welfare of the client/patient. (See also Standard 3.12, Interruption of Psychological Services.)

10.10 Terminating Therapy

(a) Psychologists terminate therapy when it becomes reasonably clear that the client/patient no longer needs the service, is not likely to benefit, or is being harmed by continued service.

(b) Psychologists may terminate therapy when threatened or otherwise endangered by the client/patient or another person with whom the client/patient has a relationship.

(c) Except where precluded by the actions of clients/patients or third-party payors, prior to termination psychologists provide pretermination counseling and suggest alternative service providers as appropriate.

History and Effective Date Footnote

This version of the APA Ethics Code was adopted by the American Psychological Association's Council of Representatives during its meeting, August 21, 2002, and is effective beginning June 1, 2003. Inquiries concerning the substance or interpretation of the APA Ethics Code should be addressed to the Director, Office of Ethics, American Psychological Association, 750 First Street, NE, Washington, DC 20002-4242. The Ethics Code and information regarding the Code can be found on the APA web site, http://www.apa.org/ethics.   The standards in this Ethics Code will be used to adjudicate complaints brought concerning alleged conduct occurring on or after the effective date. Complaints regarding conduct occurring prior to the effective date will be adjudicated on the basis of the version of the Ethics Code that was in effect at the time the conduct occurred.

The APA has previously published its Ethics Code as follows:

American Psychological Association. (1953). Ethical standards of psychologists. Washington, DC: Author.

American Psychological Association. (1959). Ethical standards of psychologists. American Psychologist, 14, 279-282.

American Psychological Association. (1963). Ethical standards of psychologists. American Psychologist, 18, 56-60.

American Psychological Association. (1968). Ethical standards of psychologists. American Psychologist, 23, 357-361.

American Psychological Association. (1977, March). Ethical standards of psychologists. APA Monitor, 22-23.

American Psychological Association. (1979). Ethical standards of psychologists. Washington, DC: Author.

American Psychological Association. (1981). Ethical principles of psychologists. American Psychologist, 36, 633-638.

American Psychological Association. (1990). Ethical principles of psychologists (Amended June 2, 1989). American Psychologist, 45, 390-395.

American Psychological Association. (1992). Ethical principles of psychologists and code of conduct. American Psychologist, 47, 1597-1611.

Request copies of the APA's Ethical Principles of Psychologists and Code of Conduct from the APA Order Department, 750 First Street, NE, Washington, DC 20002-4242, or phone (202) 336-5510.

American School Counselor Association
Ethical Standards for School Counselors

Preamble

The American School Counselor Association (ASCA) is a professional organization whose members are certified/licensed in school counseling with unique qualifications and skills to address the academic, personal/ social and career development needs of all students. Professional school counselors are advocates, leaders, collaborators and consultants who create opportunities for equity in access and success in educational opportunities by connecting their programs to the mission of schools and subscribing to the following tenets of professional responsibility:

- Each person has the right to be respected, be treated with dignity and have access to a comprehensive school counseling program that advocates for and affirms all students from diverse populations regardless of ethnic/racial status, age, economic status, special needs, English as a second language or other language group, immigration status, sexual orientation, gender, gender identity/expression, family type, religious/spiritual identity and appearance.
- Each person has the right to receive the information and support needed to move toward self-direction and self-development and affirmation within one's group identities, with special care being given to students who have historically not received adequate educational services: students of color, low socio-economic students, students with disabilities and students with nondominant language backgrounds.
- Each person has the right to understand the full magnitude and meaning of his/her educational choices and how those choices will affect future opportunities.
- Each person has the right to privacy and thereby the right to expect the counselor-student relationship to comply with all laws, policies and ethical standards pertaining to confidentiality in the school setting.

In this document, ASCA specifies the principles of ethical behavior necessary to maintain the high standards of integrity, leadership and professionalism among its members. The Ethical Standards for School Counselors were developed to clarify the nature of ethical responsibilities held in common by school counseling professionals.

The purposes of this document are to:

- Serve as a guide for the ethical practices of all professional school counselors regardless of level, area, population served or membership in this professional association;
- Provide self-appraisal and peer evaluations regarding counselor responsibilities to students, parents/guardians, colleagues and professional associates, schools, communities and the counseling profession; and
- Inform those served by the school counselor of acceptable counselor practices and expected professional behavior.

A.1. Responsibilities to Students

The professional school counselor:
a. Has a primary obligation to the student, who is to be treated with respect as a unique individual.
b. Is concerned with the educational, academic, career, personal and social needs and encourages the maximum development of every student.
c. Respects the student's values and beliefs and does not impose the counselor's personal values.
d. Is knowledgeable of laws, regulations and policies relating to students and strives to protect and inform students regarding their rights.

A.2. Confidentiality

The professional school counselor:

a. Informs students of the purposes, goals, techniques and rules of procedure under which they may receive counseling at or before the time when the counseling relationship is entered. Disclosure notice includes the limits of confidentiality such as the possible necessity for consulting with other professionals, privileged communication, and legal or authoritative restraints. The meaning and limits of confidentiality are defined in developmentally appropriate terms to students.

b. Keeps information confidential unless disclosure is required to prevent clear and imminent danger to the student or others or when legal requirements demand that confidential information be revealed. Counselors will consult with appropriate professionals when in doubt as to the validity of an exception.

c. In absence of state legislation expressly forbidding disclosure, considers the ethical responsibility to provide information to an identified third party who, by his/her relationship with the student, is at a high risk of contracting a disease that is commonly known to be communicable and fatal. Disclosure requires satisfaction of all of the following conditions:
   - Student identifies partner or the partner is highly identifiable
   - Counselor recommends the student notify partner and refrain from further high-risk behavior
   - Student refuses
   - Counselor informs the student of the intent to notify the partner
   - Counselor seeks legal consultation as to the legalities of informing the partner

d. Requests of the court that disclosure not be required when the release of confidential information may potentially harm a student or the counseling relationship.

e. Protects the confidentiality of students' records and releases personal data in accordance with prescribed laws and school policies. Student information stored and transmitted electronically is treated with the same care as traditional student records.

f. Protects the confidentiality of information received in the counseling relationship as specified by federal and state laws, written policies and applicable ethical standards. Such information is only to be revealed to others with the informed consent of the student, consistent with the counselor's ethical obligation.

g. Recognizes his/her primary obligation for confidentiality is to the student but balances that obligation with an understanding of the legal and inherent rights of parents/guardians to be the guiding voice in their children's lives.

A.3. Counseling Plans

The professional school counselor:

a. Provides students with a comprehensive school counseling program that includes a strong emphasis on working jointly with all students to develop academic and career goals. b. Advocates for counseling plans supporting students right to choose from the wide array of options when they leave secondary education. Such plans will be regularly reviewed to update students regarding critical information they need to make informed decisions.

A.4. Dual Relationships

The professional school counselor:

a. Avoids dual relationships that might impair his/her objectivity and increase the risk of harm to the student (e.g., counseling one's family members, close friends or associates). If a dual relationship is unavoidable, the counselor is responsible for taking action to eliminate or reduce the potential for harm. Such safeguards might include informed consent, consultation, supervision and documentation.

b. Avoids dual relationships with school personnel that might infringe on the integrity of the counselor/student relationship

A.5. Appropriate Referrals

The professional school counselor:

a. Makes referrals when necessary or appropriate to outside resources. Appropriate referrals may necessitate informing both parents/ guardians and students of applicable resources and making proper plans for transitions with minimal interruption of services. Students retain the right to discontinue the counseling relationship at any time.

A.6. Group Work

The professional school counselor:

a. Screens prospective group members and maintains an awareness of participants' needs and goals in relation to the goals of the group. The counselor takes reasonable precautions to protect members from physical and psychological harm resulting from interaction within the group.

b. Notifies parents/guardians and staff of group participation if the counselor deems it appropriate and if consistent with school board policy or practice.

c. Establishes clear expectations in the group setting and clearly states that confidentiality in group counseling cannot be guaranteed. Given the developmental and chronological ages of minors in schools, the counselor recognizes the tenuous nature of confidentiality for minors renders some topics inappropriate for group work in a school setting.

d. Follows up with group members and documents proceedings as appropriate.

A.7. Danger to Self or Others

The professional school counselor:

a. Informs parents/guardians or appropriate authorities when the student's condition indicates a clear and imminent danger to the student or others. This is to be done after careful deliberation and, where possible, after consultation with other counseling professionals.

b. Will attempt to minimize threat to a student and may choose to 1) inform the student of actions to be taken, 2) involve the student in a three-way communication with parents/guardians when breaching confidentiality, or 3) allow the student to have input as to how and to whom the breach will be made.

A.8. Student Records

The professional school counselor:

a. Maintains and secures records necessary for rendering professional services to the student as required by laws, regulations, institutional procedures and confidentiality guidelines.

b. Keeps sole-possession records separate from students' educational records in keeping with state laws.

c. Recognizes the limits of sole-possession records and understands these records are a memory aid for the creator and in absence of privilege communication may be subpoenaed and may become educational records when they 1) are shared with others in verbal or written form, 2) include information other than professional opinion or personal observations and/or 3) are made accessible to others.

d. Establishes a reasonable timeline for purging sole-possession records or case notes. Suggested guidelines include shredding sole possession records when the student transitions to the next level, transfers to another school or graduates. Careful discretion and deliberation should be applied before destroying sole-possession records that may be needed by a court of law such as notes on child abuse, suicide, sexual harassment or violence.

A.9. Evaluation, Assessment and Interpretation

The professional school counselor:

a. Adheres to all professional standards regarding selecting, administering and interpreting assessment measures and only utilizes assessment measures that are within the scope of practice for school counselors.

b. Seeks specialized training regarding the use of electronically based testing programs in administering, scoring and interpreting that may differ from that required in more traditional assessments.

c. onsiders confidentiality issues when utilizing evaluative or assessment instruments and electronically based programs.

d. Provides interpretation of the nature, purposes, results and potential impact of assessment/evaluation measures in language the student(s) can understand.

e. Monitors the use of assessment results and interpretations, and takes reasonable steps to prevent others from misusing the information.

f. Uses caution when utilizing assessment techniques, making evaluations and interpreting the performance of populations not represented in the norm group on which an instrument is standardized.

g. Assesses the effectiveness of his/her program in having an impact on students' academic, career and personal/social development through accountability measures especially examining efforts to close achievement, opportunity and attainment gaps.

A.10. Technology

The professional school counselor:

a. Promotes the benefits of and clarifies the limitations of various appropriate technological applications. The counselor promotes technological applications (1) that are appropriate for the student's individual needs, (2) that the student understands how to use and (3) for which follow-up counseling assistance is provided.

b. Advocates for equal access to technology for all students, especially those historically underserved.

c. Takes appropriate and reasonable measures for maintaining confidentiality of student information and educational records stored or transmitted over electronic media including although not limited to fax, electronic mail and instant messaging.

d. While working with students on a computer or similar technology, takes reasonable and appropriate measures to protect students from objectionable and/or harmful online material.

e. Who is engaged in the delivery of services involving technologies such as the telephone, videoconferencing and the Internet takes responsible steps to protect students and others from harm.

A.11. Student Peer Support Program

The professional school counselor:

Has unique responsibilities when working with student-assistance programs. The school counselor is responsible for the welfare of students participating in peer-to-peer programs under his/her direction.

B. RESPONSIBILITIES TO PARENTS/GUARDIANS

B.1. Parent Rights and Responsibilities

The professional school counselor:

a. Respects the rights and responsibilities of parents/guardians for their children and endeavors to establish, as appropriate, a collaborative relationship with parents/guardians to facilitate the student's maximum development.

b. Adheres to laws, local guidelines and ethical standards of practice when assisting parents/guardians experiencing family difficulties that interfere with the student's effectiveness and welfare.

c. Respects the confidentiality of parents/guardians.

d. Is sensitive to diversity among families and recognizes that all parents/guardians, custodial and noncustodial, are vested with certain rights and responsibilities for the welfare of their children by virtue of their role and according to law.

B.2. Parents/Guardians and Confidentiality

The professional school counselor:

a. Informs parents/guardians of the counselor's role with emphasis on the confidential nature of the counseling relationship between the counselor and student.

b. Recognizes that working with minors in a school setting may require counselors to collaborate with students' parents/guardians.

c. Provides parents/guardians with accurate, comprehensive and relevant information in an objective and caring manner, as is appropriate and consistent with ethical responsibilities to the student.

d. Makes reasonable efforts to honor the wishes of parents/guardians concerning information regarding the student, and in cases of divorce or separation exercises a good-faith effort to keep both parents informed with regard to critical information with the exception of a court order.

C. RESPONSIBILITIES TO COLLEAGUES AND PROFESSIONAL ASSOCIATES

C.1. Professional Relationships

The professional school counselor:
a. Establishes and maintains professional relationships with faculty, staff and administration to facilitate an optimum counseling program.
b. Treats colleagues with professional respect, courtesy and fairness. The qualifications, views and findings of colleagues are represented to accurately reflect the image of competent professionals.
c. Is aware of and utilizes related professionals, organizations and other resources to whom the student may be referred.

C.2. Sharing Information with Other Professionals

The professional school counselor:
a. Promotes awareness and adherence to appropriate guidelines regarding confidentiality, the distinction between public and private information and staff consultation.
b. Provides professional personnel with accurate, objective, concise and meaningful data necessary to adequately evaluate, counsel and assist the student.
c. If a student is receiving services from another counselor or other mental health professional, the counselor, with student and/or parent/ guardian consent, will inform the other professional and develop clear agreements to avoid confusion and conflict for the student.
d. Is knowledgeable about release of information and parental rights in sharing information.

D. RESPONSIBILITIES TO THE SCHOOL AND COMMUNITY

D.1. Responsibilities to the School

The professional school counselor:
a. Supports and protects the educational program against any infringement not in students' best interest.
b. Informs appropriate officials in accordance with school policy of conditions that may be potentially disruptive or damaging to the school's mission, personnel and property while honoring the confidentiality between the student and counselor.
c. Is knowledgeable and supportive of the school's mission and connects his/her program to the school's mission.
d. Delineates and promotes the counselor's role and function in meeting the needs of those served. Counselors will notify appropriate officials of conditions that may limit or curtail their effectiveness in providing programs and services.
e. Accepts employment only for positions for which he/she is qualified by education, training, supervised experience, state and national professional credentials and appropriate professional experience.
f. Advocates that administrators hire only qualified and competent individuals for professional counseling positions.
g. Assists in developing: (1) curricular and environmental conditions appropriate for the school and community, (2) educational procedures and programs to meet students' developmental needs and (3) a systematic evaluation process for comprehensive, developmental, standards-based school counseling programs, services and personnel. The counselor is guided by the findings of the evaluation data in planning programs and services.

D.2. Responsibility to the Community

The professional school counselor:
a. Collaborates with agencies, organizations and individuals in the community in the best interest of students and without regard to personal reward or remuneration.
b. Extends his/her influence and opportunity to deliver a comprehensive school counseling program to all students by collaborating with community resources for student success.

E. RESPONSIBILITIES TO SELF

E.1. Professional Competence

The professional school counselor:

a. Functions within the boundaries of individual professional competence and accepts responsibility for the consequences of his/her actions.

b. Monitors personal well-being and effectiveness and does not participate in any activity that may lead to inadequate professional services or harm to a student.

c. Strives through personal initiative to maintain professional competence including technological literacy and to keep abreast of professional information. Professional and personal growth are ongoing throughout the counselor's career.

E.2. Diversity

The professional school counselor:

a. Affirms the diversity of students, staff and families.

b. Expands and develops awareness of his/her own attitudes and beliefs affecting cultural values and biases and strives to attain cultural competence.

c. Possesses knowledge and understanding about how oppression, racism, discrimination and stereotyping affects her/him personally and professionally.

d. Acquires educational, consultation and training experiences to improve awareness, knowledge, skills and effectiveness in working with diverse populations: ethnic/racial status, age, economic status, special needs, ESL or ELL, immigration status, sexual orientation, gender, gender identity/expression, family type, religious/spiritual identity and appearance.

F. RESPONSIBILITIES TO THE PROFESSION

F.1. Professionalism

The professional school counselor:

a. Accepts the policies and procedures for handling ethical violations as a result of maintaining membership in the American School Counselor Association.

b. Conducts herself/himself in such a manner as to advance individual ethical practice and the profession.

c. Conducts appropriate research and report findings in a manner consistent with acceptable educational and psychological research practices. The counselor advocates for the protection of the individual student's identity when using data for research or program planning.

d. Adheres to ethical standards of the profession, other official policy statements, such as ASCA's position statements, role statement and the ASCA National Model, and relevant statutes established by federal, state and local governments, and when these are in conflict works responsibly for change.

e. Clearly distinguishes between statements and actions made as a private individual and those made as a representative of the school counseling profession.

f. Does not use his/her professional position to recruit or gain clients, consultees for his/her private practice or to seek and receive unjustified personal gains, unfair advantage, inappropriate relationships or unearned goods or services.

F.2. Contribution to the Profession

The professional school counselor:

a. Actively participates in local, state and national associations fostering the development and improvement of school counseling.

b. Contributes to the development of the profession through the sharing of skills, ideas and expertise with colleagues.

c. Provides support and mentoring to novice professionals.

G. MAINTENANCE OF STANDARDS

Ethical behavior among professional school counselors, association members and nonmembers, is expected at all times. When there exists serious doubt as to the ethical behavior of colleagues or if counselors are forced to work in situations or abide by policies that do not reflect the standards as outlined in these Ethical Standards for School Counselors, the counselor is obligated to take appropriate action to rectify the condition. The following procedure may serve as a guide:

1. The counselor should consult confidentially with a professional colleague to discuss the nature of a complaint to see if the professional colleague views the situation as an ethical violation.

2. When feasible, the counselor should directly approach the colleague whose behavior is in question to discuss the complaint and seek resolution.

3. If resolution is not forthcoming at the personal level, the counselor shall utilize the channels established within the school, school district, the state school counseling association and ASCA's Ethics Committee.

4. If the matter still remains unresolved, referral for review and appropriate action should be made to the Ethics Committees in the following sequence:
    *   state school counselor association
    *   American School Counselor Association

5. The ASCA Ethics Committee is responsible for:
    *   educating and consulting with the membership regarding ethical standards
    *   periodically reviewing and recommending changes in code
    *   receiving and processing questions to clarify the application of such standards; Questions must be submitted in writing to the ASCA Ethics chair.
    *   handling complaints of alleged violations of the ethical standards. At the national level, complaints should be submitted in writing to the ASCA Ethics Committee, c/o the Executive Director, American School Counselor Association, 1101 King St., Suite 625, Alexandria, VA 22314.

Revised June 26, 2004
Ethical Standards for School Counselors was adopted by the ASCA Delegate Assembly, March 19,1984, revised March 27, 1992, June 25, 1998, and June 26, 2004.

Association for Counselor Education and Supervision
Ethical Guidelines for Counseling Supervisors

Adopted by ACES Executive Counsel and Delegate Assembly
March, 1993

Preamble

The Association for Counselor Education and Supervision (ACES) is composed of people engaged in the professional preparation of counselors and people responsible for the ongoing supervision of counselors. ACES is a founding division of the American Counseling Association for (ACA) and as such adheres to ACA's current ethical standards and to general codes of competence adopted throughout the mental health community.

ACES believes that counselor educators and counseling supervisors in universities and in applied counseling settings, including the range of education and mental health delivery systems, carry responsibilities unique to their job roles. Such responsibilities may include administrative supervision, clinical supervision, or both. Administrative supervision refers to those supervisory activities which increase the efficiency of the delivery of counseling services; whereas, clinical supervision includes the supportive and educative activities of the supervisor designed to improve the application of counseling theory and technique directly to clients.

Counselor educators and counseling supervisors encounter situations which challenge the help given by general ethical standards of the profession at large. These situations require more specific guidelines that provide appropriate guidance in everyday practice.

The Ethical Guidelines for Counseling Supervisors are intended to assist professionals by helping them:

1. Observe ethical and legal protection of clients' and supervisee' rights;
2. Meet the training and professional development needs of supervisees in ways consistent with clients' welfare and programmatic requirements; and
3. Establish policies, procedures, and standards for implementing programs.

The specification of ethical guidelines enables ACES members to focus on and to clarify the ethical nature of responsibilities held in common. Such guidelines should be reviewed formally every five years, or more often if needed, to meet the needs of ACES members for guidance.

The Ethical Guidelines for Counselor Educators and Counseling Supervisors are meant to help ACES members in conducting supervision. ACES is not currently in a position to hear complaints about alleged non-compliance with these guidelines. Any complaints about the ethical behavior of any ACA member should be measured against the ACA Ethical Standards and a complaint lodged with ACA in accordance with its procedures for doing so.

One overriding assumption underlying this document is that supervision should be ongoing throughout a counselor's career and not stop when a particular level of education, certification, or membership in a professional organization is attained.

DEFINITIONS OF TERMS

Applied Counseling Settings - Public or private organizations of counselors such as community mental health centers, hospitals, schools, and group or individual private practice settings.

Supervisees - Counselors-in-training in university programs at any level who working with clients in applied settings as part of their university training program, and counselors who have completed their formal education and are employed in an applied counseling setting.

Supervisors - Counselors who have been designated within their university or agency to directly oversee the professional clinical work of counselors. Supervisors also may be persons who offer supervision to counselors seeking state licensure and so provide supervision outside of the administrative aegis of an applied counseling setting.

1. Client Welfare and Rights

1.01 The Primary obligation of supervisors is to train counselors so that they respect the integrity and promote the welfare of their clients. Supervisors should have supervisees inform clients that they are being supervised and that observation and/or recordings of the session may be reviewed by the supervisor.

1.02 Supervisors who are licensed counselors and are conducting supervision to aid a supervisee to become licensed should instruct the supervisee not to communicate or in any way convey to the supervisee's clients or to other parties that the supervisee is himself/herself licensed.

1.03 Supervisors should make supervisees aware of clients' rights, including protecting clients' right to privacy and confidentiality in the counseling relationship and the information resulting from it. Clients also should be informed that their right to privacy and confidentiality will not be violated by the supervisory relationship.

1.04 Records of the counseling relationship, including interview notes, test data, correspondence, the electronic storage of these documents, and audio and videotape recordings, are considered to be confidential professional information. Supervisors should see that these materials are used in counseling, research, and training and supervision of counselors with the full knowledge of the clients and that permission to use these materials is granted by the applied counseling setting offering service to the client. This professional information is to be used for full protection of the client. Written consent from the client (or legal guardian, if a minor) should be secured prior to the use of such information for instructional, supervisory, and/or research purposes. Policies of the applied counseling setting regarding client records also should be followed.

1.05 Supervisors shall adhere to current professional and legal guidelines when conducting research with human participants such as Section D-1 of the ACA Ethical Standards.

1.06 Counseling supervisors are responsible for making every effort to monitor both the professional actions, and failures to take action, of their supervisees.

2. Supervisory Role

Inherent and integral to the role of supervisor are responsibilities for:

a. Monitoring client welfare;
b. encouraging compliance with relevant legal, ethical, and professional standards for clinical practice;
c. monitoring clinical performance and professional development of supervisees; and
d. evaluating and certifying current performance and potential of supervisees for academic, screening, selection, placement, employment, and credentialing purposes.

2.01 Supervisors should have had training in supervision prior to initiating their role as supervisors.

2.02 Supervisors should pursue professional and personal continuing education activities such as advanced courses, seminars, and professional conferences on a regular and ongoing basis. These activities should include both counseling and supervision topics and skills.

2.03 Supervisors should make their supervisees aware of professional and ethical standards and legal responsibilities of the counseling profession.

2.04 Supervisors of post-degree counselors who are seeking state licensure should encourage these counselors to adhere to the standards for practice established by the state licensure board of the state in which they practice.

2.05 Procedures for contacting the supervisor, or an alternative supervisor, to assist in handling crisis situations should be established and communicated to supervisees.

2.06 Actual work samples via audio and/or video tape or live observation in addition to case notes should be reviewed by the supervisor as a regular part of the ongoing supervisory process.

2.07 Supervisors of counselors should meeting regularly in face-to-face sessions with their supervisees.

2.08 Supervisors should provide supervisees with ongoing feedback on their performance. This feedback should take a variety of forms, both formal and informal, and should include verbal and written evaluations. It should be formative during the supervisory experience and summative at the conclusion of the experience.

2.09 Supervisors who have multiple roles (e.g., teacher, clinical supervisor, administrative supervisor, etc.) with supervisees should minimize potential conflicts. Where possible, the roles should be divided among several supervisors. Where this is not possible, careful explanation should be conveyed to the supervisee as to the expectations and responsibilities associated with each supervisory role.

2.10 Supervisors should not participate in any form of sexual contact with supervisees. Supervisors should not engage in any form of social contact or interaction which would compromise the supervisor-supervisee relationship. Dual relationships with supervisees that might impair the supervisor's objectivity and professional judgment should be avoided and/or the supervisory relationship terminated.

2.11 Supervisors should not establish a psychotherapeutic relationship as a substitute for supervision. Personal issues should be addressed in supervision only in terms of the impact of these issues on clients and on professional functioning.

2.12 Supervisors, through ongoing supervisee assessment and evaluation, should be aware of any personal or professional limitations of supervisees which are likely to impede future professional performance. Supervisors have the responsibility of recommending remedial assistance to the supervisee and of screening from the training program, applied counseling setting, or state licensure those supervisees who are unable to provide competent professional services. These recommendations should be clearly and professionally explained in writing to the supervisees who are so evaluated.

2.13 Supervisors should not endorse a supervisee for certification, licensure, completion of an academic training program, or continued employment if the supervisor believes the supervisee is impaired in any way that would interfere with the performance of counseling duties. The presence of any such impairment should begin a process of feedback and remediation wherever possible so that the supervisee understands the nature of the impairment and has the opportunity to remedy the problem and continue with his/her professional development.

2.14 Supervisors should incorporate the principles of informed consent and participation; clarity of requirements, expectations, roles and rules; and due process and appeal into the establishment of policies and procedures of their institutions, program, courses, and individual supervisory relationships. Mechanisms for due process appeal of individual supervisory actions should be established and made available to all supervisees.

3. Program Administration Role

3.01 Supervisors should ensure that the programs conducted and experiences provided are in keeping with current guidelines and standards of ACA and its divisions.

3.02 Supervisors should teach courses and/or supervise clinical work only in areas where they are fully competent and experienced.

3.03 To achieve the highest quality of training and supervision, supervisors should be active participants in peer review and peer supervision procedures.

3.04 Supervisors should provide experiences that integrate theoretical knowledge and practical application. Supervisors also should provide opportunities in which supervisees are able to apply the knowledge they have learned and understand the rationale for the skills they have acquired. The knowledge and skills conveyed should reflect current practice, research findings, and available resources.

3.05 Professional competencies, specific courses, and/or required experiences expected of supervisees should be communicated to them in writing prior to admission to the training program or placement/employment by the applied counseling setting, and, in case of continued employment, in a timely manner.

3.06 Supervisors should accept only those persons as supervisees who meet identified entry level requirements for admission to a program of counselor training or for placement in an applied counseling setting. In the case of private supervision in search of state licensure, supervisees should have completed all necessary prerequisites as determined by the state licensure board.

3.07 Supervisors should inform supervisees of the goals, policies, theoretical orientations toward counseling, training, and supervision model or approach on which the supervision is based.

3.08 Supervisees should be encouraged and assisted to define their own theoretical orientation toward counseling, to establish supervision goals for themselves, and to monitor and evaluate their progress toward meeting these goals.

3.09 Supervisors should assess supervisees' skills and experience in order to establish standards for competent professional behavior. Supervisors should restrict supervisees' activities to those that are commensurate with their current level of skills and experiences.

3.10 Supervisors should obtain practicum and fieldwork sites that meet minimum standards for preparing student to become effective counselors. No practicum or fieldwork setting should be approved unless it truly replicates a counseling work setting.

3.11 Practicum and fieldwork classes would be limited in size according to established professional standards to ensure that each student has ample opportunity for individual supervision and feedback. Supervisors in applied counseling settings should have a limited number of supervisees.

3.12 Supervisors in university settings should establish and communicate specific policies and procedures regarding field placement of students. The respective roles of the student counselor, the university supervisor, and the field supervisor should be clearly differentiated in areas such as evaluation, requirements, and confidentiality.

3.13 Supervisors in training programs should communicate regularly with supervisors in agencies used as practicum and/or fieldwork sites regarding current professional practices, expectations of students, and preferred models and modalities of supervision.

3.14 Supervisors at the university should establish clear lines of communication among themselves, the field supervisors, and the students/supervisees.

3.15 Supervisors should establish and communicate to supervisees and to field supervisors specific procedures regarding consultation, performance review, and evaluation of supervisees.

3.16 Evaluations of supervisee performance in universities and in applied counseling settings should be available to supervisees in ways consistent with the Family Rights and Privacy Act and the Buckley Amendment.

3.17 Forms of training that focus primarily on self understanding and problem resolution (e.g., personal growth groups or individual counseling) should be voluntary. Those who conduct these forms of training should not serve simultaneously as supervisors of the supervisees involved in the training.

3.18 A supervisor may recommend participation in activities such as personal growth groups or personal counseling when it has been determined that a supervisee has deficits in the areas of self understanding and problem resolution which impede his/her professional functioning. The supervisors should not be the direct provider of these activities for the supervisee.

3.19 When a training program conducts a personal growth or counseling experience involving relatively intimate self disclosure, care should be taken to eliminate or minimize potential role conflicts for faculty and/or agency supervisors who may conduct these experiences and who also serve as teachers, group leaders, and clinical directors.

3.20 Supervisors should use the following prioritized sequence in resolving conflicts among the needs of the client, the needs of the supervisee, and the needs of the program or agency. Insofar as the client much be protected, it should be understood that client welfare is usually subsumed in federal and state laws such that these statutes should be the first point of reference. Where laws and ethical standards are not present or are unclear, the good judgment of the supervisor should be guided by the following list.

    a. Relevant legal and ethical standards (e.g., duty to warn, state child abuse laws, etc.);
    b. Client welfare;
    c. Supervisee welfare;
    d. Supervisor welfare; and
    e. Program and/or agency service and administrative needs.

Ethical Guidelines for Counseling Supervisors, Association for Counselor Education and Supervision (1993) Reprinted with permission.

Association for the Specialists in Group Work
Professional Standards for the Training of Group Workers

Revision Approved by the Executive Board, January 22, 2000
Prepared by F. Robert Wilson and Lynn S. Rapin, Co-Chairs,
and Lynn Haley-Banez, Member, ASGW Standards Committee
Consultants: Robert K. Conyne and Donald E. Ward

Preamble

For nearly two decades, the Association for Specialists in Group Work (herein referred to as ASGW or as the Association) has promulgated professional standards for the training of group workers. In the early 1980s, the Association published the ASGW Training Standards for Group Counselors (1983) which established nine knowledge competencies, seventeen skill competencies, and clock-hour baselines for various aspects of supervised clinical experience in group counseling. The focus on group counseling embodied in these standards mirrored the general conception of the time that whatever counselors did with groups of individuals should properly be referred to as group counseling.

New ground was broken in the 1990 revision of the ASGW Professional Standards for the Training of Group Workers with (a) the articulation of the term, *group work*, to capture the variety of ways in which counselors work with groups, (b) differentiation of core training, deemed essential for all counselors, from specialization training required of those intending to engage in group work as part of their professional practice, and (c) the differentiation among four distinct group work specializations: task and work group facilitation, group psychoeducation, group counseling, and group psychotherapy. Over the ten years in which these standards have been in force, commentary and criticism has been elicited through discussion groups at various regional and national conferences and through published analyses in the Association's journal, the *Journal for Specialists in Group Work*.

In this Year-2000 revision of the ASGW Professional Standards for the Training of Group Workers, the foundation established by the 1990 training standards has been preserved and refined by application of feedback received through public discussion and scholarly debate. The Year-2000 revision maintains and strengthens the distinction between core and specialization training with requirements for core training and aspirational guidelines for specialization training. Further, the definitions of group work specializations have been expanded and clarified. Evenness of application of training standards across the specializations has been assured by creating a single set of guidelines for all four specializations with specialization specific detail being supplied where necessary. Consistent with both the pattern for training standards established by the Council for Accreditation of Counseling and Related Educational Programs accreditation standards and past editions of the ASGW training standards, the Year-2000 revision addresses both content and clinical instruction. Content instruction is described in terms of both course work requirements and knowledge objectives while clinical instruction is articulated in terms of experiential requirements and skill objectives. This revision of the training standards was informed by and profits from the seminal ASGW Best Practice Guidelines (1998) and the ASGW Principles for Diversity-Competent Group Workers (1999). Although each of these documents have their own form of organization, all address the group work elements of planning, performing, and processing and the ethical and diversity-competent treatment of participants in group activities.

Purpose

The purpose of the Professional Standards for the Training of Group Workers is to provide guidance to counselor training programs in the construction of their curricula for graduate programs in counseling (e.g., masters, specialist, and doctoral degrees and other forms of advanced graduate study). Specifically, core standards express the Association's view on the minimum training in group work all programs in counseling should provide for all graduates of their entry level, master's degree programs in counseling, and specialization standards provide a framework for documenting the training philosophy, objectives, curriculum, and outcomes for each declared specialization program.

Core Training in Group Work. All counselors should possess a set of core competencies in general group work. The Association for Specialists in Group Work advocates for the incorporation of core group work competencies as part of required entry level training in all counselor preparation programs. The Association's standards for core training are consistent with and provide further elaboration of the standards for accreditation of entry level counseling programs identified by the Council for Accreditation of Counseling and Related Educational Programs (CACREP, 1994). Mastery of the core competencies detailed in the ASGW training standards will prepare the counselor to understand group process phenomena and to function more effectively in groups in which the counselor is a member. Mastery of basic knowledge and skill in group work provides a foundation which specialty training can extend but does not qualify one to independently practice any group work specialty.

Specialist Training in Group Work. The independent practice of group work requires training beyond core competencies. ASGW advocates that independent practitioners of group work must possess advanced competencies relevant to the particular kind of group work practice in which the group work student wants to specialize (e.g., facilitation of task groups, group psychoeducation, group counseling, or group psychotherapy). To encourage program creativity in development of specialization training, the specialization guidelines do not prescribe minimum trainee competencies. Rather, the guidelines establish a framework within which programs can develop unique training experiences utilizing scientific foundations and best practices to achieve their training objectives. In providing these guidelines for specialized training, ASGW makes no presumption that a graduate program in counseling must provide training in a group work specialization nor that adequate training in a specialization can be accomplished solely within a well-rounded master's degree program in counseling. To provide adequate specialization training, completion of post-master's options such as certificates of post-master's study or doctoral degrees may be required. Further, there is no presumption that an individual who may have received adequate training in a given declared specialization will be prepared to function effectively with all group situations in which the graduate may want to or be required to work. It is recognized that the characteristics of specific client populations and employment settings vary widely. Additional training beyond that which was acquired in a specific graduate program may be necessary for optimal, diversity-competent, group work practice with a given population in a given setting.

Definitions

Group Work: is a broad professional practice involving the application of knowledge and skill in group facilitation to assist an interdependent collection of people to reach their mutual goals which may be intrapersonal, interpersonal, or work-related. The goals of the group may include the accomplishment of tasks related to work, education, personal development, personal and interpersonal problem solving, or remediation of mental and emotional disorders.

Core Training in Group Work: includes knowledge, skills, and experiences deemed necessary for general competency for all master's degree prepared counselors. ASGW advocates for all counselor preparation programs to provide core training in group work regardless of whether the program intends to prepare trainees for independent practice in a group work specialization. Core training in group work is considered a necessary prerequisite for advanced practice in group work.

Specialization Training in Group Work: includes knowledge, skills, and experiences deemed necessary for counselors to engage in independent practice of group work. Four areas of advanced practice, referred to as specializations, are identified: Task Group Facilitation, Group Psychoeducation, Group Counseling, and Group Psychotherapy. This list is not presumed to be exhaustive and while there may be no sharp boundaries between the specializations, each has recognizable characteristics that have professional utility. The definitions for these group work specializations have been built upon the American Counseling Association's model definition of counseling (adopted by the ACA Governing Council in 1997), describing the methods typical of the working stage of the group being defined and the typical purposes to which those methods are put and the typical populations served by those methods. Specialized training presumes mastery of prerequisite core knowledge, skills, and experiences.

Specialization in Task and Work Group Facilitation:

- The application of principles of normal human development and functioning
- through group based educational, developmental, and systemic strategies
- applied in the context of here-and-now interaction
- that promote efficient and effective accomplishment of group tasks
- among people who are gathered to accomplish group task goals.

Specialization in Psychoeducation Group Leadership:

- The application of principles of normal human development and functioning
- through group based educational and developmental strategies
- applied in the context of here-and-now interaction
- that promote personal and interpersonal growth and development and the prevention of future difficulties
- among people who may be at risk for the development of personal or interpersonal problems or who seek enhancement of personal qualities and abilities.

Specialization in Group Counseling:

- The application of principles of normal human development and functioning
- through group based cognitive, affective, behavioral, or systemic intervention strategies
- applied in the context of here-and-now interaction
- that address personal and interpersonal problems of living and promote personal and interpersonal growth and development
- among people who may be experiencing transitory maladjustment, who are at risk for the development of personal or interpersonal problems, or who seek enhancement of personal qualities and abilities.

Specialization in Group Psychotherapy:

- The application of principles of normal and abnormal human development and functioning
- through group based cognitive, affective, behavioral, or systemic intervention strategies
- applied in the context of negative emotional arousal
- that address personal and interpersonal problems of living, remediate perceptual and cognitive distortions or repetitive patterns of dysfunctional behavior, and promote personal and interpersonal growth and development
- among people who may be experiencing severe and/or chronic maladjustment.

Core Training Standards

I. Coursework and Experiential Requirements

Coursework Requirements.

Core training shall include at least one graduate course in group work that addresses such as but not limited to scope of practice, types of group work, group development, group process and dynamics, group leadership, and standards of training and practice for group workers.

Experiential Requirements.

Core training shall include a minimum of 10 clock hours (20 clock hours recommended) observation of and participation in a group experience as a group member and/or as a group leader.

II. Knowledge and Skill Objectives

A. Nature and Scope of Practice

1. Knowledge Objectives. Identify and describe:

   a. the nature of group work and the various specializations within group work
   b. theories of group work including commonalties and distinguishing characteristics among the various specializations within group work
   c. research literature pertinent to group work and its specializations

2. Skill Objectives. Demonstrate skill in:

   a. preparing a professional disclosure statement for practice in a chosen area of specialization
   b. applying theoretical concepts and scientific findings to the design of a group and the interpretation of personal experiences in a group

B. Assessment of Group Members and the Social Systems in which they Live and Work

1. Knowledge Objectives. Identify and describe:

   a. principles of assessment of group functioning in group work
   b. use of personal contextual factors (e.g., family-of-origin, neighborhood-of-residence, organizational membership, cultural membership) in interpreting behavior of members in a group

2. Skill Objectives. Demonstrate skill in:

   a. observing and identifying group process
   b. observing the personal characteristics of individual members in a group
   c. developing hypotheses about the behavior of group members
   d. employing contextual factors (e.g., family of origin, neighborhood of residence, organizational membership, cultural membership) in interpretation of individual and group data

C. Planning Group Interventions

1. <u>Knowledge Objectives</u>. Identify and describe:

   a. environmental contexts, which affect planning for, group interventions
   b. the impact of group member diversity (e.g., gender, culture, learning style, group climate preference) on group member behavior and group process and dynamics in group work
   c. principles of planning for group work

2. <u>Skill Objectives</u>. Demonstrate skill in:

   a. collaborative consultation with targeted populations to enhance ecological validity of planned group interventions
   b. planning for a group work activity including such aspects as developing overarching purpose, establishing goals and objectives, detailing methods to be used in achieving goals and objectives, determining methods for outcome assessment, and verifying ecological validity of plan

D. Implementation of Group Interventions

1. <u>Knowledge Objectives</u>. Identify and describe:
   a. principles of group formation including recruiting, screening, and selecting group members
   b. principles for effective performance of group leadership functions
   c. therapeutic factors within group work and when group work approaches are indicated and contraindicated
   d. principles of group dynamics including group process components, developmental stage theories, group member roles, group member behaviors

2. <u>Skill Objectives</u>. Demonstrate skill in:
   a. encouraging participation of group members
   b. attending to, describing, acknowledging, confronting, understanding, and responding empathically to group member behavior
   c. attending to, acknowledging, clarifying, summarizing, confronting, and responding empathically to group member statements
   d. attending to, acknowledging, clarifying, summarizing, confronting, and responding empathically to group themes
   e. eliciting information from and imparting information to group members
   f. providing appropriate self-disclosure
   g. maintaining group focus; keeping a group on task
   h. giving and receiving feedback in a group setting

E. Leadership and Co-Leadership

1. <u>Knowledge Objectives</u>. Identify and describe:
   a. group leadership styles and approaches
   b. group work methods including group worker orientations and specialized group leadership behaviors
   c. principles of collaborative group processing

2. <u>Skill Objectives</u>. To the extent opportunities for leadership or co-leadership are provided, demonstrate skill in:
   a. engaging in reflective evaluation of one's personal leadership style and approach
   b. working cooperatively with a co-leader and/or group members
   c. engaging in collaborative group processing.

F. Evaluation

    1. <u>Knowledge Objectives</u>. Identify and describe:
       a. methods for evaluating group process in group work
       b. methods for evaluating outcomes in group work
    2. <u>Skill Objectives</u>. Demonstrate skill in:
       a. contributing to evaluation activities during group participation
       b. engaging in self-evaluation of personally selected performance goals

G. Ethical Practice, Best Practice, Diversity-Competent Practice

    1. <u>Knowledge Objectives</u>. Identify and describe:
       a. ethical considerations unique to group work
       b. best practices in group work
       c. diversity competent group work
    2. <u>Skill Objectives</u>. Demonstrate skill in:
       a. evidencing ethical practice in planning, observing, and participating in group activities
       b. evidencing best practice in planning, observing, and participating in group activities
       c. evidencing diversity-competent practice in planning, observing, and participating in group activities

<u>Specialization Guidelines</u>
I. Overarching Program Characteristics

A. The program has a clearly specified philosophy of training for the preparation of specialists for independent practice of group work in one of the forms of group work recognized by the Association (i.e., task and work group facilitation, group psychoeducation, group counseling, or group psychotherapy).

    1. The program states an explicit intent to train group workers in one or more of the group work specializations.
    2. The program states an explicit philosophy of training, based on the science of group work, by which it intends to prepare students for independent practice in the declared specialization(s).

B. For each declared specialization, the program specifies education and training objectives in terms of the competencies expected of students completing the specialization training. These competencies are consistent with

    1. the program's philosophy and training model,
    2. the substantive area(s) relevant for best practice of the declared specialization area, and
    3. standards for competent, ethical, and diversity sensitive practice of group work

C. For each declared specialization, the program specifies a sequential, cumulative curriculum, expanding in breadth and depth, and designed to prepare students for independent practice of the specialization and relevant credentialing.

D. For each declared specialization, the program documents achievement of training objectives in terms of student competencies.

II. Recommended Coursework and Experience

A. <u>Coursework</u>. Specialization training may include coursework which provide the student with a broad foundation in the group work domain in which the student seeks specialized training:

1. Task/Work Group Facilitation: coursework includes but is not limited to organizational development, management, and consultation, theory and practice of task/work group facilitation
2. Group Psychoeducation: coursework includes but is not limited to organizational development, school and community counseling/psychology, health promotion, marketing, program development and evaluation, organizational consultation, theory and practice of group psychoeducation
3. Group Counseling: coursework includes but is not limited to normal human development, health promotion, theory and practice of group counseling
4. Group Psychotherapy: coursework includes but is not be limited to normal and abnormal human development, assessment and diagnosis of mental and emotional disorders, treatment of psychopathology, theory and practice of group psychotherapy

B. Experience. Specialization training includes

1. Task/Work Group Facilitation: a minimum of 30 clock hours (45 clock hours recommended) supervised practice facilitating or conducting an intervention with a task or work group appropriate to the age and clientele of the group leader's specialty area (e.g., school counseling, student development counseling, community counseling, mental health counseling)
2. Group Psychoeducation: a minimum of 30 clock hours (45 clock hours recommended) supervised practice conducting a psychoeducation group appropriate to the age and clientele of the group leader's specialty area (e.g., school counseling, student development counseling, community counseling, mental health counseling)
3. Group Counseling: a minimum of 45 clock hours (60 clock hours recommended) supervised practice conducting a counseling group appropriate to the age and clientele of the group leader's specialty area (e.g., school counseling, student development counseling, community counseling, mental health counseling)
Group Psychotherapy: a minimum of 45 clock hours (60 clock hours recommended) supervised practice conducting a psychotherapy group appropriate to the age and clientele of the group leader's specialty area (e.g., mental health counseling)

III. Knowledge and Skill Elements

In achieving its objectives, the program has and implements a clear and coherent curriculum plan that provides the means whereby all students can acquire and demonstrate substantial understanding of and competence in the following areas:

A. Nature and Scope of Practice

The program states a clear expectation that its students will limit their independent practice of group work to those specialization areas for which they have been appropriately trained and supervised.

B. Assessment of Group Members and the Social Systems in Which they Live and Work

All graduates of specialization training will understand and demonstrate competence in the use of assessment instruments and methodologies for assessing individual group member characteristics and group development, group dynamics, and process phenomena relevant for the program's declared specialization area(s). Studies should include but are not limited to:

1. methods of screening and assessment of populations, groups, and individual members who are or may be targeted for intervention
2. methods for observation of group member behavior during group interventions
3. methods of assessment of group development, process, and outcomes

C. Planning Group Interventions

All graduates of specialization training will understand and demonstrate competence in planning group interventions consistent with the program's declared specialization area(s). Studies should include but are not limited to:

1. establishing the overarching purpose for the intervention
2. identifying goals and objectives for the intervention
3. detailing methods to be employed in achieving goals and objectives during the intervention
4. selecting methods for examining group process during group meetings, between group sessions, and at the completion of the group intervention
5. preparing methods for helping members derive meaning from their within-group experiences and transfer within-group learning to real-world circumstances
6. determining methods for measuring outcomes during and following the intervention
7. verifying ecological validity of plans for the intervention

D. Implementation of Group Interventions

All graduates of specialization training will understand and demonstrate competence in implementing group interventions consistent with the program's declared specialization area(s). Studies should include but are not limited to:

1. principles of group formation including recruiting, screening, selection, and orientation of group members
2. standard methods and procedures for group facilitation
3. selection and use of referral sources appropriate to the declared specialization
4. identifying and responding constructively to extra-group factors which may influence the success of interventions
5. applying the major strategies, techniques, and procedures
6. adjusting group pacing relative to the stage of group development
7. identifying and responding constructively to critical incidents
8. identifying and responding constructively to disruptive members
9. helping group members attribute meaning to and integrate and apply learning
10. responding constructively to psychological emergencies
11. involving group members in within group session processing and on-going planning

E. Leadership and Co-Leadership

All graduates of specialization training will understand and demonstrate competence in pursuing personal competence as a leader and in selecting and managing the interpersonal relationship with a co-leader for group interventions consistent with the program's declared specialization area(s). Studies should include but are not limited to:

1. characteristics and skills of effective leaders
2. relationship skills required of effective co-leaders
3. processing skills required of effective co-leaders

F. Evaluation

All graduates of specialization training will understand and demonstrate competence in evaluating group interventions consistent with the program's declared specialization area(s). Studies should include but are not limited to methods for evaluating participant outcomes and participant satisfaction.

G. Ethical Practice, Best Practice, Diversity-Competent Practice

All graduates of specialization training will understand and demonstrate consistent effort to comply with principles of ethical, best practice, and diversity-competent practice of group work consistent with the program's declared specialization area(s). Studies should include but are not limited to:

1. ethical considerations unique to the program's declared specialization area
2. best practices for group work within the program's declared specialization area
3. diversity issues unique to the program's declared specialization area

Implementation Guidelines

Implementation of the Professional Standards for the Training of Group Workers requires a commitment by a program's faculty and a dedication of program resources to achieve excellence in preparing all counselors at core competency level and in preparing counselors for independent practice of group work. To facilitate implementation of the training standards, the Association offers the following guidelines.

Core Training in Group Work

Core training in group work can be provided through a single, basic course in group theory and process. This course should include the elements of content instruction detailed below and may also include the required clinical instruction component.

Content Instruction

Consistent with accreditation standards (CACREP, 1994; Standard II.J.4), study in the area of group work should provide an understanding of the types of group work (e.g., facilitation of task groups, psychoeducation groups, counseling groups, psychotherapy groups); group development, group dynamics, and group leadership styles; and group leadership methods and skills. More explicitly, studies should include, but not be limited to the following:

- principles of group dynamics including group process components, developmental stage theories, and group member's roles and behaviors;

- group leadership styles and approaches including characteristics of various types of group leaders and leadership styles;

- theories of group counseling including commonalties, distinguishing characteristics, and pertinent research and literature;

- group work methods including group leader orientations and behaviors, ethical standards, appropriate selection criteria and methods, and methods of evaluating effectiveness;

- approaches used for other types of group work, including task groups, prevention groups, support groups, and therapy groups; and,

- skills in observing member behavior and group process, empathic responding, confronting, self-disclosing, focusing, protecting, recruiting and selecting members, opening and closing sessions, managing, explicit and implicit teaching, modeling, giving and receiving feedback

Clinical Instruction

Core group work training requires a minimum of 10 clock hours of supervised practice (20 clock hours of supervised practice is recommended). Consistent with CACREP standards for accreditation, the supervised experience provides the student with direct experiences as a participant in a small group, and may be met either in the basic course in group theory and practice or in a specially conducted small group designed for the purpose of meeting this standard. (CACREP, 1994; Standard II.D). In arranging for and conducting this group experience, care must be taken by program faculty to assure that the ACA ethical standard for dual relationships and ASGW standards for best practice are observed.

Specialist Training in Group Work

Though ASGW advocates that all counselor training programs provide all counseling students with core group work training, specialization training is elective. If a counselor training program chooses to offer specialization training (e.g., task group facilitation, group psychoeducation, group counseling, group psychotherapy), ASGW urges institutions to develop their curricula consistent with the ASGW standards for that specialization.

Content Instruction

Each area of specialization has its literature. In addition to basic course work in group theory and process, each specialization requires additional coursework providing specialized knowledge necessary for professional application of the specialization:

- **Task Group Facilitation:** course work in such areas as organization development, consultation, management, or sociology so students gain a basic understanding of organizations and how task groups function within them.

- **Group Psychoeducation:** course work in community psychology, consultation, health promotion, marketing, curriculum design to prepare students to conduct structured consciousness raising and skill training groups in such areas as stress management, wellness, anger control and assertiveness training, problem solving.

- **Group Counseling:** course work in normal human development, family development and family counseling, assessment and problem identification of problems in living, individual counseling, and group counseling, including training experiences in personal growth or counseling group.

- **Group Psychotherapy:** coursework in abnormal human development, family pathology and family therapy, assessment and diagnosis of mental and emotional disorders, individual therapy, and group therapy, including training experiences in a therapy group.

Clinical Instruction

For Task Group Facilitation and Group Psychoeducation, group specialization training recommends a minimum of 30 clock hours of supervised practice (45 clock hours of supervised practice is strongly suggested). Because of the additional difficulties presented by Group Counseling and Group Psychotherapy, a minimum of 45 clock hours of supervised practice is recommended (60 clock hours of supervised practice is strongly suggested). Consistent with CACREP standards for accreditation, supervised experience should provide an opportunity for the student to perform under supervision a variety of activities that a professional counselor would perform in conducting group work consistent with a given specialization (i.e., assessment of group members and the social systems in which they live and work, planning group interventions, implementing group interventions, leadership and co-leadership, and within-group, between-group, and end-of-group processing and evaluation).

In addition to courses offering content and experience related to a given specialization, supervised clinical experience should be obtained in practica and internship experiences. Following the model provided by

CACREP for master's practica, we recommend that one quarter of all required supervised clinical experience be devoted to group work:

- **Master's Practicum:** At least 10 clock hours of the required 40 clock hours of direct service should be spent in supervised leadership or co-leadership experience in group work, typically in Task Group Facilitation, Group Psychoeducation, or Group Counseling (at the master's practicum level, experience in Group Psychotherapy would be unusual) (CACREP, 1994; Standard III.H.1).

- **Master's Internship:** At least 60 clock hours of the required 240 clock hours of direct services should be spent in supervised leadership or co-leadership in group work consistent with the program's specialization offering(s) (i.e., in Task Group Facilitation, Group Psychoeducation, Group Counseling, or Group Psychotherapy).

- **Doctoral Internship:** At least 150 clock hours of the required 600 clock hours of direct service should be spent in supervised leadership or co-leadership in group work consistent with the program's specialization offering(s) (i.e., in Task Group Facilitation, Group Psychoeducation, Group Counseling, or Group Psychotherapy).

References

Association for Specialists in Group Work (1998). ASGW Best Practice Guidelines. Journal for Specialists in Group Work, 23, 237-244.

Association for Specialists in Group Work (1999). ASGW Principles for Diversity-Competent Group Workers. Journal for Specialists in Group Work, 24, 7-14.

Association for Specialists in Group Work (1983). ASGW Professional Standards for Group Counseling. Alexandria VA: Author.

Association for Specialists in Group Work (1990). Professional Standards for the Training of Group Workers. Alexandria VA: Author.

Council for Accreditation of Counseling and Related Educational Programs (CACREP) (1994). CACREP accreditation standards and procedures manual. Alexandria, VA: Author.

Professional Standards for the Training of Group Workers (ASGW, 1999).
Reprinted with permission.

Association for Specialists in Group Work
Best Practice Guidelines
Approved by the ASGW Executive Board, March 29, 1998
Prepared by: Lynn Rapin and Linda Keel ASGW Ethics Committee Co-Chairs

The Association for Specialists in Group Work (ASGW) is a division of the American Counseling Association whose members are interested in and specialize in group work. We value the creation of community; service to our members, clients, and the profession; and value leadership as a process to facilitate the growth and development of individuals and groups.

The Association for Specialists in Group Work recognizes the commitment of its members to the Code of Ethics and Standards of Practice (as revised in 1995) of its parent organization, the American Counseling Association, and nothing in this document shall be construed to supplant that code. These Best Practice Guidelines are intended to clarify the application of the ACA Code of Ethics and Standards of Practice to the field of group work by defining Group Workers' responsibility and scope of practice involving those activities, strategies and interventions that are consistent and current with effective and appropriate professional ethical and community standards. ASGW views ethical process as being integral to group work and views Group Workers as ethical agents. Group Workers, by their very nature in being responsible and responsive to their group members, necessarily embrace a certain potential for ethical vulnerability. It is incumbent upon Group Workers to give considerable attention to the intent and context of their actions because the attempts of Group Workers to influence human behavior through group work always have ethical implications. These Best Practice Guidelines address Group Workers' responsibilities in planning, performing and processing groups.

Section A: Best Practice in Planning
A.1. Professional Context and Regulatory Requirements
Group Workers actively know, understand and apply the ACA Code of Ethics and Standards of Best Practice, the ASGW Professional Standards for the Training of Group Workers, these ASGW Best Practice Guidelines, the ASGW diversity competencies, the ACA Multicultural Guidelines, relevant state laws, accreditation requirements, relevant National Board for Certified Counselors Codes and Standards, their organization's standards, and insurance requirements impacting the practice of group work.

A.2. Scope of Practice and Conceptual Framework
Group Workers define the scope of practice related to the core and specialization competencies defined in the ASGW Training Standards. Group Workers are aware of personal strengths and weaknesses in leading groups. Group Workers develop and are able to articulate a general conceptual framework to guide practice and a rationale for use of techniques that are to be used. Group Workers limit their practice to those areas for which they meet the training criteria established by the ASGW Training Standards.

A.3. Assessment
a. <u>Assessment of self</u>. Group Workers actively assess their knowledge and skills related to the specific group(s) offered. Group Workers assess their values, beliefs and theoretical orientation and how these impact upon the group, particularly when working with a diverse and multicultural population.

b. <u>Ecological assessment</u>. Group Workers assess community needs, agency or organization resources, sponsoring organization mission, staff competency, attitudes regarding group work, professional training levels of potential group leaders regarding group work; client attitudes regarding group work, and multicultural and diversity considerations. Group Workers use this information as the basis for making decisions related to their group practice, or to the implementation of groups for which they have supervisory, evaluation, or oversight responsibilities.

A.4. Program Development and Evaluation
a. Group Workers identify the type(s) of group(s) to be offered and how they relate to community needs.

b. Group Workers concisely state in writing the purpose and goals of the group. Group Workers also identify the role of the group members in influencing or determining the group goals.

c. Group Workers set fees consistent with the organization's fee schedule, taking into consideration the financial status and locality of prospective group members.

d. Group Workers choose techniques and a leadership style appropriate to the type(s) of group(s) being offered.

e. Group Workers have an evaluation plan consistent with regulatory, organization and insurance requirements, where appropriate.

f. Group Workers take into consideration current professional guidelines when using technology, including but not limited to Internet communication.

A.5. Resources

Group Workers coordinate resources related to the kind of group(s) and group activities to be provided, such as: adequate funding; the appropriateness and availability of a trained co-leader; space and privacy requirements for the type(s) of group(s) being offered; marketing and recruiting; and appropriate collaboration with other community agencies and organizations.

A.6. Professional Disclosure Statement

Group Workers have a professional disclosure statement which includes information on confidentiality and exceptions to confidentiality, theoretical orientation, information on the nature, purpose(s) and goals of the group, the group services that can be provided, the role and responsibility of group members and leaders, Group Workers; qualifications to conduct the specific group(s), specific licenses, certifications and professional affiliations, and address of licensing/credentialing body.

A.7. Group and Member Preparation

a. Group Workers screen prospective group members if appropriate to the type of group being offered. When selection of group members is appropriate, Group Workers identify group members whose needs and goals are compatible with the goals of the group.

b. Group Workers facilitate informed consent. Group Workers provide in oral and written form to prospective members (when appropriate to group type): the professional disclosure statement; group purpose and goals; group participation expectations including voluntary and involuntary membership; role expectations of members and leader(s); policies related to entering and exiting the group; policies governing substance use; policies and procedures governing mandated groups (where relevant); documentation requirements; disclosure of information to others; implications of out-of-group contact or involvement among members; procedures for consultation between group leader(s) and group member(s); fees and time parameters; and potential impacts of group participation.

c. Group Workers obtain the appropriate consent forms for work with minors and other dependent group members.

d. Group Workers define confidentiality and its limits (for example, legal and ethical exceptions and expectations; waivers implicit with treatment plans, documentation and insurance usage). Group Workers have the responsibility to inform all group participants of the need for confidentiality, potential consequences of breaching confidentiality and that legal privilege does not apply to group discussions (unless provided by state statute).

A.8. Professional Development

Group Workers recognize that professional growth is a continuous, ongoing, developmental process throughout their career.

a. Group Workers remain current and increase knowledge and skill competencies through activities such as continuing education, professional supervision, and participation in personal and professional development activities.

b. Group Workers seek consultation and/or supervision regarding ethical concerns that interfere with effective functioning as a group leader. Supervisors have the responsibility to keep abreast of consultation, group theory, process, and adhere to related ethical guidelines.

c. Group Workers seek appropriate professional assistance for their own personal problems or conflicts that are likely to impair their professional judgement or work performance.

d. Group Workers seek consultation and supervision to ensure appropriate practice whenever working with a group for which all knowledge and skill competencies have not been achieved.

e. Group Workers keep abreast of group research and development.

A.9. Trends and Technological Changes

Group Workers are aware of and responsive to technological changes as they affect society and the profession. These include but are not limited to changes in mental health delivery systems; legislative and insurance industry reforms; shifting population demographics and client needs; and technological advances in Internet and other communication and delivery systems. Group Workers adhere to ethical guidelines related to the use of developing technologies.

Section B: Best Practice in Performing

B.1. Self Knowledge

Group Workers are aware of and monitor their strengths and weaknesses and the effects these have on group members.

B.2. Group Competencies

Group Workers have a basic knowledge of groups and the principles of group dynamics, and are able to perform the core group competencies, as described in the ASGW Professional Standards for the Training of Group Workers. Additionally, Group Workers have adequate understanding and skill in any group specialty area chosen for practice (psychotherapy, counseling, task, psychoeducation, as described in the ASGW Training Standards).

B.3. Group Plan Adaptation

    a. Group Workers apply and modify knowledge, skills and techniques appropriate to group type and stage, and to the unique needs of various cultural and ethnic groups.

    b. Group Workers monitor the group's progress toward the group goals and plan.

    c. Group Workers clearly define and maintain ethical, professional, and social relationship boundaries with group members as appropriate to their role in the organization and the type of group being offered.

B.4. Therapeutic Conditions and Dynamics

Group Workers understand and are able to implement appropriate models of group development, process observation and therapeutic conditions.

B.5. Meaning

Group Workers assist members in generating meaning from the group experience.

B.6. Collaboration

Group Workers assist members in developing individual goals and respect group members as co-equal partners in the group experience.

B.7. Evaluation

Group Workers include evaluation (both formal and informal) between sessions and at the conclusion of the group.

B.8. Diversity

Group Workers practice with broad sensitivity to client differences including but not limited to ethnic, gender, religious, sexual, psychological maturity, economic class, family history, physical characteristics or limitations, and geographic location. Group Workers continuously seek information regarding the cultural issues of the diverse population with whom they are working both by interaction with participants and from using outside resources.

B.9. Ethical Surveillance

Group Workers employ an appropriate ethical decision making model in responding to ethical challenges and issues and in determining courses of action and behavior for self and group members. In addition, Group Workers employ applicable standards as promulgated by ACA, ASGW, or other appropriate professional organizations.

Section C: Best Practice in Group Processing

C.1. Processing Schedule

Group Workers process the workings of the group with themselves, group members, supervisors or other colleagues, as appropriate. This may include assessing progress on group and member goals, leader behaviors and techniques, group dynamics and interventions; developing understanding and acceptance of meaning. Processing may occur both within sessions and before and after each session, at time of termination, and later follow up, as appropriate .

C.2. Reflective Practice

Group Workers attend to opportunities to synthesize theory and practice and to incorporate learning outcomes into ongoing groups. Group Workers attend to session dynamics of members and their interactions and also attend to the relationship between session dynamics and leader values, cognition and affect.

C.3. Evaluation and Follow-Up

a. Group Workers evaluate process and outcomes. Results are used for ongoing program planning, improvement and revisions of current group and/or to contribute to professional research literature. Group Workers follow all applicable policies and standards in using group material for research and reports.

b. Group Workers conduct follow-up contact with group members, as appropriate, to assess outcomes or when requested by a group member(s).

C.4. Consultation and Training with Other Organizations

Group Workers provide consultation and training to organizations in and out of their setting, when appropriate. Group Workers seek out consultation as needed with competent professional persons knowledgeable about group work

Best Practice Guidelines for Group Workers (ASGW, 1998).
Reprinted with permission.

Association for Specialists in Group Work
Principles for Diversity-Competent Group Workers
Approved by the Executive Board, August 1, 1998
Prepared by Lynn Haley-Banez, Sherlon Brown, and Bogusia Molina
Consultants: Michael D'Andrea, Patricia Arrendondo,
Niloufer Merchant, and Sandra Wathen

Preamble

The Association for Specialists in Group Work (ASGW) is committed to understanding how issues of diversity affect all aspects of group work. This includes but is not limited to: training diversity-competent group workers; conducting research that will add to the literature on group work with diverse populations; understanding how diversity affects group process and dynamics; and assisting group facilitators in various settings to increase their awareness, knowledge, and skills as they relate to facilitating groups with diverse memberships.

As an organization, ASGW has endorsed this document with the recognition that issues of diversity affect group process and dynamics, group facilitation, training, and research. As an organization, we recognize that racism, classism, sexism, heterosexism, ableism, and so forth, affect everyone. As individual members of this organization, it is our personal responsibility to address these issues through awareness, knowledge, and skills. As members of ASGW, we need to increase our awareness of our own biases, values, and beliefs and how they impact the groups we run. We need to increase our awareness of our group members' biases, values, and beliefs and how they also impact and influence group process and dynamics. Finally, we need to increase our knowledge in facilitating, with confidence, competence, and integrity, groups that are diverse on many dimensions.

Definitions

For the purposes of this document, it is important that the language used is understood. Terms such as "dominant," "nondominant," and "target" persons and/or populations are used to define a person or groups of persons who historically, in the United States, do not have equal access to power, money, certain privileges (such as access to mental health services because of financial constraints, or the legal right to marry, in the case of a gay or lesbian couple), and/or the ability to influence or initiate social policy because of unequal representation in government and politics. These terms are not used to denote a lack of numbers in terms of representation in the overall U.S. population. Nor are these terms used to continue to perpetuate the very biases and forms of oppression, both overt and covert, that this document attempts to address.

For the purposes of this document, the term "disabilities" refers to differences in physical, mental, emotional, and learning abilities and styles among people. It is not meant as a term to define a person, such as a learning disabled person, but rather in the context of a person with a learning disability.

Given the history and current cultural, social, and political context in which this document is written, the authors of this document are limited to the language of this era. With this in mind, we have attempted to construct a "living document" that can and will change as the sociopolitical and cultural context changes.

The Principles

I. Awareness of Self
A. Attitudes and Beliefs

Diversity-competent group workers demonstrate movement from being unaware to being increasingly aware and sensitive to their own race, ethnic and cultural heritage, gender, socioeconomic status (SES), sexual orientation, abilities, and religion and spiritual beliefs, and to valuing and respecting differences.

Diversity-competent group workers demonstrate increased awareness of how their own race, ethnicity, culture, gender, SES, sexual orientation, abilities, and religion and spiritual beliefs are impacted by their own experiences and histories, which in turn influence group process and dynamics.

Diversity-competent group workers can recognize the limits of their competencies and expertise with regard to working with group members who are different from them in terms of race, ethnicity, culture (including language), SES, gender, sexual orientation, abilities, religion, and spirituality and their beliefs, values, and biases. (For further clarification on limitations, expertise, and type of group work, refer to the training standards and best practice guidelines, Association for Specialists in Group Work, 1998; and the ethical guidelines, American Counseling Association, 1995.)

Diversity-competent group workers demonstrate comfort, tolerance, and sensitivity with differences that exist between themselves and group members in terms of race, ethnicity, culture, SES, gender, sexual orientation, abilities, religion, and spirituality and their beliefs, values, and biases.

B. Knowledge

Diversity-competent group workers can identify specific knowledge about their own race, ethnicity, SES, gender, sexual orientation, abilities, religion, and spirituality, and how they personally and professionally affect their definitions of "normality" and the group process.

Diversity-skilled group workers demonstrate knowledge and understanding regarding how oppression in any form-such as, racism, classism, sexism, heterosexism, ableism, discrimination, and stereotyping-affects them personally and professionally.

Diversity-skilled group workers demonstrate knowledge about their social impact on others. They are knowledgeable about communication style differences, how their style may inhibit or foster the group process with members who are different from themselves along the different dimensions of diversity, and how to anticipate the impact they may have on others.

C. Skills

Diversity-competent group workers seek out educational, consultative, and training experiences to improve their understanding and effectiveness in working with group members who self-identify as Indigenous Peoples, African Americans, Asian Americans, Hispanics, Latinos/Latinas, gays, lesbians, bisexuals, or transgendered persons and persons with physical, mental/emotional, and/or learning disabilities, particularly with regard to race and ethnicity. Within this context, group workers are able to recognize the limits of their competencies and : (a) seek consultation, (b) seek further training or education, (c) refer members to more qualified group workers, or (d) engage in a combination of these.

Group workers who exhibit diversity competence are constantly seeking to understand themselves within their multiple identities (apparent and unapparent differences), for example, gay, Latina, Christian, working-class and female, and are constantly and actively striving to unlearn the various behaviors and processes they covertly and overtly communicate that perpetuate oppression, particularly racism.

II. Group Worker's Awareness of Group Member's Worldview

A. Attitudes and Beliefs

Diversity-skilled group workers exhibit awareness of any possible negative emotional reactions toward Indigenous Peoples, African Americans, Asian Americans, Hispanics, Latinos/Latinas, gays, lesbians, bisexuals, or transgendered persons and persons with physical, mental/emotional, and/or learning disabilities that they may hold. They are willing to contrast in a nonjudgmental manner their own beliefs and attitudes with those of Indigenous Peoples, African Americans, Asian Americans, Hispanics, Latinos/Latinas, gays, lesbians, bisexuals, or transgendered persons and persons with physical, mental/emotional, and/or learning disabilities who are group members.

Diversity-competent group workers demonstrate awareness of their stereotypes and preconceived notions that they may hold toward Indigenous Peoples, African Americans, Asian Americans, Hispanics, Latinos/Latinas, gays, lesbians, bisexuals, or transgendered persons and persons with physical, mental/emotional, and/or learning disabilities.

B. Knowledge

Diversity-skilled group workers possess specific knowledge and information about Indigenous Peoples, African Americans, Asian Americans, Hispanics, Latinos/Latinas, gays, lesbians, bisexuals, and transgendered people and group members who have mental/emotional, physical, and/or learning disabilities with whom they are working. They are aware of the life experiences, cultural heritage, and sociopolitical background of Indigenous Peoples, African Americans, Asian Americans, Hispanics, Latinos/Latinas, gays, lesbians, bisexuals, or transgendered persons and group members with physical, mental/emotional, and/or learning disabilities. This particular knowledge-based competency is strongly linked to the various racial/minority and sexual identity development models available in the literature (Atkinson, Morten, & Sue, 1993; Cass, 1979; Cross, 1995; D'Augelli & Patterson, 1995; Helms, 1992).

Diversity-competent group workers exhibit an understanding of how race, ethnicity, culture, gender, sexual identity, different abilities, SES, and other immutable personal characteristics may affect personality formation, vocational choices, manifestation of psychological disorders, physical "dis-ease" or somatic symptoms, help-seeking behavior(s), and the appropriateness or inappropriateness of the various types of and theoretical approaches to group work.

Group workers who demonstrate competency in diversity in groups understand and have the knowledge about sociopolitical influences that impinge upon the lives of Indigenous Peoples, African Americans, Asian Americans, Hispanics, Latinos/Latinas, gays, lesbians, bisexuals, or transgendered persons and persons with physical, mental/emotional, and/or learning disabilities. Immigration issues, poverty, racism, oppression, stereotyping, and/or powerlessness adversely impacts many of these individuals and therefore impacts group process or dynamics.

C. Skills

Diversity-skilled group workers familiarize themselves with relevant research and the latest findings regarding mental health issues of Indigenous Peoples, African Americans, Asian Americans, Hispanics, Latinos/Latinas, gays, lesbians, bisexuals, or transgendered persons and persons with physical, mental/emotional, and/or learning disabilities. They actively seek out educational experiences that foster their knowledge and understanding of skills for facilitating groups across differences.

Diversity-competent group workers become actively involved with Indigenous Peoples, African Americans, Asian Americans, Hispanics, Latinos/Latinas, gays, lesbians, bisexuals, or transgendered persons and persons with physical, mental/emotional, and/or learning disabilities outside of their group work/counseling setting (community events, social and political functions, celebrations, friendships, neighborhood groups, etc.) so that their perspective of minorities is more than academic or experienced through a third party.

III. Diversity-Appropriate Intervention Strategies

A. Attitudes and Beliefs

Diversity-competent group workers respect clients' religious and/or spiritual beliefs and values, because they affect worldview, psychosocial functioning, and expressions of distress.

Diversity-competent group workers respect indigenous helping practices and respect Indigenous Peoples, African Americans, Asian Americans, Hispanics, Latinos/Latinas, gays, lesbians, bisexuals, or transgendered persons and persons with physical, mental/emotional, and/or learning disabilities and can identify and utilize community intrinsic help-giving networks.

Diversity-competent group workers value bilingualism and sign language and do not view another language as an impediment to group work.

B. Knowledge

Diversity-competent group workers demonstrate a clear and explicit knowledge and understanding of generic characteristics of group work and theory and how they may clash with the beliefs, values, and traditions of Indigenous Peoples, African Americans, Asian Americans, Hispanics, Latinos/Latinas, gays, lesbians, bisexuals, or transgendered persons and persons with physical, mental/emotional, and/or learning disabilities.

Diversity-competent group workers exhibit an awareness of institutional barriers that prevent Indigenous Peoples, African Americans, Asian Americans, Hispanics, Latinos/Latinas, gays, lesbians, bisexuals, or transgendered members and members with physical, mental/emotional, and/or learning disabilities from actively participating in or using various types of groups, that is, task groups, psychoeducational groups, counseling groups, and psychotherapy groups or the settings in which the services are offered.

Diversity-competent group workers demonstrate knowledge of the potential bias in assessment instruments and use procedures and interpret findings, or actively participate in various types of evaluations of group outcome or success, keeping in mind the linguistic, cultural, and other self-identified characteristics of the group member.

Diversity-competent group workers exhibit knowledge of the family structures, hierarchies, values, and beliefs of Indigenous Peoples, African Americans, Asian Americans, Hispanics, Latinos/Latinas, gays, lesbians, bisexuals, or transgendered persons and persons with physical, mental/emotional, and/or learning disabilities. They are knowledgeable about the community characteristics and the resources in the community as well as about the family.

Diversity-competent group workers demonstrate an awareness of relevant discriminatory practices at the social and community level that may be affecting the psychological welfare of persons and access to services of the population being served.

C. Skills

Diversity-competent group workers are able to engage in a variety of verbal and nonverbal group-facilitating functions, dependent upon the type of group (task, counseling, psychoeducational, psychotherapy), and the multiple, self-identified status of various group members (such as Indigenous Peoples, African Americans, Asian Americans, Hispanics, Latinos/Latinas, gays, lesbians, bisexuals, or transgendered persons and persons with physical, mental/emotional, and/or learning disabilities). They demonstrate the ability to send and receive both verbal and nonverbal messages accurately, appropriately, and across/between the differences represented in the group. They are not tied down to one method or approach to group facilitation and recognize that helping styles and approaches may be culture-bound. When they sense that their group facilitation style is limited and potentially inappropriate, they can anticipate and ameliorate its negative impact by drawing upon other culturally relevant skill sets.

Diversity-competent group workers have the ability to exercise institutional intervention skills on behalf of their group members. They can help a member determine whether a "problem" with the institution stems from the oppression of Indigenous Peoples, African Americans, Asian Americans, Hispanics, Latinos/Latinas, gays, lesbians, bisexuals, or transgendered persons and persons with physical, mental/emotional, and/or learning disabilities, such as in the case of developing or having a "healthy" paranoia, so that group members do not inappropriately personalize problems.

Diversity-competent group workers do not exhibit a reluctance to seek consultation with traditional healers and religious and spiritual healers and practitioners in the treatment of members who are self-identified Indigenous Peoples, African Americans, Asian Americans, Hispanics, Latinos/Latinas, gays, lesbians, bisexuals, and transgendered persons and/or group members with mental/emotional, physical, and/or learning disabilities when appropriate.

Diversity-competent group workers take responsibility for interacting in the language requested by the group member(s) and, if not feasible, make an appropriate referral. A serious problem arises when the linguistic skills of a group worker and a group member or members, including sign language, do not match. The same problem occurs when the linguistic skills of one member or several members do not match. This being the case, the group worker, should (a) seek a translator with cultural knowledge and appropriate professional background, and (b) refer to a knowledgeable, competent bilingual group worker or a group worker competent or certified in sign language. In some cases, it may be necessary to have a group for group members of similar languages or to refer the group member for individual counseling.

Diversity-competent group workers are trained and have expertise in the use of traditional assessment and testing instruments related to group work, such as in screening potential members, and they also are aware of the cultural bias/limitations of these tools and processes.

This allows them to use the tools for the welfare of diverse group members following culturally appropriate procedures.

Diversity-competent group workers attend to as well as work to eliminate biases, prejudices, oppression, and discriminatory practices. They are cognizant of how sociopolitical contexts may affect evaluation and provision of group work and should develop sensitivity to issues of oppression, racism, sexism, heterosexism, classism, and so forth.

Diversity-competent group workers take responsibility in educating their group members to the processes of group work, such as goals, expectations, legal rights, sound ethical practice, and the group worker's theoretical orientation with regard to facilitating groups with diverse membership.

Conclusion

This document is the "starting point" for group workers as we become increasingly aware, knowledgeable, and skillful in facilitating groups whose memberships represent the diversity of our society. It is not intended to be a "how to" document. It is written as a call to action and/or a guideline and represents ASGW's commitment to moving forward with an agenda for addressing and understanding the needs of the populations we serve. As a "living document," the Association for Specialists in Group Work acknowledges the changing world in which we live and work and therefore recognizes that this is the first step in working with diverse group members with competence, compassion, respect, and integrity. As our awareness, knowledge, and skills develop, so too will this document evolve. As our knowledge as a profession grows in this area and as the sociopolitical context in which this document was written, changes, new editions of these Principles for Diversity-Competent Group Workers will arise. The operationalization of this document (article in process) will begin to define appropriate group leadership skills and interventions as well as make recommendations for research in understanding how diversity in group membership affects group process and dynamics.

References

American Counseling Association. (1995). Code of ethics and standards. Alexandria, VA: Author.

Association for Multicultural Counseling and Development. (1996).Multicultural competencies. Alexandria, VA: American Counseling Association.

Association for Specialists in Group Work (1991). Professional standards for training of group workers. Together, 20, 9-14.

Association for Specialists in Group Work (1998). Best practice guidelines. Journal for Specialists in Group Work, 23, 237-244.

Atkinson, D.R., Morten, G., & Sue, D.W. (Eds.).(1993). Counseling American minorities (4th ed.). Madison, WI:Brown & Benchmark.

Cass, V.C. (1979).Homosexual identity formation: A theoretical model. Journal of Homosexuality, 4, 219-236.

Cross, W.E. (1995). The psychology of Nigrescence: Revising the cross model. In J.G. Ponterotto, J.M. Casas, L.A. Suzuki, & C.M. Alexander (Eds.), Handbook of multicultural counseling (pp. 93-122). Thousand Oaks, CA:Sage.

D'Augelli, A.R.,& Patterson, C.J. (Eds.). (1995). Lesbian, gay and bisexual identities over the lifespan. New York: Oxford University Press.

Helms, J.E. (1992). A race is a nice thing to have. Topeka, KS: Context Communications.

Principles for Diversity-Competent Group Workers (ASGW, 1999).
Reprinted with permission.

Canadian Counselling Association
Code of Ethics

Preamble

This Code of Ethics expresses the ethical principles and values of the Canadian Counselling Association and serves as a guide to the professional conduct of all its members. It also informs the public which they serve of the standards of ethical conduct for which members are to be responsible and accountable. The Code reflects such values as integrity, competence, responsibility and an understanding of and respect for the cultural diversity of society. It is part of a social contract, based on attitudes of mutual respect and trust by which society supports the autonomy of the profession in return for the commitment of its members to act ethically in the provision of professional services.

Members of CCA have a responsibility to ensure that they are familiar with this Code of Ethics, understand its application to their professional conduct, and strive to adhere to its principles and values. Counsellors should also be familiar with other sources of information which will assist them in making informed professional decisions. These include; the laws, regulations, and policies which are professionally relevant to their working environment.

Members are accountable to both the public and their peers and are therefore subject to the complaints and disciplinary procedures of the Canadian Counselling Association. Violations of this Code, however, do not automatically imply legal liability. Such a determination can only be made by legal and judicial proceedings. This peer review process is intended to enable the Association to advise and discipline its members in response to complaints originating either with peers or the public.

Although a Code of Ethics is essential to the maintenance of ethical integrity and accountability, it cannot be a substitute for the active process of ethical decision-making. Members increasingly confront challenging ethical demands and dilemmas in a complex and dynamic society to which a simple and direct application of this code may not be possible. Also, reasonable differences of opinion can and do exist among members with respect to how ethical principles and values should be rank-ordered when they are in conflict. Therefore, members must develop the ability and the courage to exercise a high level of ethical judgement. For these reasons, the code includes a section on ethical decision making.

This Code is not a static document but will need revisions over time because of the continuing development of ethical knowledge and the emergence of consensus on challenging ethical issues.Therefore, members and others, including members of the public, are invited to submit comments and suggestions at any time to CCA.

Ethical Principles

The expectations for ethical conduct as expressed in this Code are based on the following fundamental principles:

a. respect for the dignity of persons

b. not wilfully harming others

c. integrity in relationships

d. responsible caring

e. responsibility to society

f. respect for self-determination

The CCA Process of Ethical Decision-Making

This brief overview of a process of ethical decision-making is provided here so that counsellors will have a sequence of steps to follow when making ethical decisions and resolving ethical dilemmas.

Step One - What are the key ethical issues in this situation?

This first step consists of the counsellor clearly identifying the ethical issues and/or behaviours which are of concern in the particular situation.

Step Two - What ethical guidelines are relevant to this situation?

The second important step consists of referring to the CCA Code of Ethics to see if the situation is dealt with under one or more of the articles in the Code. If there are appropriate articles (for example, on confidentiality or informed consent), following it may be sufficient to address the ethical issue. If the ethical problem is more complex, however, the following further steps will be needed.

Step Three - What ethical principles are of major importance in this situation?

The third step consists of examining the ethical principles that are important in the situation including those that may be in conflict. This would include a review of the six ethical principles as stated in this Code of Ethics.

Step Four - What are the most important principles, and what are the risks and benefits if these principles are acted upon?

The fourth step consists of choosing the most important principles and relevant ethical articles and beginning to implement some possible action by:

(a) generating alternatives and examining the risks and benefits of each,

(b) securing additional information,including possible discussion with the client

(c) consulting with knowledgeable colleagues, with provincial or CCA ethics committees, or with other appropriate sources, and

(d) examining the probable outcomes of various courses of action.

Step Five - Will I feel the same about this situation if I think about it a little longer?

Until this point, this decision-making process has concentrated on fairly cognitive, rational steps, so at the fifth step counsellors should acknowledge and include in their decision making process the feelings and intuitions evoked by the ethical challenge. In so doing, they could use such techniques as:

Quest - a solitary walk in the woods or park where your emotions evoked by the ethical challenge are

(a) brought into full awareness,

(b) Incubation - "sleep on it",

(c) Time projection - projecting the ethical situation into the future and thinking about the various probable scenarios.

Step Six - What plan of action will be most helpful in this situation?

The sixth step consists of taking some action. Counsellors should follow a concrete action plan, evaluate the plan, and be prepared to correct any negative consequences that might occur from the action taken.

> *For a more comprehensive treatment of Ethical Decision-Making, members are directed to the CCA Counselling Ethics Casebook, available from the CCA National Office*

A. Professional Responsibility

A1. General Responsibility

Counsellors maintain high standards of professional competence and ethical behaviour, and recognize the need for continuing education and personal care in order to meet this responsibility.

A2. Respect for Rights

Counsellors participate in only those practices which are respectful of the legal, civic, and moral rights of others, and act to safeguard the dignity and rights of their clients, students, and research participants.

A3. Boundaries of Competence

Counsellors limit their counselling services and practices to those which are within their professional competence by virtue of their education and professional experience, and consistent with any requirements for provincial and national credentials. They refer to other professionals, when the counselling needs of clients exceed their level of competence.

A4. Supervision and Consultation

Counsellors take reasonable steps to obtain supervision and/or consultation with respect to their counselling practices and, particularly, with respect to doubts or uncertainties which may arise during their professional work.

A5. Representation of Professional Qualifications

Counsellors claim or imply only those professional qualifications which they possess, and are responsible for correcting any known misrepresentation of their qualifications by others.

A6. Responsibility to Counsellors and other Professionals

Counsellors understand that ethical behaviour among themselves and with other professionals is expected at all time.

A7. Unethical Behaviour by Other Counsellors

Counsellors have an obligation when they have serious doubts as to the ethical behaviour of another counsellor, to seek an informal resolution with the counsellor, when feasible and appropriate. When an informal resolution is not appropriate or feasible,or is unsuccessful, counsellors report their concerns to the CCA Ethics Committee. When the counsellors are members of a CCA Affiliate organization that has agreed to manage Complaints and Disciplinary Procedures for its members, counsellors will report their concerns to the appropriate committee of the CCA Affiliate.

A8. Sexual Harassment

Counsellors do not condone or engage in sexual harassment, which is defined as deliberate or repeated verbal or written comments, gestures, or physical contacts of a sexual nature.

A9. Sensitivity to Diversity

Counsellors strive to understand and respect the diversity of their clients, including differences related to age, ethnicity, culture, gender, disability, religion, sexual orientation and social-economic status.

A10. Extension of Ethical Responsibilities

Counselling services and products provided by counsellors through classroom instruction, public lectures, demonstrations, publications, radio and television programs, computer technology and other media must meet the appropriate ethical standards of this Code of Ethics.

B. Counselling Relationships

B1. Primary Responsibility

Counsellors have a primary responsibility to respect the integrity and promote the welfare of their clients. They work collaboratively with clients to devise integrated, individual counselling plans that offer reasonable promise of success and are consistent with the abilities and circumstances of clients.

B2. Confidentiality

Counselling relationships and information resulting therefrom are kept confidential. However, there are the following exceptions to confidentiality:

(i) when disclosure is required to prevent clear and imminent danger to the client or others;

(ii) when legal requirements demand that confidential material be revealed;

(iii) when a child is in need of protection

B3. Duty to Warn

When counsellors become aware of their clients intent or potential to place others in clear or imminent danger, they use reasonable care to give threatened persons such warnings as are essential to avert foreseeable dangers.

B4. Client 's Rights and Informed Consent

When counselling is initiated, and throughout the counselling process as necessary, counsellors inform clients of the purposes, goals, techniques, procedures, limitations, potential risks and benefits of services to be performed, and other such pertinent information. Counsellors make sure that clients understand the implications of diagnosis, fees and fee collection arrangements, record keeping, and limits to confidentiality. Clients have the right to participate in the ongoing counselling plans, to refuse any recommended services, and to be advised of the consequences of such refusal.

B5. Children and Persons with Diminished Capacity

Counsellors conduct the informed consent process with those legally appropriate to give consent when counselling, assessing, and having as research subjects children and/or persons with diminished capacity. These clients also give consent to such services or involvement commensurate with their capacity to do so.

B6. Maintenance of Records

Counsellors maintain records in sufficient detail to track the sequence and nature of professional services rendered and consistent with any legal, regulatory, agency, or institutional requirement. They secure the safety of such records and, create, maintain, transfer, and dispose of them in a manner compliant with the requirements of confidentiality and the other articles of this Code of Ethics.

B7. Access to Records

Counsellors understand that clients have a right of access to their counselling records, and that disclosure to others of information from these records only occurs with the written consent of the client and/or when required by law.

B8. Dual Relationships

Counsellors make every effort to avoid dual relationships with clients that could impair professional judgment or increase the risk of harm to clients. Examples of dual relationships include, but are not limited to, familial, social, financial, business, or close personal relationships. When a dual relationship can not be avoided, counsellors take appropriate professional precautions such as informed consent, consultation, supervision, and documentation to ensure that judgment is not impaired and no exploitation occurs.

B9. Respecting Diversity

Counsellors actively work to understand the diverse cultural background of the clients with whom they work, and do not condone or engage in discrimination based on age, colour, culture, ethnicity, disability, gender, religion, sexual orientation, marital, or socioeconomic status.

B10. Consulting With Other Professionals

Counsellors may consult with other professionally competent persons about the client. However, if the identity of the client is to be revealed, it is done with the written consent of the client. Counsellors choose professional consultants in a manner which will avoid placing the consultant in a conflict of interest situation.

B11. Relationships with Former Clients

Counsellors remain accountable for any relationships established with former clients. Those relationships could include, but are not limited to those of a friendship, social, financial, and business nature. Counsellors exercise caution about entering any such relationships and take into account whether or not the issues and relational dynamics present during the counselling have been fully resolved and properly terminated. In any case, counsellors seek consultation on such decisions.

B12. Sexual Intimacies

Counsellors avoid any type of sexual intimacies with clients and they do not counsel persons with whom they have had a sexual relationship. Counsellors do not engage in sexual intimacies with former clients within a minimum of three years after terminating the counselling relationship. This prohibition is not limited to the three year period but extends indefinitely if the client is clearly vulnerable, by reason of emotional or cognitive disorder, to exploitative influence by the counsellor. Counsellors, in all such circumstances, clearly bear the burden to ensure that no such exploitative influence has occurred, and to seek consultative assistance.

B13. Multiple Clients

When counsellors agree to provide counselling to two or more persons who have a relationship (such as husband and wife, or parents and children), counsellors clarify at the outset which person or persons are clients and the nature of the relationship they will have with each person. If conflicting roles emerge for counsellors, they must clarify, adjust, or withdraw from roles appropriately.

B14. Multiple Helpers

If, after entering a counselling relationship, a counsellor discovers the client is already in a counselling relationship then, the counsellor is responsible for discussing the issues related to continuing or terminating counselling with the client. It may be necessary, with client consent, to discuss these issues with the other helper.

B15. Group Work

Counsellors have the responsibility to screen prospective group members, especially when group goals focus on self-understanding and growth through self-disclosure. They take reasonable precautions to protect group members from physical and/or psychological harm resulting from interaction within the group, both during and following the group experience.

B16. Computer Use

When computer applications are used as a component of counselling services, counsellors ensure that: (a) client and counsellor identity is verified; (b) the client is capable of using the computer application; (c) the computer application is appropriate to the needs of the client; (d) the client understands the purpose and operation of client-assisted and/or self-help computer applications; and (e) a follow-up of client use of a computer application is provided to assist subsequent needs. In any case, computer applications do not diminish the counsellor's responsibility to act in accordance with the CCA Code of Ethics, and in particular, to ensure adherence to the principles of confidentiality, informed consent, and safeguarding against harmful effects.

B17. Referral

When counsellors determine their inability to be of professional assistance to clients, they avoid initiating a counselling relationship, or immediately terminate it. In either event, members suggest appropriate alternatives, including making a referral to resources about which they are knowledgeable. Should clients decline the suggested referral, counsellors are not obligated to continue the relationship.

B18. Termination of Counselling

Counsellors terminate counselling relationships, with client agreement whenever possible, when it is reasonably clear that: the goals of counselling have been met, the client is no longer benefitting from counselling, when clients do not pay fees charged, when previously disclosed agency or institutional limits do not allow for the provision of further counselling services.

However, counsellors make reasonable efforts to facilitate the continuation of counselling services when services are interrupted by such factors as counsellor illness, client or counsellor relocation, client financial diicultities, and so forth.

C. Consulting and Private Practice

C1. General Responsibility

Counsellors provide consultative services only in those areas in which they have demonstrated competency by virtue of their education and experience.

C2. Undiminished Responsibility and Liability

Counsellors who work in private practice, whether incorporated or not, must ensure that there is no diminishing of their individual professional responsibility to act in accordance with the CCA Code of Ethics, or in their liability for any failure to do so.

C3. Accurate Advertising

Counsellors, when advertising services as private practitioners, do so in a manner that accurately and clearly informs the public of their services and areas of expertise.

C4. Consultative Relationships

Counsellors ensure that consultation occurs within a voluntary relationship between a counsellor and a help-seeking individual, group, or organization, and that the goals are understood by all parties concerned.

C5. Informed Consent

Counsellors who provide services for the use of third parties, acknowledge and clarify for the informed consent of clients, all obligations of such multiple relationships, including purpose(s), entitlement to information, and any restrictions on confidentiality. Third parties include, courts, public and private institutions, funding agencies, employees, and so forth.

C6. Respect for Privacy

Counsellors limit any discussion of client information obtained from a consulting relationship to persons clearly involved with the case. Any written and oral reports restrict data to the purposes of the consultation and, every effort is made to protect client identity and to avoid undue invasion of privacy.

C7. Conflict of Interest

Counsellors who engage in consultation avoid circumstances where the duality of relationships, or the prior possession of information could lead to a conflict of interest.

C8. Sponsorship and Recruitment

Counsellors present any of their organizational affiliations or membership in such a way as to avoid misunderstanding regarding sponsorship or certification. They also avoid the use of any institutional affiliation to recruit private practice clients.

D. Evaluation and Assessment

D1. General Orientation

Counsellors adequately orient and inform clients so that evaluation and assessment results can be placed in proper perspective along with other relevant information.

D2. Purposes and Results of Evaluation and Assessment

Counsellors take responsibility to inform clients about the purpose of any evaluation and assessment instruments and procedures and the meaning of evaluation and assessment results.

D3. Evaluation and Assessment Competence

Counsellors recognize the limits of their competence and offer only those evaluation and assessment services for which they have appropriate preparation and which meet established professional standards.

D4. Administrative and Supervisory Conditions

Counsellors ensure that evaluation and assessment instruments and procedures are administered and supervised under established conditions consistent with professional standards. They note any departures from standard conditions, and any unusual behavior or irregularities which may affect the interpretation of results.

D5. Use of Technology

Counsellors recognize that their ethical responsibilities are not altered, or in any way diminished, by the use of technology for the administration of evaluation and assessment instruments. Counsellors retain their responsibility for the maintenance of the ethical principles of privacy, confidentiality, and responsibility for decisions regardless of the technology used.

D6. Appropriateness of Evaluation and Assessment

Counsellors ensure that evaluation and assessment instruments and procedures are valid, reliable, and appropriate to both the client and the intended purposes.

D7. Reporting Evaluation and Assessment Results

Counsellors ensure that when reporting evaluation and assessment results to clients and other individuals care is taken to provide, in an appropriate manner, accurate and sufficient information for an understanding of any conclusions and recommendations made, and to identify the basis for any reservations which might exist.

D8. Release of Evaluation and Assessment Data

Counsellors ensure that evaluation and assessment data are released only to persons qualified to interpret and use them properly.

D9. Integrity of Evaluation and Assessment Instruments and Procedures

Counsellors who use psychological tests and other assessment instruments, the value of which depends on their novelty to the client, ensure that they are limited to and safeguarded by those with the professional interest and competence to do so.

D10. Sensitivity to Diversity when Assessing and Evaluating

Counsellors proceed with caution when judging and interpreting the performance of minority group members and any other persons not represented in the group on which the evaluation and assessment instruments and procedures were standardized. They recognize and take into account the potential effects of age, ethnicity, disability, culture, gender, religion, sexual orientation, and social-economic status on both the administration of, and the interpretation of date from, such instruments and procedures.

D11. Security Maintenance

Counsellors ensure the integrity and security of evaluation and assessment instruments and procedures consistent with any legal and contractual obligations. They refrain from appropriating, reproducing, or modifying established evaluation and assessment instruments without the expressed permission and adequate recognition of the original author, publisher, and copy right holder.

E. Research and Publications

E1. Researcher Responsibility

Counsellors plan, conduct, and report on research in a manner consistent with relevant ethical principles, professional standards of practice, federal and provincial laws, institutional regulations, cultural norms, and standards governing research with human subjects.

E2. Subject Welfare

Counsellors are responsible for protecting the welfare of their research subjects during research, and avoid causing injurious psychological, physical or social effects to persons who participate in their research activities.

E3. Principal Researcher Responsibility

Counsellors when in the role of principal researcher are responsible for ensuring that appropriate ethical research practices are followed and, with respect to research involving human subjects, they obtain an independent and appropriate ethical review before proceeding with the research. Research associates involved in the research activities share ethical obligations and full responsibility for their own actions.

E4. Voluntary Participation

Counsellors ensure that participation in research is voluntary. However, involuntary participation may be appropriate when it can be shown that participation will have no harmful effects on subjects, is essential to the research, and meets ethical review requirements.

E5. Informed Consent of Research Subjects

Counsellors inform all research subjects of the purpose(s) of their research. In addition, subjects are made aware of any experimental procedures, possible risks, disclosures and limitations on confidentiality. Subjects are also told they are free to ask questions and to discontinue at any time.

E6. Research Confidentiality

Counsellors ensure that research information on subjects is confidential and the identity of participants is protected unless otherwise authorized by them, consistent with all informed consent procedures.

E7. Further Research

Counsellors have an obligation to collaborate with colleagues by making available original research data to qualified researchers who may wish to replicate or verify the research.

E8. Research Sponsors

Counsellors when conducting research obtain informed consent form sponsors and institutions and ensure that sponsors and institutions are given feedback information and proper acknowledgment.

E9. Review of Manuscripts

Counsellors who review material submitted for publication, research or other scholarly purposes respect the confidentiality and proprietary rights of those who submitted the research.

E10. Reporting Results

In reporting research results, counsellors mention any variables and conditions that might affect the outcome of the investigation or the interpretation of the results, and provide information sufficient for others who might wish to replicate the research.

E11. Research Contributions

Counsellors give due credit through joint authorship, acknowledgment, footnote statements, or other appropriate means to those who have contributed significantly to the research and/or publication, and to those who have done previous work on the topic. For an article that is based mainly on a student thesis or dissertation, the student is listed as principal author.

E12. Submission for Publication

Counsellors do not submit the same manuscript or one essentially similar in content for simultaneous publication consideration by two or more journals. In addition, manuscripts published in whole or in substantial part in another journal or published work should not be submitted for publication without acknowledgment and permission from the previous publication.

F. Counsellor Education, Training, and Supervision

F1. General Responsibility

Counsellors who are responsible for counsellor education, training, and supervision adhere to current CCA guidelines and standards with respect to such activities and conduct themselves in a manner consistent with the CCA Code of Ethics and Standards of Practice.

F2. Boundaries of Competence

Counsellors who conduct counsellor education, training, and supervision have the necessary knowledge and skills to do so, and limit their involvement to such competencies.

F3. Ethical Orientation

Counsellors who are responsible for counsellor education, training, and supervision have an obligation to make their students, trainees, and supervisees aware of their ethical responsibilities as expressed in the CCA Code of Ethics, and Standards of Practice.

F4. Clarification of Roles and Responsibilities

Counsellors who engage in counselling supervision of students or trainees take responsibility for clarifying their respective roles and obligations.

F5. Welfare of Clients

Counsellors who engage in counselling supervision of students or trainees take steps to ensure the welfare of clients during the supervised practice period, and intervene, when necessary, to ensure that this obligation is met.

F6. Program Orientation

Counsellors responsible for counsellor education programs and training activities take responsibility to orient perspective students and trainees to all core elements of such programs and activities, including to a clear policy with respect to all supervised practice components, both those simulated and real.

F7. Relational Boundaries

Counsellors who work as counsellor educators, trainers, and supervisors establish relationships with their students, trainees, and supervisees such that appropriate relational boundaries are clarified and maintained, and dual relationships avoided.

F8. Obligation to Inform

Counsellors who work as counsellor educators, trainers, and supervisors take steps to inform students, trainees, and supervisees, at the beginning of activities associated with these roles, of all reasonably foreseeable circumstances under which confidentiality may be breached during such activities.

F9. Self-Development and Self-Awareness

Counsellors who work as counsellor educators, trainers, and supervisors, encourage and facilitate the self-development and self-awareness of students, trainees, and supervisees, so that they learn to integrate their professional practice and personal insight.

F10. Dealing with Personal Issues

Counsellors responsible for counsellor education, training, and supervision recognize when such activities evoke significant personal issues for students, trainees, and supervisees and refer to other sources when necessary to avoid counselling those for whom they hold administrative, or evaluative responsibility.

F11. Self Growth Activities

Counsellors who work as counsellor educators, trainees, and supervisors ensure that any professional experiences which require self-disclosure, and engagement in self-growth activities are managed in a manner consistent with the principles of informed consent, confidentiality, and safeguarding against any harmful effects.

Code of Ethics, Canadian Counselling Association, (CCA, 1999).
Reprinted with Permission

Canadian Psychological Association
Canadian Code of Ethics for Psychologists

Introduction

Every discipline that has relatively autonomous control over its entry requirements, training, development of knowledge, standards, methods, and practices does so only within the context of a contract with the society in which it functions. This social contract is based on attitudes of mutual respect and trust, with society granting support for the autonomy of a discipline in exchange for a commitment by the discipline to do everything it can to assure that its members act ethically in conducting the affairs of the discipline within society; in particular, a commitment to try to assure that each member will place the welfare of the society and individual members of that society above the welfare of the discipline and its own members. By virtue of this social contract, psychologists have a higher duty of care to members of society than the general duty of care that all members of society have to each other.

The Canadian Psychological Association recognizes its responsibility to help assure ethical behaviour and attitudes on the part of psychologists. Attempts to assure ethical behaviour and attitudes include articulating ethical principles, values, and standards; promoting those principles, values, and standards through education, peer modelling, and consultation; developing and implementing methods to help psychologists monitor the ethics of their behaviour and attitudes; adjudicating complaints of unethical behaviour; and, taking corrective action when warranted.

This *Code* articulates ethical principles, values, and standards to guide all members of the Canadian Psychological Association, whether scientists, practitioners, or scientist practitioners, or whether acting in a research, direct service, teaching, student, trainee, administrative, management, employer, employee, supervisory, consultative, peer review, editorial, expert witness, social policy, or any other role related to the discipline of psychology.

Structure and Derivation of *Code*

Structure. Four ethical principles, to be considered and balanced in ethical decision making, are presented. Each principle is followed by a statement of those values that are included in and give definition to the principle. Each values statement is followed by a list of ethical standards that illustrate the application of the specific principle and values to the activities of psychologists. The standards range from minimal behavioural expectations (e.g., Standards I.28, II.28, III.33, IV.27) to more idealized, but achievable, attitudinal and behavioural expectations (e.g., Standards I.12, II.12, III.10, IV.6). In the margin, to the left of the standards, key words are placed to guide the reader through the standards and to illustrate the relationship of the specific standards to the values statement.

Derivation. The four principles represent those ethical principles used most consistently by Canadian psychologists to resolve hypothetical ethical dilemmas sent to them by the CPA Committee on Ethics during the initial development of the *Code*. In addition to the responses provided by Canadian psychologists, the values statements and ethical standards have been derived from interdisciplinary and international ethics codes, provincial and specialty codes of conduct, and ethics literature.

When Principles Conflict

- **Principle I: Respect for the Dignity of Persons.** This principle, with its emphasis on moral rights, generally should be given the highest weight, except in circumstances in which there is a clear and imminent danger to the physical safety of any person.

- **Principle II: Responsible Caring.** This principle generally should be given the second highest weight. Responsible caring requires competence and should be carried out only in ways that respect the dignity of persons.
- **Principle III: Integrity in Relationships.** This principle generally should be given the third highest weight. Psychologists are expected to demonstrate the highest integrity in all of their relationships. However, in rare circumstances, values such as openness and straightforwardness might need to be subordinated to the values contained in the Principles of Respect for the Dignity of Persons and Responsible Caring.
- **Principle IV: Responsibility to Society.** This principle generally should be given the lowest weight of the four principles when it conflicts with one or more of them. Although it is necessary and important to consider responsibility to society in every ethical decision, adherence to this principle must be subject to and guided by Respect for the Dignity of Persons, Responsible Caring, and Integrity in Relationships. When a person's welfare appears to conflict with benefits to society, it is often possible to find ways of working for the benefit of society that do not violate respect and responsible caring for the person. However, if this is not possible, the dignity and well-being of a person should not be sacrificed to a vision of the greater good of society, and greater weight must be given to respect and responsible caring for the person.

Even with the above ordering of the principles, psychologists will be faced with ethical dilemmas that are difficult to resolve. In these circumstances, psychologists are expected to engage in an ethical decision-making process that is explicit enough to bear public scrutiny. In some cases, resolution might be a matter of personal conscience. However, decisions of personal conscience are also expected to be the result of a decision-making process that is based on a reasonably coherent set of ethical principles and that can bear public scrutiny. If the psychologist can demonstrate that every reasonable effort was made to apply the ethical principles of this *Code* and resolution of the conflict has had to depend on the personal conscience of the psychologist, such a psychologist would be deemed to have followed this *Code*.

The Ethical Decision-Making Process

The ethical decision-making process might occur very rapidly, leading to an easy resolution of an ethical issue. This is particularly true of issues for which clear-cut guidelines or standards exist and for which there is no conflict between principles. On the other hand, some ethical issues (particularly those in which ethical principles conflict) are not easily resolved, might be emotionally distressful, and might require time-consuming deliberation.

The following basic steps typify approaches to ethical decision making:

1. Identification of the individuals and groups potentially affected by the decision.
2. Identification of ethically relevant issues and practices, including the interests, rights, and any relevant characteristics of the individuals and groups involved and of the system or circumstances in which the ethical problem arose.
3. Consideration of how personal biases, stresses, or self-interest might influence the development of or choice between courses of action.
4. Development of alternative courses of action.
5. Analysis of likely short-term, ongoing, and long-term risks and benefits of each course of action on the individual(s)/group(s) involved or likely to be affected (e.g., client, client's family or employees, employing institution, students, research participants, colleagues, the discipline, society, self).
6. Choice of course of action after conscientious application of existing principles, values, and standards.
7. Action, with a commitment to assume responsibility for the consequences of the action.
8. Evaluation of the results of the course of action.

9. Assumption of responsibility for consequences of action, including correction of negative consequences, if any, or re-engaging in the decision-making process if the ethical issue is not resolved.
10. Appropriate action, as warranted and feasible, to prevent future occurrences of the dilemma (e.g., communication and problem solving with colleagues; changes in procedures and practices).

Psychologists engaged in time-consuming deliberation are encouraged and expected to consult with parties affected by the ethical problem, when appropriate, and with colleagues and/or advisory bodies when such persons can add knowledge or objectivity to the decision-making process. Although the decision for action remains with the individual psychologist, the seeking and consideration of such assistance reflects an ethical approach to ethical decision making.

Uses of the *Code*

This *Code* is intended to guide psychologists in their everyday conduct, thinking, and planning, and in the resolution of ethical dilemmas; that is, it advocates the practice of both proactive and reactive ethics.

The *Code* also is intended to serve as an umbrella document for the development of codes of conduct or other more specific codes. For example, the *Code* could be used as an ethical framework for the identification of behaviours that would be considered enforceable in a jurisdiction, the violation of which would constitute misconduct; or, jurisdictions could identify those standards in the *Code* that would be considered of a more serious nature and, therefore, reportable and subject to possible discipline. In addition, the principles and values could be used to help specialty areas develop standards that are specific to those areas. Some work in this direction has already occurred within CPA (e.g., *Guidelines for the Use of Animals in Research and Instruction in Psychology, Guidelines for Non-Discriminatory Practice, Guidelines for Psychologists in Addressing Recovered Memories*). The principles and values incorporated into this *Code*, insofar as they come to be reflected in other documents guiding the behaviour of psychologists, will reduce inconsistency and conflict between documents.

A third use of the *Code* is to assist in the adjudication of complaints against psychologists. A body charged with this responsibility is required to investigate allegations, judge whether unacceptable behaviour has occurred, and determine what corrective action should be taken. In judging whether unacceptable conduct has occurred, many jurisdictions refer to a code of conduct. Some complaints, however, are about conduct that is not addressed directly in a code of conduct. The *Code* provides an ethical framework for determining whether the complaint is of enough concern, either at the level of the individual psychologist or at the level of the profession as a whole, to warrant corrective action (e.g., discipline of the individual psychologist, general educational activities for members, or incorporation into the code of conduct). In determining corrective action for an individual psychologist, one of the judgments the adjudicating body needs to make is whether an individual conscientiously engaged in an ethical decision-making process and acted in good faith, or whether there was a negligent or willful disregard of ethical principles. The articulation of the ethical decision-making process contained in this *Code* provides guidance for making such judgements.

Responsibility of the Individual Psychologist

The discipline's contract with society commits the discipline and its members to act as a moral community that develops its ethical awareness and sensitivity, educates new members in the ethics of the discipline, manages its affairs and its members in an ethical manner, is as self-correcting as possible, and is accountable both internally and externally.

However, responsibility for ethical action depends foremost on the integrity of each individual psychologist; that is, on each psychologist's commitment to behave as ethically as possible in every situation. Acceptance to membership in the Canadian Psychological Association, a scientific and professional association of psychologists, commits members:

1. To adhere to the Association's *Code* in all current activities as a psychologist.
2. To apply conscientiously the ethical principles and values of the *Code* to new and emerging areas of activity.
3. To assess and discuss ethical issues and practices with colleagues on a regular basis.
4. To bring to the attention of the Association ethical issues that require clarification or the development of new guidelines or standards.
5. To bring concerns about possible unethical actions by a psychologist directly to the psychologist when the action appears to be primarily a lack of sensitivity, knowledge, or experience, and attempt to reach an agreement on the issue and, if needed, on the appropriate action to be taken.
6. To bring concerns about possible unethical actions of a more serious nature (e.g., actions that have caused or could cause serious harm, or actions that are considered misconduct in the jurisdiction) to the person(s) or body(ies) best suited to investigating the situation and to stopping or offsetting the harm.
7. To consider seriously others' concerns about one's own possibly unethical actions and attempt to reach an agreement on the issue and, if needed, take appropriate action.
8. In bringing or in responding to concerns about possible unethical actions, not to be vexatious or malicious.
9. To cooperate with duly constituted committees of the Association that are concerned with ethics and ethical conduct.

Relationship of *Code* to Personal Behaviour

This *Code* is intended to guide and regulate only those activities a psychologist engages in by virtue of being a psychologist. There is no intention to guide or regulate a psychologist's activities outside of this context. Personal behaviour becomes a concern of the discipline only if it is of such a nature that it undermines public trust in the discipline as a whole or if it raises questions about the psychologist's ability to carry out appropriately his/her responsibilities as a psychologist.

Relationship of *Code* to Provincial Regulatory Bodies

In exercising its responsibility to articulate ethical principles, values, and standards for those who wish to become and remain members in good standing, the Canadian Psychological Association recognizes the multiple memberships that some psychologists have (both regulatory and voluntary). The *Code* has attempted to encompass and incorporate those ethical principles most prevalent in the discipline as a whole, thereby minimizing the possibility of variance with provincial/territorial regulations and guidelines. Psychologists are expected to respect the requirements of their provincial/territorial regulatory bodies. Such requirements might define particular behaviours that constitute misconduct, are reportable to the regulatory body, and/or are subject to discipline.

Definition of Terms

For the purposes of this *Code:*

a. **"Psychologist"** means any person who is a Fellow, Member, Student Affiliate or Foreign Affiliate of the Canadian Psychological Association, or a member of any psychology voluntary association or regulatory body adopting this *Code*. (Readers are reminded that provincial/territorial jurisdictions might restrict the legal use of the term psychologist in their jurisdiction and that such restrictions are to be honoured.)
b. **"Client"** means an individual, family, or group (including an organization or community) receiving service from a psychologist.

c. Clients, research participants, students, and any other persons with whom psychologists come in contact in the course of their work, are **"independent"** if they can independently contract or give informed consent. Such persons are **"partially dependent"** if the decision to contract or give informed consent is shared between two or more parties (e.g., parents and school boards, workers and Workers' Compensation Boards, adult members of a family). Such persons are considered to be **"fully dependent"** if they have little or no choice about whether or not to receive service or participate in an activity (e.g., patients who have been involuntarily committed to a psychiatric facility, or very young children involved in a research project).

d. **"Others"** means any persons with whom psychologists come in contact in the course of their work. This may include, but is not limited to: clients seeking help with individual, family, organizational, industrial, or community issues; research participants; employees; students; trainees; supervisees; colleagues; employers; third party payers; and, members of the general public.

e. **"Legal or civil rights"** means those rights protected under laws and statutes recognized by the province or territory in which the psychologist is working.

f. **"Moral rights"** means fundamental and inalienable human rights that might or might not be fully protected by existing laws and statutes. Of particular significance to psychologists, for example, are rights to: distributive justice; fairness and due process; and, developmentally appropriate privacy, self-determination, and personal liberty. Protection of some aspects of these rights might involve practices that are not contained or controlled within current laws and statutes. Moral rights are not limited to those mentioned in this definition.

g. **"Unjust discrimination"** or **"unjustly discriminatory"** means activities that are prejudicial or promote prejudice to persons because of their culture, nationality, ethnicity, colour, race, religion, sex, gender, marital status, sexual orientation, physical or mental abilities, age, socio-economic status, or any other preference or personal characteristic, condition, or status.

h. **"Sexual harassment"** includes either or both of the following: (i) The use of power or authority in an attempt to coerce another person to engage in or tolerate sexual activity. Such uses include explicit or implicit threats of reprisal for noncompliance, or promises of reward for compliance. (ii) Engaging in deliberate and/or repeated unsolicited sexually oriented comments, anecdotes, gestures, or touching, if such behaviours: are offensive and unwelcome; create an offensive, hostile, or intimidating working, learning, or service environment; or, can be expected to be harmful to the recipient.[1]

i. The **"discipline of psychology"** refers to the scientific and applied methods and knowledge of psychology, and to the structures and procedures used by its members for conducting their work in relationship to society, to members of the public, to students or trainees, and to each other.

Review Schedule

To maintain the relevance and responsiveness of this *Code*, it will be reviewed regularly by the CPA Board of Directors, and revised as needed. You are invited to forward comments and suggestions, at any time, to the CPA office. In addition to psychologists, this invitation is extended to all readers, including members of the public and other disciplines.

Principle I: Respect for the Dignity of Persons

Values Statement

In the course of their work as scientists, practitioners, or scientist-practitioners, psychologists come into contact with many different individuals and groups, including: research participants; clients seeking help with individual, family, organizational, industrial, or community issues; students; trainees; supervisees; employees; business partners; business competitors; colleagues; employers; third party payers; and, the general public.

In these contacts, psychologists accept as fundamental the principle of respect for the dignity of persons; that is, the belief that each person should be treated primarily as a person or an end in him/herself, not as an object or a means to an end. In so doing, psychologists acknowledge that all persons have a right to have their innate worth as human beings appreciated and that this worth is not dependent upon their culture, nationality, ethnicity, colour, race, religion, sex, gender, marital status, sexual orientation, physical or mental abilities, age, socio-economic status, or any other preference or personal characteristic, condition, or status.

Although psychologists have a responsibility to respect the dignity of all persons with whom they come in contact in their role as psychologists, the nature of their contract with society demands that their greatest responsibility be to those persons in the most vulnerable position. Normally, persons directly receiving or involved in the psychologist's activities are in such a position (e.g., research participants, clients, students). This responsibility is almost always greater than their responsibility to those indirectly involved (e.g., employers, third party payers, the general public).

Adherence to the concept of moral rights is an essential component of respect for the dignity of persons. Rights to privacy, self-determination, personal liberty, and natural justice are of particular importance to psychologists, and they have a responsibility to protect and promote these rights in all of their activities. As such, psychologists have a responsibility to develop and follow procedures for informed consent, confidentiality, fair treatment, and due process that are consistent with those rights.

As individual rights exist within the context of the rights of others and of responsible caring (see Principle II), there might be circumstances in which the possibility of serious detrimental consequences to themselves or others, a diminished capacity to be autonomous, or a court order, would disallow some aspects of the rights to privacy, self-determination, and personal liberty. Indeed, such circumstances might be serious enough to create a duty to warn or protect others (see Standards I.45 and II.39). However, psychologists still have a responsibility to respect the rights of the person(s) involved to the greatest extent possible under the circumstances, and to do what is necessary and reasonable to reduce the need for future disallowances.

Psychologists recognize that, although all persons possess moral rights, the manner in which such rights are promoted, protected, and exercised varies across communities and cultures. For instance, definitions of what is considered private vary, as does the role of families and other community members in personal decision making. In their work, psychologists acknowledge and respect such differences, while guarding against clear violations of moral rights.

In addition, psychologists recognize that as individual, family, group, or community vulnerabilities increase, or as the power of persons to control their environment or their lives decreases, psychologists have an increasing responsibility to seek ethical advice and to establish safeguards to protect the rights of the persons involved. For this reason, psychologists consider it their responsibility to increase safeguards to protect and promote the rights of persons involved in their activities proportionate to the degree of dependency and the lack of voluntary initiation. For example, this would mean that there would be more safeguards to protect and promote the rights of fully dependent persons than partially dependent persons, and more safeguards for partially dependent than independent persons.

Respect for the dignity of persons also includes the concept of distributive justice. With respect to psychologists, this concept implies that all persons are entitled to benefit equally from the contributions of psychology and to equal quality in the processes, procedures, and services being conducted by psychologists, regardless of the person's characteristics, condition, or status. Although individual psychologists might specialize and direct their activities to particular populations, or might decline to engage in activities based on the limits of their competence or acknowledgment of problems in some relationships, psychologists must not exclude persons on a capricious or unjustly discriminatory basis.

By virtue of the social contract that the discipline has with society, psychologists have a higher duty of care to members of society than the general duty of care all members of society have to each other. However, psychologists are entitled to protect themselves from serious violations of their own moral rights (e.g., privacy, personal liberty) in carrying out their work as psychologists.

Ethical Standards

In adhering to the Principle of Respect for the Dignity of Persons, psychologists would:

General respect

I.1 Demonstrate appropriate respect for the knowledge, insight, experience, and areas of expertise of others.

I.2 Not engage publicly (e.g., in public statements, presentations, research reports, or with clients) in degrading comments about others, including demeaning jokes based on such characteristics as culture, nationality, ethnicity, colour, race, religion, sex, gender, or sexual orientation.

I.3 Strive to use language that conveys respect for the dignity of persons as much as possible in all written or oral communication.

I.4 Abstain from all forms of harassment, including sexual harassment.

General rights

I.5 Avoid or refuse to participate in practices disrespectful of the legal, civil, or moral rights of others.

I.6 Refuse to advise, train, or supply information to anyone who, in the psychologist's judgement, will use the knowledge or skills to infringe on human rights.

I.7 Make every reasonable effort to ensure that psychological knowledge is not misused, intentionally or unintentionally, to infringe on human rights.

I.8 Respect the right of research participants, clients, employees, supervisees, students, trainees, and others to safeguard their own dignity.

Non-discrimination

I.9 Not practice, condone, facilitate, or collaborate with any form of unjust discrimination.

I.10 Act to correct practices that are unjustly discriminatory.

I.11 Seek to design research, teaching, practice, and business activities in such a way that they contribute to the fair distribution of benefits to individuals and groups, and that they do not unfairly exclude those who are vulnerable or might be disadvantaged.

Fair treatment/due process

I.12 Work and act in a spirit of fair treatment to others.

I.13 Help to establish and abide by due process or other natural justice procedures for employment, evaluation, adjudication, editorial, and peer review activities.

I.14 Compensate others fairly for the use of their time, energy, and knowledge, unless such compensation is refused in advance.

I.15 Establish fees that are fair in light of the time, energy, and knowledge of the psychologist and any associates or employees, and in light of the market value of the product or service. (Also see Standard IV.12.)

Informed consent

I.16 Seek as full and active participation as possible from others in decisions that affect them, respecting and integrating as much as possible their opinions and wishes.

I.17 Recognize that informed consent is the result of a process of reaching an agreement to work collaboratively, rather than of simply having a consent form signed.

I.18 Respect the expressed wishes of persons to involve others (e.g., family members, community members) in their decision making regarding informed consent. This would include respect for written and clearly expressed unwritten advance directives.

I.19 Obtain informed consent from all independent and partially dependent persons for any psychological services provided to them except in circumstances of urgent need (e.g., disaster or other crisis). In urgent circumstances, psychologists would proceed with the assent of such persons, but fully informed consent would be obtained as soon as possible. (Also see Standard I.29.)

I.20 Obtain informed consent for all research activities that involve obtrusive measures, invasion of privacy, more than minimal risk of harm, or any attempt to change the behaviour of research participants.

I.21 Establish and use signed consent forms that specify the dimensions of informed consent or that acknowledge that such dimensions have been explained and are understood, if such forms are required by law or if such forms are desired by the psychologist, the person(s) giving consent, or the organization for whom the psychologist works.

I.22 Accept and document oral consent, in situations in which signed consent forms are not acceptable culturally or in which there are other good reasons for not using them.

I.23 Provide, in obtaining informed consent, as much information as reasonable or prudent persons would want to know before making a decision or consenting to the activity. The psychologist would relay this information in language that the persons understand (including providing translation into another language, if necessary) and would take whatever reasonable steps are needed to ensure that the information was, in fact, understood.

I.24 Ensure, in the process of obtaining informed consent, that at least the following points are understood: purpose and nature of the activity; mutual responsibilities; confidentiality protections and limitations; likely benefits and risks; alternatives; the likely consequences of non-action; the option to refuse or withdraw at any time, without prejudice; over what period of time the consent applies; and, how to rescind consent if desired. (Also see Standards III.23-30.)

I.25 Provide new information in a timely manner, whenever such information becomes available and is significant enough that it reasonably could be seen as relevant to the original or ongoing informed consent.

I.26 Clarify the nature of multiple relationships to all concerned parties before obtaining consent, if providing services to or conducting research at the request or for the use of third parties. This would include, but not be limited to: the purpose of the service or research; the reasonably anticipated use that will be made of information collected; and, the limits on confidentiality. Third parties may include schools, courts, government agencies, insurance companies, police, and special funding bodies.

Freedom of consent

I.27 Take all reasonable steps to ensure that consent is not given under conditions of coercion, undue pressure, or undue reward. (Also see Standard III.32.)

I.28 Not proceed with any research activity, if consent is given under any condition of coercion, undue pressure, or undue reward. (Also see Standard III.32.)

I.29 Take all reasonable steps to confirm or re-establish freedom of consent, if consent for service is given under conditions of duress or conditions of extreme need.

I.30 Respect the right of persons to discontinue participation or service at any time, and be responsive to non-verbal indications of a desire to discontinue if a person has difficulty with verbally communicating such a desire (e.g., young children, verbally disabled persons) or, due to culture, is unlikely to communicate such a desire orally.

Protections for vulnerable persons

I.31 Seek an independent and adequate ethical review of human rights issues and protections for any research involving members of vulnerable groups, including persons of diminished capacity to give informed consent, before making a decision to proceed.

I.32 Not use persons of diminished capacity to give informed consent in research studies, if the research involved may be carried out equally well with persons who have a fuller capacity to give informed consent.

I.33 Seek to use methods that maximize the understanding and ability to consent of persons of diminished capacity to give informed consent, and that reduce the need for a substitute decision maker.

I.34 Carry out informed consent processes with those persons who are legally responsible or appointed to give informed consent on behalf of persons not competent to consent on their own behalf, seeking to ensure respect for any previously expressed preferences of persons not competent to consent.

I.35 Seek willing and adequately informed participation from any person of diminished capacity to give informed consent, and proceed without this assent only if the service or research activity is considered to be of direct benefit to that person.

I.36 Be particularly cautious in establishing the freedom of consent of any person who is in a dependent relationship to the psychologist (e.g., student, employee). This may include, but is not limited to, offering that person an alternative activity to fulfill their educational or employment goals, or offering a range of research studies or experience opportunities from which the person can select, none of which is so onerous as to be coercive.

Privacy

I.37 Seek and collect only information that is germane to the purpose(s) for which consent has been obtained.

I.38 Take care not to infringe, in research, teaching, or service activities, on the personally, developmentally, or culturally defined private space of individuals or groups, unless clear permission is granted to do so.

I.39 Record only that private information necessary for the provision of continuous, coordinated service, or for the goals of the particular research study being conducted, or that is required or justified by law. (Also see Standards IV.17 and IV.18.)

I.40 Respect the right of research participants, employees, supervisees, students, and trainees to reasonable personal privacy.

I.41 Collect, store, handle, and transfer all private information, whether written or unwritten (e.g., communication during service provision, written records, e-mail or fax communication, computer files, video-tapes), in a way that attends to the needs for privacy and security. This would include having adequate plans for records in circumstances of one's own serious illness, termination of employment, or death.

I.42 Take all reasonable steps to ensure that records over which they have control remain personally identifiable only as long as necessary in the interests of those to whom they refer and/or to the research project for which they were collected, or as required or justified by law (e.g., the possible need to defend oneself against future allegations), and render anonymous or destroy any records under their control that no longer need to be personally identifiable. (Also see Standards IV.17 and IV.18.)

Confidentiality

I.43 Be careful not to relay information about colleagues, colleagues' clients, research participants, employees, supervisees, students, trainees, and members of organizations, gained in the process of their activities as psychologists, that the psychologist has reason to believe is considered confidential by those persons, except as required or justified by law. (Also see Standards IV.17 and IV.18.)

I.44 Clarify what measures will be taken to protect confidentiality, and what responsibilities family, group, and community members have for the protection of each other's confidentiality, when engaged in services to or research with individuals, families, groups, or communities.

I.45 Share confidential information with others only with the informed consent of those involved, or in a manner that the persons involved cannot be identified, except as required or justified by law, or in circumstances of actual or possible serious physical harm or death. (Also see Standards II.39, IV.17, and IV.18.)

Extended responsibility

I.46 Encourage others, in a manner consistent with this *Code*, to respect the dignity of persons and to expect respect for their own dignity.

I.47 Assume overall responsibility for the scientific and professional activities of their assistants, employees, students, supervisees, and trainees with regard to Respect for the Dignity of Persons, all of whom, however, incur similar obligations.

Principle II: Responsible Caring

Values Statement

A basic ethical expectation of any discipline is that its activities will benefit members of society or, at least, do no harm. Therefore, psychologists demonstrate an active concern for the welfare of any individual, family, group, or community with whom they relate in their role as psychologists. This concern includes both those directly involved and those indirectly involved in their activities. However, as with Principle I, psychologists' greatest responsibility is to protect the welfare of those in the most vulnerable position. Normally, persons directly involved in their activities (e.g., research participants, clients, students) are in such a position. Psychologists' responsibility to those indirectly involved (e.g., employers, third party payers, the general public) normally is secondary.

As persons usually consider their own welfare in their personal decision making, obtaining informed consent (see Principle I) is one of the best methods for ensuring that their welfare will be protected. However, it is only when such consent is combined with the responsible caring of the psychologist that there is considerable ethical protection of the welfare of the person(s) involved.

Responsible caring leads psychologists to take care to discern the potential harm and benefits involved, to predict the likelihood of their occurrence, to proceed only if the potential benefits outweigh the potential harms, to develop and use methods that will minimize harms and maximize benefits, and to take responsibility for correcting clearly harmful effects that have occurred as a direct result of their research, teaching, practice, or business activities.

In order to carry out these steps, psychologists recognize the need for competence and self-knowledge. They consider incompetent action to be unethical per se, as it is unlikely to be of benefit and likely to be harmful. They engage only in those activities in which they have competence or for which they are receiving supervision, and they perform their activities as competently as possible. They acquire, contribute to, and use the existing knowledge most relevant to the best interests of those concerned. They also engage in self-reflection regarding how their own values, attitudes, experiences, and social context (e.g., culture, ethnicity, colour, religion, sex, gender, sexual orientation, physical and mental abilities, age, and socio-economic status) influence their actions, interpretations, choices, and recommendations. This is done with the intent of increasing the probability that their activities will benefit and not harm the individuals, families, groups, and communities to whom they relate in their role as psychologists. Psychologists define harm and benefit in terms of both physical and psychological dimensions. They are concerned about such factors as: social, family, and community relationships; personal and cultural identity; feelings of self-worth, fear, humiliation, interpersonal trust, and cynicism; self-knowledge and general knowledge; and, such factors as physical safety, comfort, pain, and injury. They are concerned about immediate, short-term, and long-term effects.

Responsible caring recognizes and respects (e.g., through obtaining informed consent) the ability of individuals, families, groups, and communities to make decisions for themselves and to care for themselves and each other. It does not replace or undermine such ability, nor does it substitute one person's opinion about what is in the best interests of another person for that other person's competent decision making. However, psychologists recognize that, as vulnerabilities increase or as power to control one's own life decreases, psychologists have an increasing responsibility to protect the well-being of the individual, family, group, or community involved. For this reason, as in Principle I, psychologists consider it their responsibility to increase safeguards proportionate to the degree of dependency and the lack of voluntary initiation on the part of the persons involved. However, for Principle II, the safeguards are for the well-being of persons rather than for the rights of persons.

Psychologists' treatment and use of animals in their research and teaching activities are also a component of responsible caring. Although animals do not have the same moral rights as persons (e.g., privacy), they do have the right to be treated humanely and not to be exposed to unnecessary discomfort, pain, or disruption.

By virtue of the social contract that the discipline has with society, psychologists have a higher duty of care to members of society than the general duty of care all members of society have to each other. However, psychologists are entitled to protect their own basic well-being (e.g., physical safety, family relationships) in their work as psychologists.

Ethical Standards

In adhering to the Principle of Responsible Caring, psychologists would:

General caring

II.1 Protect and promote the welfare of clients, research participants, employees, supervisees, students, trainees, colleagues, and others.

II.2 Avoid doing harm to clients, research participants, employees, supervisees, students, trainees, colleagues, and others.

II.3 Accept responsibility for the consequences of their actions.

II.4 Refuse to advise, train, or supply information to anyone who, in the psychologist's judgment, will use the knowledge or skills to harm others.

II.5 Make every reasonable effort to ensure that psychological knowledge is not misused, intentionally or unintentionally, to harm others.

Competence and self-knowledge

II.6 Offer or carry out (without supervision) only those activities for which they have established their competence to carry them out to the benefit of others.

II.7 Not delegate activities to persons not competent to carry them out to the benefit of others.

II.8 Take immediate steps to obtain consultation or to refer a client to a colleague or other appropriate professional, whichever is more likely to result in providing the client with competent service, if it becomes apparent that a client's problems are beyond their competence.

II.9 Keep themselves up to date with a broad range of relevant knowledge, research methods, and techniques, and their impact on persons and society, through the reading of relevant literature, peer consultation, and continuing education activities, in order that their service or research activities and conclusions will benefit and not harm others.

II.10 Evaluate how their own experiences, attitudes, culture, beliefs, values, social context, individual differences, specific training, and stresses influence their interactions with others, and integrate this awareness into all efforts to benefit and not harm others.

II.11 Seek appropriate help and/or discontinue scientific or professional activity for an appropriate period of time, if a physical or psychological condition reduces their ability to benefit and not harm others.

II.12 Engage in self-care activities that help to avoid conditions (e.g., burnout, addictions) that could result in impaired judgment and interfere with their ability to benefit and not harm others.

Risk/benefit analysis

II.13 Assess the individuals, families, groups, and communities involved in their activities adequately enough to ensure that they will be able to discern what will benefit and not harm the persons involved.

II.14 Be sufficiently sensitive to and knowledgeable about individual, group, community, and cultural differences and vulnerabilities to discern what will benefit and not harm persons involved in their activities.

II.15 Carry out pilot studies to determine the effects of all new procedures and techniques that might carry more than minimal risk, before considering their use on a broader scale.

II.16 Seek an independent and adequate ethical review of the balance of risks and potential benefits of all research and new interventions that involve procedures of unknown consequence, or where pain, discomfort, or harm are possible, before making a decision to proceed.

II.17 Not carry out any scientific or professional activity unless the probable benefit is proportionately greater than the risk involved.

Maximize benefit

II.18 Provide services that are coordinated over time and with other service providers, in order to avoid duplication or working at cross purposes.

II.19 Create and maintain records relating to their activities that are sufficient to support continuity and appropriate coordination of their activities with the activities of others.

II.20 Make themselves aware of the knowledge and skills of other disciplines (e.g., law, medicine, business administration) and advise the use of such knowledge and skills, where relevant to the benefit of others.

II.21 Strive to provide and/or obtain the best possible service for those needing and seeking psychological service. This may include, but is not limited to: selecting interventions that are relevant to the needs and characteristics of the client and that have reasonable theoretical or empirically-supported efficacy in light of those needs and characteristics; consulting with, or including in service delivery, persons relevant to the culture or belief systems of those served; advocating on behalf of the client; and, recommending professionals other than psychologists when appropriate.

II.22 Monitor and evaluate the effect of their activities, record their findings, and communicate new knowledge to relevant others.

II.23 Debrief research participants in such a way that the participants' knowledge is enhanced and the participants have a sense of contribution to knowledge. (Also see Standards III.26 and III.27.)

II.24 Perform their teaching duties on the basis of careful preparation, so that their instruction is current and scholarly.

II.25 Facilitate the professional and scientific development of their employees, supervisees, students, and trainees by ensuring that these persons understand the values and ethical prescriptions of the discipline, and by providing or arranging for adequate working conditions, timely evaluations, and constructive consultation and experience opportunities.

II.26 Encourage and assist students in publication of worthy student papers.

Minimize harm

II.27 Be acutely aware of the power relationship in therapy and, therefore, not encourage or engage in sexual intimacy with therapy clients, neither during therapy, nor for that period of time following therapy during which the power relationship reasonably could be expected to influence the client's personal decision making. (Also see Standard III.31.)

II.28 Not encourage or engage in sexual intimacy with students or trainees with whom the psychologist has an evaluative or other relationship of direct authority. (Also see Standard III.31.)

II.29 Be careful not to engage in activities in a way that could place incidentally involved persons at risk.

II.30 Be acutely aware of the need for discretion in the recording and communication of information, in order that the information not be misinterpreted or misused to the detriment of others. This includes, but is not limited to: not recording information that could lead to misinterpretation and misuse; avoiding conjecture; clearly labelling opinion; and, communicating information in language that can be understood clearly by the recipient of the information.

II.31 Give reasonable assistance to secure needed psychological services or activities, if personally unable to meet requests for needed psychological services or activities.

II.32 Provide a client, if appropriate and if desired by the client, with reasonable assistance to find a way to receive needed services in the event that third party payments are exhausted and the client cannot afford the fees involved.

II.33 Maintain appropriate contact, support, and responsibility for caring until a colleague or other professional begins service, if referring a client to a colleague or other professional.

II.34 Give reasonable notice and be reasonably assured that discontinuation will cause no harm to the client, before discontinuing services.

II.35 Screen appropriate research participants and select those least likely to be harmed, if more than minimal risk of harm to some research participants is possible.

II.36 Act to minimize the impact of their research activities on research participants' personalities, or on their physical or mental integrity.

Offset/correct harm

II.37 Terminate an activity when it is clear that the activity carries more than minimal risk of harm and is found to be more harmful than beneficial, or when the activity is no longer needed.

II.38 Refuse to help individuals, families, groups, or communities to carry out or submit to activities that, according to current knowledge, or legal or professional guidelines, would cause serious physical or psychological harm to themselves or others.

II.39 Do everything reasonably possible to stop or offset the consequences of actions by others when these actions are likely to cause serious physical harm or death. This may include reporting to appropriate authorities (e.g., the police), an intended victim, or a family member or other support person who can intervene, and would be done even when a confidential relationship is involved. (Also see Standard I.45.)

II.40 Act to stop or offset the consequences of seriously harmful activities being carried out by another psychologist or member of another discipline, when there is objective information about the activities and the harm, and when these activities have come to their attention outside of a confidential client relationship between themselves and the psychologist or member of another discipline. This may include reporting to the appropriate regulatory body, authority, or committee for action, depending on the psychologist's judgment about the person(s) or body(ies) best suited to stop or offset the harm, and depending upon regulatory requirements and definitions of misconduct.

II.41 Act also to stop or offset the consequences of harmful activities carried out by another psychologist or member of another discipline, when the harm is not serious or the activities appear to be primarily a lack of sensitivity, knowledge, or experience, and when the activities have come to their attention outside of a confidential client relationship between themselves and the psychologist or member of another discipline. This may include talking informally with the psychologist or member of the other discipline, obtaining objective information and, if possible and relevant, the assurance that the harm will discontinue and be corrected. If in a vulnerable position (e.g., employee, trainee) with respect to the other psychologist or member of the other discipline, it may include asking persons in less vulnerable positions to participate in the meeting(s).

II.42 Be open to the concerns of others about perceptions of harm that they as a psychologist might be causing, stop activities that are causing harm, and not punish or seek punishment for those who raise such concerns in good faith.

II.43 Not place an individual, group, family, or community needing service at a serious disadvantage by offering them no service in order to fulfill the conditions of a research design, when a standard service is available.

II.44 Debrief research participants in such a way that any harm caused can be discerned, and act to correct any resultant harm. (Also see Standards III.26 and III.27.)

Care of animals

II.45 Not use animals in their research unless there is a reasonable expectation that the research will increase understanding of the structures and processes underlying behaviour, or increase understanding of the particular animal species used in the study, or result eventually in benefits to the health and welfare of humans or other animals.

II.46 Use a procedure subjecting animals to pain, stress, or privation only if an alternative procedure is unavailable and the goal is justified by its prospective scientific, educational, or applied value.

II.47 Make every effort to minimize the discomfort, illness, and pain of animals. This would include performing surgical procedures only under appropriate anaesthesia, using techniques to avoid infection and minimize pain during and after surgery and, if disposing of experimental animals is carried out at the termination of the study, doing so in a humane way.

II.48 Use animals in classroom demonstrations only if the instructional objectives cannot be achieved through the use of video-tapes, films, or other methods, and if the type of demonstration is warranted by the anticipated instructional gain.

Extended responsibility

II.49 Encourage others, in a manner consistent with this *Code*, to care responsibly.

II.50 Assume overall responsibility for the scientific and professional activities of their assistants, employees, supervisees, students, and trainees with regard to the Principle of Responsible Caring, all of whom, however, incur similar obligations.

Principle III: Integrity in Relationships

Values Statement

The relationships formed by psychologists in the course of their work embody explicit and implicit mutual expectations of integrity that are vital to the advancement of scientific knowledge and to the maintenance of public confidence in the discipline of psychology. These expectations include: accuracy and honesty; straightforwardness and openness; the maximization of objectivity and minimization of bias; and, avoidance of conflicts of interest. Psychologists have a responsibility to meet these expectations and to encourage reciprocity.

In addition to accuracy, honesty, and the obvious prohibitions of fraud or misrepresentation, meeting expectations of integrity is enhanced by self-knowledge and the use of critical analysis. Although it can be argued that science is value-free and impartial, scientists are not. Personal values and self-interest can affect the questions psychologists ask, how they ask those questions, what assumptions they make, their selection of methods, what they observe and what they fail to observe, and how they interpret their data.

Psychologists are not expected to be value-free or totally without self-interest in conducting their activities. However, they are expected to understand how their backgrounds, personal needs, and values interact with their activities, to be open and honest about the influence of such factors, and to be as objective and unbiased as possible under the circumstances.

The values of openness and straightforwardness exist within the context of Respect for the Dignity of Persons (Principle I) and Responsible Caring (Principle II). As such, there will be circumstances in which openness and straightforwardness will need to be tempered. Fully open and straightforward disclosure might not be needed or desired by others and, in some circumstances, might be a risk to their dignity or well-being, or considered culturally inappropriate. In such circumstances, however, psychologists have a responsibility to ensure that their decision not to be fully open or straightforward is justified by higher-order values and does not invalidate any informed consent procedures.

Of special concern to psychologists is the provision of incomplete disclosure when obtaining informed consent for research participation, or temporarily leading research participants to believe that a research project has a purpose other than its actual purpose. These actions sometimes occur in research where full disclosure would be likely to influence the responses of the research participants and thus invalidate the results. Although research that uses such techniques can lead to knowledge that is beneficial, such benefits must be weighed against the research participant's right to self-determination and the importance of public and individual trust in psychology. Psychologists have a serious obligation to avoid as much as possible the use of such research procedures. They also have a serious obligation to consider the need for, the possible consequences of, and their responsibility to correct any resulting mistrust or other harmful effects from their use.

As public trust in the discipline of psychology includes trusting that psychologists will act in the best interests of members of the public, situations that present real or potential conflicts of interest are of concern to psychologists. Conflict-of-interest situations are those that can lead to distorted judgment and can motivate psychologists to act in ways that meet their own personal, political, financial, or business interests at the expense of the best interests of members of the public. Although avoidance of all conflicts of interest and potential exploitation of others is not possible, some are of such a high risk to protecting the interests of members of the public and to maintaining the trust of the public, that they are considered never acceptable (see Standard III.31). The risk level of other conflicts of interest (e.g., dual or multiple relationships) might be partially dependent on cultural factors and the specific type of professional relationship (e.g., long-term psychotherapy vs. community development activities). It is the responsibility of psychologists to avoid dual or multiple relationships and other conflicts of interest when appropriate and possible. When such situations cannot be avoided or are inappropriate to avoid, psychologists have a responsibility to declare that they have a conflict of interest, to seek advice, and to establish safeguards to ensure that the best interests of members of the public are protected.

Integrity in relationships implies that psychologists, as a matter of honesty, have a responsibility to maintain competence in any specialty area for which they declare competence, whether or not they are currently practising in that area. It also requires that psychologists, in as much as they present themselves as members and representatives of a specific discipline, have a responsibility to actively rely on and be guided by that discipline and its guidelines and requirements.

Ethical Standards

In adhering to the Principle of Integrity in Relationships, psychologists would:

Accuracy/honesty

III.1 Not knowingly participate in, condone, or be associated with dishonesty, fraud, or misrepresentation.

III.2 Accurately represent their own and their colleagues' credentials, qualifications, education, experience, competence, and affiliations, in all spoken, written, or printed communications, being careful not to use descriptions or information that could be misinterpreted (e.g., citing membership in a voluntary association of psychologists as a testament of competence).

III.3 Carefully protect their own and their colleagues' credentials from being misrepresented by others, and act quickly to correct any such misrepresentation.

III.4 Maintain competence in their declared area(s) of psychological competence, as well as in their current area(s) of activity. (Also see Standard II.9.)

III.5 Accurately represent their own and their colleagues' activities, functions, contributions, and likely or actual outcomes of their activities (including research results) in all spoken, written, or printed communication. This includes, but is not limited to: advertisements of services or products; course and workshop descriptions; academic grading requirements; and, research reports.

III.6 Ensure that their own and their colleagues' activities, functions, contributions, and likely or actual outcomes of their activities (including research results) are not misrepresented by others, and act quickly to correct any such misrepresentation.

III.7 Take credit only for the work and ideas that they have actually done or generated, and give credit for work done or ideas contributed by others (including students), in proportion to their contribution.

III.8 Acknowledge the limitations of their own and their colleagues' knowledge, methods, findings, interventions, and views.

III 9. Not suppress disconfirming evidence of their own and their colleagues' findings and views, acknowledging alternative hypotheses and explanations.

Objectivity/lack of bias

III.10 Evaluate how their personal experiences, attitudes, values, social context, individual differences, stresses, and specific training influence their activities and thinking, integrating this awareness into all attempts to be objective and unbiased in their research, service, and other activities.

III.11 Take care to communicate as completely and objectively as possible, and to clearly differentiate facts, opinions, theories, hypotheses, and ideas, when communicating knowledge, findings, and views.

III.12 Present instructional information accurately, avoiding bias in the selection and presentation of information, and publicly acknowledge any personal values or bias that influence the selection and presentation of information.

III.13 Act quickly to clarify any distortion by a sponsor, client, agency (e.g., news media), or other persons, of the findings of their research.

Straightforwardness/openness

III.14 Be clear and straightforward about all information needed to establish informed consent or any other valid written or unwritten agreement (for example: fees, including any limitations imposed by third-party payers; relevant business policies and practices; mutual concerns; mutual responsibilities; ethical responsibilities of psychologists; purpose and nature of the relationship, including research participation; alternatives; likely experiences; possible conflicts; possible outcomes; and, expectations for processing, using, and sharing any information generated).

III.15 Provide suitable information about the results of assessments, evaluations, or research findings to the persons involved, if appropriate and if asked. This information would be communicated in understandable language.

III.16 Fully explain reasons for their actions to persons who have been affected by their actions, if appropriate and if asked.

III.17 Honour all promises and commitments included in any written or verbal agreement, unless serious and unexpected circumstances (e.g., illness) intervene. If such circumstances occur, then the psychologist would make a full and honest explanation to other parties involved.

III.18 Make clear whether they are acting as private citizens, as members of specific organizations or groups, or as representatives of the discipline of psychology, when making statements or when involved in public activities.

III.19 Carry out, present, and discuss research in a way that is consistent with a commitment to honest, open inquiry, and to clear communication of any research aims, sponsorship, social context, personal values, or financial interests that might affect or appear to affect the research.

III.20 Submit their research, in some accurate form and within the limits of confidentiality, to persons with expertise in the research area, for their comments and evaluations, prior to publication or the preparation of any final report.

III.21 Encourage and not interfere with the free and open exchange of psychological knowledge and theory between themselves, their students, colleagues, and the public.

III.22 Make no attempt to conceal the status of a trainee and, if a trainee is providing direct client service, ensure that the client is informed of that fact.

Avoidance of incomplete disclosure

III.23 Not engage in incomplete disclosure, or in temporarily leading research participants to believe that a research project or some aspect of it has a different purpose, if there are alternative procedures available or if the negative effects cannot be predicted or offset.

III.24 Not engage in incomplete disclosure, or in temporarily leading research participants to believe that a research project or some aspect of it has a different purpose, if it would interfere with the person's understanding of facts that clearly might influence a decision to give adequately informed consent (e.g., withholding information about the level of risk, discomfort, or inconvenience).

III.25 Use the minimum necessary incomplete disclosure or temporary leading of research participants to believe that a research project or some aspect of it has a different purpose, when such research procedures are used.

III.26 Debrief research participants as soon as possible after the participants' involvement, if there has been incomplete disclosure or temporary leading of research participants to believe that a research project or some aspect of it has a different purpose.

III.27 Provide research participants, during such debriefing, with a clarification of the nature of the study, seek to remove any misconceptions that might have arisen, and seek to re-establish any trust that might have been lost, assuring the participants that the research procedures were neither arbitrary nor capricious, but necessary for scientifically valid findings. (Also see Standards II.23 and II.44.)

III.28 Act to re-establish with research participants any trust that might have been lost due to the use of incomplete disclosure or temporarily leading research participants to believe that the research project or some aspect of it had a different purpose.

III.29 Give a research participant the option of removing his or her data, if the research participant expresses concern during the debriefing about the incomplete disclosure or the temporary leading of the research participant to believe that the research project or some aspect of it had a different purpose, and if removal of the data will not compromise the validity of the research design and hence diminish the ethical value of the participation of the other research participants.

III.30 Seek an independent and adequate ethical review of the risks to public or individual trust and of safeguards to protect such trust for any research that plans to provide incomplete disclosure or temporarily lead research participants to believe that the research project or some aspect of it has a different purpose, before making a decision to proceed.

Avoidance of conflict of interest

III.31 Not exploit any relationship established as a psychologist to further personal, political, or business interests at the expense of the best interests of their clients, research participants, students, employers, or others. This includes, but is not limited to: soliciting clients of one's employing agency for private practice; taking advantage of trust or dependency to encourage or engage in sexual intimacies (e.g., with clients not included in Standard II.27, with clients' partners or relatives, with students or trainees not included in Standard II.28, or with research participants); taking advantage of trust or dependency to frighten clients into receiving services; misappropriating students' ideas, research or work; using the resources of one's employing institution for purposes not agreed to; giving or receiving kickbacks or bonuses for referrals; seeking or accepting loans or investments from clients; and, prejudicing others against a colleague for reasons of personal gain.

III.32 Not offer rewards sufficient to motivate an individual or group to participate in an activity that has possible or known risks to themselves or others. (Also see Standards I.27, I.28, II.2, and II.49.)

III.33 Avoid dual or multiple relationships (e.g.. with clients, research participants, employees, supervisees, students, or trainees) and other situations that might present a conflict of interest or that might reduce their ability to be objective and unbiased in their determinations of what might be in the best interests of others.

III.34 Manage dual or multiple relationships that are unavoidable due to cultural norms or other circumstances in such a manner that bias, lack of objectivity, and risk of exploitation are minimized. This might include obtaining ongoing supervision or consultation for the duration of the dual or multiple relationship, or involving a third party in obtaining consent (e.g., approaching a client or employee about becoming a research participant).

III.35 Inform all parties, if a real or potential conflict of interest arises, of the need to resolve the situation in a manner that is consistent with Respect for the Dignity of Persons (Principle I) and Responsible Caring (Principle II), and take all reasonable steps to resolve the issue in such a manner.

Reliance on the discipline

III.36 Familiarize themselves with their discipline's rules and regulations, and abide by them, unless abiding by them would be seriously detrimental to the rights or welfare of others as demonstrated in the Principles of Respect for the Dignity of Persons or Responsible Caring. (See Standards IV.17 and IV.18 for guidelines regarding the resolution of such conflicts.)

III.37 Familiarize themselves with and demonstrate a commitment to maintaining the standards of their discipline.

III.38 Seek consultation from colleagues and/or appropriate groups and committees, and give due regard to their advice in arriving at a responsible decision, if faced with difficult situations.

Extended responsibility

III.39 Encourage others, in a manner consistent with this *Code*, to relate with integrity.

III.40 Assume overall responsibility for the scientific and professional activities of their assistants, employees, supervisees, students, and trainees with regard to the Principle of Integrity in Relationships, all of whom, however, incur similar obligations.

Principle IV: Responsibility to Society

Values Statement

Psychology functions as a discipline within the context of human society[2]. Psychologists, both in their work and as private citizens, have responsibilities to the societies in which they live and work, such as the neighbourhood or city, and to the welfare of all human beings in those societies.

Two of the legitimate expectations of psychology as a science and a profession are that it will increase knowledge and that it will conduct its affairs in such ways that it will promote the welfare of all human beings.

Freedom of enquiry and debate (including scientific and academic freedom) is a foundation of psychological education, science, and practice. In the context of society, the above expectations imply that psychologists will exercise this freedom through the use of activities and methods that are consistent with ethical requirements.

The above expectations also imply that psychologists will do whatever they can to ensure that psychological knowledge, when used in the development of social structures and policies, will be used for beneficial purposes, and that the discipline's own structures and policies will support those beneficial purposes. Within the context of this document, social structures and policies that have beneficial purposes are defined as those that more readily support and reflect respect for the dignity of persons, responsible caring, integrity in relationships, and responsibility to society. If psychological knowledge or structures are used against these purposes, psychologists have an ethical responsibility to try to draw attention to and correct the misuse. Although this is a collective responsibility, those psychologists having direct involvement in the structures of the discipline, in social development, or in the theoretical or research data base that is being used (e.g., through research, expert testimony, or policy advice) have the greatest responsibility to act. Other psychologists must decide for themselves the most appropriate and beneficial use of their time and talents to help meet this collective responsibility.

In carrying out their work, psychologists acknowledge that many social structures have evolved slowly over time in response to human need and are valued by the societies that have developed them. In such circumstances, psychologists convey respect for such social structures and avoid unwarranted or unnecessary disruption. Suggestions for and action toward changes or enhancement of such structures are carried out through processes that seek to achieve a consensus within those societies and/or through democratic means.

On the other hand, if structures or policies seriously ignore or oppose the principles of respect for the dignity of persons, responsible caring, integrity in relationships, or responsibility to society, psychologists involved have a responsibility to speak out in a manner consistent with the principles of this *Code*, and advocate for appropriate change to occur as quickly as possible.

In order to be responsible and accountable to society, and to contribute constructively to its ongoing development, psychologists need to be willing to work in partnership with others, be self-reflective, and be open to external suggestions and criticisms about the place of the discipline of psychology in society. They need to engage in even-tempered observation and interpretation of the effects of societal structures and policies, and their process of change, developing the ability of psychologists to increase the beneficial use of psychological knowledge and structures, and avoid their misuse. The discipline needs to be willing to set high standards for its members, to do what it can to assure that such standards are met, and to support its members in their attempts to maintain the standards. Once again, individual psychologists must decide for themselves the most appropriate and beneficial use of their time and talents in helping to meet these collective responsibilities.

Ethical Standards

In adhering to the Principle of Responsibility to Society, psychologists would:

Development of knowledge

IV.1 Contribute to the discipline of psychology and of society's understanding of itself and human beings generally, through free enquiry and the acquisition, transmission, and expression of knowledge and ideas, unless such activities conflict with other basic ethical requirements.

IV.2 Not interfere with, or condone interference with, free enquiry and the acquisition, transmission, and expression of knowledge and ideas that do not conflict with other basic ethical requirements.

IV.3 Keep informed of progress in their area(s) of psychological activity, take this progress into account in their work, and try to make their own contributions to this progress.

Beneficial activities

IV.4 Participate in and contribute to continuing education and the professional and scientific growth of self and colleagues.

IV.5 Assist in the development of those who enter the discipline of psychology by helping them to acquire a full understanding of their ethical responsibilities, and the needed competencies of their chosen area(s), including an understanding of critical analysis and of the variations, uses, and possible misuses of the scientific paradigm.

IV.6 Participate in the process of critical self-evaluation of the discipline's place in society, and in the development and implementation of structures and procedures that help the discipline to contribute to beneficial societal functioning and changes.

IV.7 Provide and/or contribute to a work environment that supports the respectful expression of ethical concern or dissent, and the constructive resolution of such concern or dissent.

IV.8 Engage in regular monitoring, assessment, and reporting (e.g., through peer review, and in programme reviews, case management reviews, and reports of one's own research) of their ethical practices and safeguards.

IV.9 Help develop, promote, and participate in accountability processes and procedures related to their work.

IV.10 Uphold the discipline's responsibility to society by promoting and maintaining the highest standards of the discipline.

IV.11 Protect the skills, knowledge, and interpretations of psychology from being misused, used incompetently, or made useless (e.g., loss of security of assessment techniques) by others.

IV.12 Contribute to the general welfare of society (e.g., improving accessibility of services, regardless of ability to pay) and/or to the general welfare of their discipline, by offering a portion of their time to work for which they receive little or no financial return.

IV.13 Uphold the discipline's responsibility to society by bringing incompetent or unethical behaviour, including misuses of psychological knowledge and techniques, to the attention of appropriate authorities, committees, or regulatory bodies, in a manner consistent with the ethical principles of this *Code*, if informal resolution or correction of the situation is not appropriate or possible.

IV.14 Enter only into agreements or contracts that allow them to act in accordance with the ethical principles and standards of this *Code*.

Respect for society

IV.15 Acquire an adequate knowledge of the culture, social structure, and customs of a community before beginning any major work there.

IV.16 Convey respect for and abide by prevailing community mores, social customs, and cultural expectations in their scientific and professional activities, provided that this does not contravene any of the ethical principles of this *Code*.

IV.17 Familiarize themselves with the laws and regulations of the societies in which they work, especially those that are related to their activities as psychologists, and abide by them. If those laws or regulations seriously conflict with the ethical principles contained herein, psychologists would do whatever they could to uphold the ethical principles. If upholding the ethical principles could result in serious personal consequences (e.g., jail or physical harm), decision for final action would be considered a matter of personal conscience.

IV.18 Consult with colleagues, if faced with an apparent conflict between abiding by a law or regulation and following an ethical principle, unless in an emergency, and seek consensus as to the most ethical course of action and the most responsible, knowledgeable, effective, and respectful way to carry it out.

Development of society

IV.19 Act to change those aspects of the discipline of psychology that detract from beneficial societal changes, where appropriate and possible.

IV.20 Be sensitive to the needs, current issues, and problems of society, when determining research questions to be asked, services to be developed, content to be taught, information to be collected, or appropriate interpretation of results or findings.

IV.21 Be especially careful to keep well informed of social issues through relevant reading, peer consultation, and continuing education, if their work is related to societal issues.

IV.22 Speak out, in a manner consistent with the four principles of this *Code*, if they possess expert knowledge that bears on important societal issues being studied or discussed.

IV.23 Provide thorough discussion of the limits of their data with respect to social policy, if their work touches on social policy and structure.

IV.24 Consult, if feasible and appropriate, with groups, organizations, or communities being studied, in order to increase the accuracy of interpretation of results and to minimize risk of misinterpretation or misuse.

IV.25 Make themselves aware of the current social and political climate and of previous and possible future societal misuses of psychological knowledge, and exercise due discretion in communicating psychological information (e.g., research results, theoretical knowledge), in order to discourage any further misuse.

IV.26 Exercise particular care when reporting the results of any work regarding vulnerable groups, ensuring that results are not likely to be misinterpreted or misused in the development of social policy, attitudes, and practices (e.g., encouraging manipulation of vulnerable persons or reinforcing discrimination against any specific population).

IV.27 Not contribute to nor engage in research or any other activity that contravenes international humanitarian law, such as the development of methods intended for use in the torture of persons, the development of prohibited weapons, or destruction of the environment.

IV.28 Provide the public with any psychological knowledge relevant to the public's informed participation in the shaping of social policies and structures, if they possess expert knowledge that bears on the social policies and structures.

IV.29 Speak out and/or act, in a manner consistent with the four principles of this *Code*, if the policies, practices, laws, or regulations of the social structure within which they work seriously ignore or contradict any of the principles of this *Code*.

Extended responsibility

IV.30 Encourage others, in a manner consistent with this *Code*, to exercise responsibility to society.

IV.31 Assume overall responsibility for the scientific and professional activities of their assistants, employees, supervisees, students, and trainees with regard to the Principle of Responsibility to Society, all of whom, however, incur similar obligations.

Footnotes

1 Adapted from: Canadian Psychological Association. (1985). *Guidelines for the elimination of sexual harassment.* Ottawa, Author.

2 Society is used here in the broad sense of a group of persons living as members of one or more human communities, rather than in the limited sense of state or government.

Permission is granted to copy this document for educational use.

Canadian Psychological Association
Société canadienne de psychologie
151 Slater St., Suite 205
Ottawa, Ontario
K1P 5H3

Commission on Rehabilitation Counselor Certification
Code of Professional Ethics for Rehabilitation Counselors

Adopted in June 2001 by the Commission on Rehabilitation Counselor Certification for its Certified Rehabilitation Counselors. This Code is effective as of January 1, 2002.

TABLE OF CONTENTS

Preamble

Rehabilitation counselors are committed to facilitating the personal, social, and economic independence of individuals with disabilities. In fulfilling this commitment, rehabilitation counselors work with people, programs, institutions, and service delivery systems. Rehabilitation counselors provide services within the Scope of Practice for Rehabilitation Counseling (see the Scope of Practice document) and recognize that both action and inaction can be facilitating or debilitating. It is essential that rehabilitation counselors demonstrate adherence to ethical standards and ensure that the standards are enforced vigorously. The Code of Professional Ethics for Rehabilitation Counselors, henceforth referred to as the Code, is designed to facilitate these goals.

The fundamental spirit of caring and respect with which the Code is written is based upon five principles of ethical behavior 1 . These include autonomy, beneficence, nonmaleficence, justice, and fidelity, as defined below:

Autonomy: To honor the right to make individual decisions.
Beneficence: To do good to others.
Nonmaleficence: To do no harm to others.
Justice: To be fair and give equally to others.
Fidelity: To be loyal, honest, and keep promises.

The primary obligation of rehabilitation counselors is to their clients, defined in the Code as individuals with disabilities who are receiving services from rehabilitation counselors. Regardless of whether direct client contact occurs or whether indirect services are provided, rehabilitation counselors are obligated to adhere to the Code. At times, rehabilitation counseling services may be provided to individuals other than those with disabilities, such as a student population. In all instances, the primary obligation remains with the client and adherence to the Code is required.

The basic objective of the Code is to promote public welfare by specifying ethical behavior expected of rehabilitation counselors. The Enforceable Standards within the Code are the exacting standards intended to provide guidance in specific circumstances and will serve as the basis for processing ethical complaints initiated against certificants.

Rehabilitation counselors who violate the Code are subject to disciplinary action. Since the use of the Certified Rehabilitation Counselor (CRC) designation is a privilege granted by the Commission on Rehabilitation Counselor Certification (CRCC), CRCC reserves unto itself the power to suspend or to revoke the privilege or to approve other penalties for a violation. Disciplinary penalties are imposed as warranted by the severity of the offense and its attendant circumstances. All disciplinary actions are undertaken in accordance with published procedures and penalties designed to assure the proper enforcement of the Code within the framework of due process and equal protection under the law.

1 Beauchamp, T. L., & Childress, J. F. (1994), 4 th Ed. Principles of Biomedical Ethics. Oxford: Oxford University Press. Kitchener, K. S. (1984). Ethics in Counseling Psychology: Distinctions and Directions. Counseling Psychologists, 12 (3), 43-55.

ENFORCEABLE STANDARDS OF ETHICAL PRACTICE

SECTION A: THE COUNSELING RELATIONSHIP

A.1. CLIENT WELFARE

a. DEFINITION OF CLIENT
The primary obligation of rehabilitation counselors will be to their clients, defined as individuals with disabilities who are receiving services from rehabilitation counselors.

b. REHABILITATION AND COUNSELING PLANS
Rehabilitation counselors will work jointly with their clients in devising and revising integrated, individual rehabilitation and counseling plans that contain realistic and mutually agreed upon goals and are consistent with abilities and circumstances of clients.

c. CAREER AND EMPLOYMENT NEEDS
Rehabilitation counselors will work with their clients in considering employment that is consistent with the overall abilities, vocational limitations, physical restrictions, psychological limitations, general temperament, interest and aptitude patterns, social skills, education, general qualifications, and cultural and other relevant characteristics and needs of clients. Rehabilitation counselors will neither place nor participate in placing clients in positions that will result in damaging the interest and the welfare of clients, employers, or the public.

d. AUTONOMY
Rehabilitation counselors will respect the autonomy of the client if actions such as involuntary commitment or initiation of guardianship are taken that diminish client autonomy. The assumption of responsibility for decision-making on behalf of the client will be taken only after careful deliberation. The rehabilitation counselor will advocate for client resumption of responsibility as quickly as possible.

A.2. RESPECTING DIVERSITY

a. RESPECTING CULTURE
Rehabilitation counselors will demonstrate respect for clients ' cultural backgrounds..

b. INTERVENTIONS
Rehabilitation counselors will develop and adapt interventions and services to incorporate consideration of clients ' cultural perspectives and recognition of barriers external to clients that may interfere with achieving effective rehabilitation outcomes.

c. NON-DISCRIMINATION. Rehabilitation counselors will not condone or engage in discrimination based on age, color, culture, disability, ethnic group, gender, race, religion, sexual orientation, marital status, or socioeconomic status.

A.3. CLIENT RIGHTS

a. DISCLOSURE TO CLIENTS
When counseling is initiated, and throughout the counseling process as necessary, rehabilitation counselors will inform clients, preferably through both written and oral means, of their credentials, the purposes, goals, techniques, procedures, limitations, potential risks, and benefits of services to be performed, and other pertinent information. Rehabilitation counselors will take steps to ensure that clients understand the implications of diagnosis, the intended use of tests and reports, fees, and billing arrangements. Clients have the right to (1)expect confidentiality and will be provided with an explanation of its limitations, including disclosure to supervisors and/or treatment team professionals;(2)obtain clear

information about their case records;(3)actively participate in the development and implementation of rehabilitation counseling plans;and (4)refuse any recommended services and be advised of the consequences of such refusal.

b. THIRD PARTY REFERRAL
Rehabilitation counselors who have direct contact with a client at the request of a third party will define the nature of their relationships and role to all rightful, legal parties with whom they have direct contact. Direct contact is defined as any written, oral, or electronic communication. Legal parties may include clients, legal guardians, referring third parties, and attorneys actively involved in a matter directly related to rehabilitation services.

c. INDIRECT SERVICE PROVISION
Rehabilitation counselors who are employed by third parties as case consultants or expert witnesses, and who engage in communication with the individual with a disability, will fully disclose to the individual with a disability and/or his or her designee their role and limits of their relationship. Communication includes all forms of written or oral interactions regardless of the type of communication tool used. When there is no pretense or intent to provide rehabilitation counseling services directly to the individual with a disability, and where there will be no communication, disclosure by the rehabilitation counselor is not required. When serving as case consultants or expert witnesses, rehabilitation counselors will provide unbiased, objective opinions. Rehabilitation counselors acting as expert witnesses will generate written documentation, either in the form of case notes or a report, as to their involvement and/or conclusions.

d. FREEDOM OF CHOICE
To the extent possible, rehabilitation counselors will offer clients the freedom to choose whether to enter into a counseling relationship and to determine which professional(s)will provide counseling. Restrictions that limit choices of clients will be fully explained. Rehabilitation counselors will honor the rights of clients to consent to participate and the right to make decisions with regard to rehabilitation services. Rehabilitation counselors will inform clients or the clients ' legal guardians of factors that may affect decisions to participate in rehabilitation services, and they will obtain written consent or will acknowledge consent in writing after clients or legal guardians are fully informed of such factors.

e. INABILITY TO GIVE CONSENT
When counseling minors or persons unable to give voluntary informed consent, rehabilitation counselors will obtain written informed consent from legally responsible parties. Where no legally responsible parties exist, rehabilitation counselors will act in the best interest of clients.

f. INVOLVEMENT OF SIGNIFICANT OTHERS
Rehabilitation counselors will attempt to enlist family understanding and involvement of family and/or significant others as a positive resource if (or when)appropriate. The client or legal guardian's permission will be secured prior to any involvement of family and/or significant others.

A.4. PERSONAL NEEDS AND VALUES
In the counseling relationship, rehabilitation counselors will be aware of the intimacy and responsibilities inherent in the counseling relationship, maintain respect for clients, and avoid actions that seek to meet their personal needs at the expense of clients.

A.5. SEXUAL INTIMACIES WITH CLIENTS

a. CURRENT CLIENTS
Rehabilitation counselors will not have any type of sexual intimacies with clients and will not counsel persons with whom they have had a sexual relationship.

b. FORMER CLIENTS
Rehabilitation counselors will not engage in sexual intimacies with former clients within a minimum of 5 years after terminating the counseling relationship. Rehabilitation counselors who engage in such

relationship after 5 years following termination will have the responsibility to examine and document thoroughly that such relations do not have an exploitative nature, based on factors such as duration of counseling, amount of time since counseling, termination circumstances, client's personal history and mental status, adverse impact on the client, and actions by the counselor suggesting a plan to initiate a sexual relationship with the client after termination. Rehabilitation counselors will seek peer consultation prior to engaging in a sexual relationship with a former client.

A.6. NON-PROFESSIONAL RELATIONSHIPS WITH CLIENTS

a. POTENTIAL FOR HARM
Rehabilitation counselors will be aware of their influential positions with respect to clients, and will avoid exploiting the trust and dependency of clients. Rehabilitation counselors will make every effort to avoid non-professional relationships with clients that could impair professional judgment or increase the risk of harm to clients.(Examples of such relationships include, but are not limited to, familial, social, financial, business, close personal relationships with clients, or volunteer or paid work within an office in which the client is actively receiving services.)When a non-professional relationship cannot be avoided, rehabilitation counselors will take appropriate professional precautions such as informed consent, consultation, supervision, and documentation to ensure that judgment is not impaired and no exploitation occurs.

b. SUPERIOR/SUBORDINATE RELATIONSHIPS. Rehabilitation counselors will not accept as clients, superiors or subordinates with whom they have administrative, supervisory, or evaluative relationships.

A.7. MULTIPLE CLIENTS

When rehabilitation counselors agree to provide counseling services to two or more persons who have a relationship (such as husband and wife, or parents and children),rehabilitation counselors will clarify at the outset, which person or persons are clients and the nature of the relationships they will have with each involved person. If it becomes apparent that rehabilitation counselors may be called upon to perform potentially conflicting roles, they will clarify, adjust, or withdraw from such roles appropriately.

A.8. GROUP WORK

a. SCREENING
Rehabilitation counselors will screen prospective group counseling/therapy participants. To the extent possible, rehabilitation counselors will select members whose needs and goals are compatible with goals of the group, who will not impede the group process, and whose well being will not be jeopardized by the group experience.

b. PROTECTING CLIENTS
In a group setting, rehabilitation counselors will take reasonable precautions to protect clients from physical or psychological trauma.

A.9. TERMINATION AND REFERRAL

a. ABANDONMENT PROHIBITED
Rehabilitation counselors will not abandon or neglect clients in counseling. Rehabilitation counselors will assist in making appropriate arrangements for the continuation of treatment, when necessary, during interruptions such as vacations, and following termination.

b. INABILITY TO ASSIST CLIENTS
If rehabilitation counselors determine an inability to be of professional assistance to clients, they will avoid entering or immediately terminate a counseling relationship.

c. APPROPRIATE TERMINATION

Rehabilitation counselors will terminate a counseling relationship, securing client agreement when possible, when it is reasonably clear that the client is no longer benefiting, when services are no longer required, when counseling no longer serves the client's needs or interests, or when there is failure to pay fees according to Section J of this document.

d. REFERRAL UPON TERMINATION

Rehabilitation counselors will be knowledgeable about referral resources and suggest appropriate alternatives. If clients decline the suggested referral, rehabilitation counselors have the right to discontinue the relationship.

A.10. COMPUTER TECHNOLOGY

a. USE OF COMPUTERS

When computer applications are used in counseling services, rehabilitation counselors will ensure that (1)the client is intellectually, emotionally, and physically capable of using the computer application;(2)the computer application is appropriate for the needs of the client;(3)the client understands the purpose and operation of the computer applications; and (4)a follow-up of client use of a computer application is provided to correct possible misconceptions, discover inappropriate use, and assess subsequent needs.

b. EXPLANATION OF LIMITATIONS

Rehabilitation counselors will ensure that clients are provided information as a part of the counseling relationship that adequately explains the limitations of computer technology.

c. ACCESS TO COMPUTER APPLICATIONS

Rehabilitation counselors will provide reasonable access to computer applications in counseling services.

SECTION B: CONFIDENTIALITY

B.1. RIGHT TO PRIVACY

a. RESPECT FOR PRIVACY

Rehabilitation counselors will respect clients ' rights to privacy and will avoid illegal and unwarranted disclosures of confidential information.

b. CLIENT WAIVER

Rehabilitation counselors will respect the right of the client or his/her legally recognized representative to waive the right to privacy.

c. EXCEPTIONS

When disclosure is required to prevent clear and imminent danger to the client or others, or when legal requirements demand that confidential information be revealed, the general requirement that rehabilitation counselors keep information confidential will not apply. Rehabilitation counselors will consult with other professionals when in doubt as to the validity of an exception.

d. CONTAGIOUS, FATAL DISEASES.

Rehabilitation counselors will become aware of the legal requirements for disclosure of contagious and fatal diseases in their jurisdiction. In jurisdictions where allowable, a rehabilitation counselor who receives information will confirm that a client has a disease known to be communicable and/or fatal. If allowable by law, the rehabilitation counselor will disclose this information to a third party, who by his or her relationship with the client is at high risk of contracting the disease. Prior to disclosure, the rehabilitation counselor will ascertain that the client has not already informed the third party about his or her disease and that the client is not intending to inform the third party in the immediate future.

e. COURT-ORDERED DISCLOSURE. When court ordered to release confidential information without a client's permission, rehabilitation counselors will request to the court that the disclosure not be required due to potential harm to the client or counseling relationship.

f. MINIMAL DISCLOSURE
When circumstances require the disclosure of confidential information, rehabilitation counselors will endeavor to reveal only essential information. To the extent possible, clients will be informed before confidential information is disclosed.

g. EXPLANATION OF LIMITATIONS
When counseling is initiated and throughout the counseling process as necessary, rehabilitation counselors will inform clients of the limitations of confidentiality and will identify foreseeable situations in which confidentiality must be breached.

h. WORK ENVIRONMENT
Rehabilitation counselors will make every effort to ensure that a confidential work environment exists and that subordinates including employees, supervisees, clerical assistants, and volunteers maintain the privacy and confidentiality of clients.

i. TREATMENT TEAMS
If client treatment will involve the sharing of client information among treatment team members, the client will be advised of this fact and will be informed of the team's existence and composition.

j. CLIENT ASSISTANTS
When a client is accompanied by an individual providing assistance to the client (e. g., interpreter, personal care assistant, etc.),rehabilitation counselors will ensure that the assistant is apprised of the need to maintain confidentiality.

B.2. GROUPS AND FAMILIES

a. GROUP WORK
In group work, rehabilitation counselors will clearly define confidentiality and the parameters for the specific group being entered, explain its importance, and discuss the difficulties related to confidentiality involved in group work. The fact that confidentiality cannot be guaranteed will be clearly communicated to group members.

b. FAMILY COUNSELING
In family counseling, unless otherwise directed by law, information about one family member will not be disclosed to another member without permission. Rehabilitation counselors will protect the privacy rights of each family member.

B.3. RECORDS

a. REQUIREMENT OF RECORDS
Rehabilitation counselors will maintain records necessary for rendering professional services to their clients and as required by laws, regulations, or agency or institution procedures.

b. CONFIDENTIALITY OF RECORDS
Rehabilitation counselors will be responsible for securing the safety and confidentiality of any counseling records they create, maintain, transfer, or destroy whether the records are written, taped, computerized, or stored in any other medium.

c. PERMISSION TO RECORD OR OBSERVE
Rehabilitation counselors will obtain and document written or recorded permission from clients prior to electronically recording or observing sessions. When counseling clients who are minors or individuals

who are unable to give voluntary, informed consent, written or recorded permission of guardians must be obtained.

d. CLIENT ACCESS

Rehabilitation counselors will recognize that counseling records are kept for the benefit of clients, and therefore provide access to records and copies of records when requested by clients, unless prohibited by law. In instances where the records contain information that may be sensitive or detrimental to the client, the rehabilitation counselor has a responsibility to adequately interpret such information to the client. In situations involving multiple clients, access to records will be limited to those parts of records that do not include confidential information related to another client.

e. DISCLOSURE OR TRANSFER

Rehabilitation counselors will obtain written permission from clients to disclose or transfer records to legitimate third parties unless exceptions to confidentiality exist as listed in Section B.1.

B.4. CONSULTATION

a. RESPECT FOR PRIVACY

Information obtained in a consulting relationship will be discussed for professional purposes only with persons clearly concerned with the case. Written and oral reports will present data germane to the purposes of the consultation, and every effort will be made to protect client identity and to avoid undue invasion of privacy.

b. COOPERATING AGENCIES

Before sharing information, rehabilitation counselors will make efforts to ensure that there are defined policies in other agencies serving the counselor's clients that effectively protect the confidentiality of information.

B.5. ALTERNATIVE COMMUNICATION

Rehabilitation counselors will make every effort to ensure that methods of exchanging information that utilize alternative means of communication (i. e.,facsimile, cellular telephone, computer, or videoconferencing)will be conducted in such a manner that ensures protection of client confidentiality. If confidentiality cannot be ensured, client or guardian permission must be obtained.

SECTION C: ADVOCACY AND ACCESSIBILITY

C.1. ADVOCACY

a. ATTITUDINAL BARRIERS

Rehabilitation counselors will strive to eliminate attitudinal barriers, including stereotyping and discrimination, toward individuals with disabilities and to increase their own awareness and sensitivity to such individuals.

b. ADVOCACY WITH COOPERATING AGENCIES

Rehabilitation counselors will remain aware of actions taken by cooperating agencies on behalf of their clients and will act as advocates of such clients to ensure effective service delivery.

c. EMPOWERMENT

Rehabilitation counselors will provide the client with appropriate information and will support their efforts at self-advocacy both on an individual and an organizational level.

C.2. ACCESSIBILITY

a. COUNSELING PRACTICE

Rehabilitation counselors will demonstrate, in their practice, an appreciation of the need to provide necessary accommodations, including accessible facilities and services, to individuals with disabilities.

b. BARRIERS TO ACCESS
Rehabilitation counselors will identify physical, communication, and transportation barriers to clients and will communicate information on barriers to public and private authorities to facilitate removal of barriers to access.

c. REFERRAL ACCESSIBILITY
Rehabilitation counselors, as advocates for individuals with disabilities, will ensure, prior to referring clients to programs, facilities, or employment settings, that they are appropriately accessible.

SECTION D: PROFESSIONAL RESPONSIBILITY

D.1. PROFESSIONAL COMPETENCE

a. BOUNDARIES OF COMPETENCE
Rehabilitation counselors will practice only within the boundaries of their competence, based on their education, training, supervised experience, state and national professional credentials, and appropriate professional experience. Rehabilitation counselors will demonstrate a commitment to gain knowledge, personal awareness, sensitivity, and skills pertinent to working with a diverse client population. Rehabilitation counselors will not misrepresent their role or competence to clients.

b. REFERRAL
Rehabilitation counselors will refer clients to other specialists as the needs of the clients dictate.

c. NEW SPECIALTY AREAS OF PRACTICE
Rehabilitation counselors will practice in specialty areas new to them only after appropriate education, training, and supervised experience. While developing skills in new specialty areas, rehabilitation counselors will take steps to ensure the competence of their work and to protect clients from possible harm.

d. RESOURCES
Rehabilitation counselors will ensure that the resources used or accessed in counseling are credible and valid (e. g., web link, books used in Bibliotherapy, etc.).

e. QUALIFIED FOR EMPLOYMENT
Rehabilitation counselors will accept employment only for positions for which they are qualified by education, training, supervised experience, state and national professional credentials, and appropriate professional experience. Rehabilitation counselors will hire only individuals who are qualified and competent for professional rehabilitation counseling positions.

f. MONITOR EFFECTIVENESS
Rehabilitation counselors will take reasonable steps to seek peer supervision to evaluate their efficacy as rehabilitation counselors.

g. ETHICAL ISSUES CONSULTATION
Rehabilitation counselors will take reasonable steps to consult with other rehabilitation counselors or related professionals when they have questions regarding their ethical obligations or professional practice.

h. CONTINUING EDUCATION
Rehabilitation counselors will engage in continuing education to maintain a reasonable level of awareness of current scientific and professional information in their fields of activity. They will take steps to maintain

competence in the skills they use, will be open to new techniques, and will develop and maintain competence for practice with the diverse and/or special populations with whom they work.

i. IMPAIRMENT

Rehabilitation counselors will refrain from offering or rendering professional services when their physical, mental, or emotional problems are likely to harm the client or others. They will seek assistance for problems, and, if necessary, will limit, suspend, or terminate their professional responsibilities.

D.2. LEGAL STANDARDS

a. LEGAL VERSUS ETHICAL

Rehabilitation counselors will obey the laws and statutes of the legal jurisdiction in which they practice unless there is a conflict with the Code, in which case they should seek immediate consultation and advice.

b. LEGAL LIMITATIONS

Rehabilitation counselors will be familiar with and observe the legal limitations of the services they offer to clients. They will discuss these limitations as well as all benefits available to clients they serve in order to facilitate open, honest communication and avoid unrealistic expectations.

D.3. ADVERTISING AND SOLICITING CLIENTS

a. ACCURATE ADVERTISING

Advertising by rehabilitation counselors shall not be restricted. Rehabilitation counselors will advertise or will represent their services to the public by identifying their credentials in an accurate manner that is not false, misleading, deceptive, or fraudulent. Rehabilitation counselors will only advertise the highest degree earned which is in counseling or a closely related field from a college or university that was accredited when the degree was awarded by one of the regional accrediting bodies recognized by the Council on Higher Education Accreditation.

b. TESTIMONIALS

Rehabilitation counselors who use testimonials will not solicit them from clients or other persons who, because of their particular circumstances, may be vulnerable to undue influence. Full disclosure of uses and the informed consent of the client or guardian will be obtained. Use of testimonials will be for a specified and agreed upon period of time.

c. STATEMENTS BY OTHERS

Rehabilitation counselors will make reasonable efforts to ensure that statements made by others about them or the profession of rehabilitation counseling are accurate.

d. RECRUITING THROUGH EMPLOYMENT

Employed rehabilitation counselors will not use their institutional affiliations or relationship with their employers to recruit clients, supervisees, or consultees for their separate private practices.

e. PRODUCTS AND TRAINING ADVERTISEMENTS

Rehabilitation counselors who develop products related to their profession or conduct workshops or training events will ensure that the advertisements concerning these products or events are accurate and disclose adequate information for consumers to make informed choices.

f. PROMOTING TO THOSE SERVED

Rehabilitation counselors will not use counseling, teaching, training, or supervisory relationships to promote their products or training events in a manner that is deceptive or would exert undue influence on individuals who may be vulnerable. Rehabilitation counselors may adopt textbooks they have authored for instructional purposes.

D.4. CREDENTIALS

a. CREDENTIALS CLAIMED
Rehabilitation counselors will claim or will imply only professional credentials possessed and are responsible for correcting any known misrepresentations of their credentials by others. Professional credentials include graduate degrees in counseling or closely related fields, accreditation of graduate programs, national voluntary certifications, government-issued certifications or licenses, or any other credential that might indicate to the public specialized knowledge or expertise in counseling.

b. CREDENTIAL GUIDELINES
Rehabilitation counselors will follow the guidelines for use of credentials that have been established by the entities that issue the credentials.

c. MISREPRESENTATION OF CREDENTIALS
Rehabilitation counselors will not attribute more to their credentials than the credentials represent, and will not imply that other rehabilitation counselors are not qualified because they do not possess certain credentials.

d. DOCTORAL DEGREES FROM OTHER FIELDS
Rehabilitation counselors who hold a master's degree in counseling or a closely related field, but hold a doctoral degree from other than counseling or a closely related field, will not use the title "Dr." in their practices and will not announce to the public in relation to their practice or status as a rehabilitation counselor that they hold a doctorate.

D.5. CRC CREDENTIAL

a. ACTING ON BEHALF OF CRCC
Certified Rehabilitation Counselors will not write, speak, nor act in ways that lead others to believe the counselor is officially representing CRCC unless the Commission has granted permission in writing.

b. SUPPORT OF CANDIDATES
Certified Rehabilitation Counselors will not initiate or support the candidacy of an individual for certification by CRCC if the individual is known to engage in professional practices that violate the Code of Professional Ethics for Rehabilitation Counselors.

D.6. PUBLIC RESPONSIBILITY

a. SEXUAL HARASSMENT
Rehabilitation counselors will not engage in sexual harassment. Sexual harassment is defined as sexual solicitation, physical advances, or verbal or nonverbal conduct that is sexual in nature, that occurs in connection with professional activities or roles, and that either (1)the rehabilitation counselor knows or is told the act is unwelcome, offensive, or creates a hostile workplace environment; or (2)is sufficiently severe or intense to be perceived as harassment to a reasonable person within the context in which it occurs. Sexual harassment may consist of a single intense or severe act or multiple persistent or pervasive acts.

b. REPORTS TO THIRD PARTIES
Rehabilitation counselors will be accurate, timely, and objective in reporting their professional activities and opinions to appropriate third parties including courts, health insurance companies, those who are the recipients of evaluation reports, and others.

c. MEDIA PRESENTATIONS
When rehabilitation counselors provide advice or comment by means of public lectures, demonstrations, radio or television programs, prerecorded tapes, printed articles, mailed material, or other media, they will take reasonable precautions to ensure that (1)the statements are based on appropriate professional

counseling literature and practice;(2)the statements are otherwise consistent with the Code of Professional Ethics for Rehabilitation Counselors; and (3)the recipients of the information are not encouraged to infer that a professional rehabilitation counseling relationship has been established.

d. CONFLICTS OF INTEREST
Rehabilitation counselors will not use their professional positions to seek or receive unjustified personal gains, sexual favors, unfair advantage, or unearned goods or services.

e. DISHONESTY
Rehabilitation counselors will not engage in any act or omission of a dishonest, deceitful or fraudulent nature in the conduct of their professional activities.

D.7. RESPONSIBILITY TO OTHER PROFESSIONALS

a. DISPARAGING COMMENTS
Rehabilitation counselors will not discuss in a disparaging way the competency of other professionals or agencies, or the findings made, the methods used, or the quality of rehabilitation plans.

b. PERSONAL PUBLIC STATEMENTS
When making personal statements in a public context, rehabilitation counselors will clarify that they are speaking from their personal perspectives and that they are not speaking on behalf of all rehabilitation counselors or the profession.

c. CLIENTS SERVED BY OTHERS
When rehabilitation counselors learn that their clients have an ongoing professional relationship with another rehabilitation or treating professional, they will request release from clients to inform the other professionals and strive to establish positive and collaborative professional relationships. File reviews, second-opinion services, and other indirect services are not considered ongoing professional services.

SECTION E: RELATIONSHIPS WITH OTHER PROFESSIONALS

E.1. RELATIONSHIPS WITH EMPLOYERS AND EMPLOYEES

a. NEGATIVE CONDITIONS
Rehabilitation counselors will alert their employers to conditions that may be potentially disruptive or damaging to the counselor's professional responsibilities or that may limit their effectiveness.

b. EVALUATION
Rehabilitation counselors will submit regularly to professional review and evaluation by their supervisor or the appropriate representative of the employer.

c. DISCRIMINATION
Rehabilitation counselors, as either employers or employees, will engage in fair practices with regard to hiring, promotion, or training.

d. EXPLOITATIVE RELATIONSHIPS
Rehabilitation counselors will not engage in exploitative relationships with individuals over whom they have supervisory, evaluative, or instructional control or authority.

e. EMPLOYER POLICIES
In those instances where rehabilitation counselors are critical of policies, they will attempt to affect change through constructive action within the organization. Where such change cannot be affected, rehabilitation counselors will take appropriate further action. Such action may include referral to appropriate certification, accreditation, or state licensure organizations or termination of employment.

E.2. CONSULTATION

a. CONSULTATION AS AN OPTION
Rehabilitation counselors may choose to consult with professionally competent persons about their clients. In choosing consultants, rehabilitation counselors will avoid placing the consultant in a conflict of interest situation that will preclude the consultant from being a proper party to the counselor's efforts to help the client. If rehabilitation counselors are engaged in a work setting that compromises this consultation standard, they will consult with other professionals whenever possible to consider justifiable alternatives.

b. CONSULTANT COMPETENCY
Rehabilitation counselors will be reasonably certain that they have, or the organization represented has, the necessary competencies and resources for giving the kind of consulting services needed and that appropriate referral resources are available.

E.3. AGENCY AND TEAM RELATIONSHIPS

a. CLIENT AS A TEAM MEMBER
Rehabilitation counselors will ensure that clients and/or their legally recognized representative are afforded the opportunity for full participation in their own treatment team.

b. COMMUNICATION
Rehabilitation counselors will ensure that there is fair mutual understanding of the rehabilitation plan by all agencies cooperating in the rehabilitation of clients and that any rehabilitation plan is developed with such mutual understanding.

c. DISSENT
Rehabilitation counselors will abide by and help to implement team decisions in formulating rehabilitation plans and procedures, even when not personally agreeing with such decisions, unless these decisions breach the Code.

d. REPORTS
Rehabilitation counselors will attempt to secure from other specialists appropriate reports and evaluations, when such reports are essential for rehabilitation planning and/or service delivery.

SECTION F: EVALUATION, ASSESSMENT, AND INTERPRETATION

F.1. INFORMED CONSENT

a. EXPLANATION TO CLIENTS
Prior to assessment, rehabilitation counselors will explain the nature and purposes of assessment and the specific use of results in language the client (or other legally authorized person on behalf of the client)can understand. Regardless of whether scoring and interpretation are completed by rehabilitation counselors, by assistants, or by computer or other outside services, rehabilitation counselors will take reasonable steps to ensure that appropriate explanations are given to the client.

b. RECIPIENTS OF RESULTS
The client's welfare, explicit understanding, and prior agreement will determine the recipients of test results. Rehabilitation counselors will include accurate and appropriate interpretations with any release of test results.

F.2. RELEASE OF INFORMATION TO COMPETENT PROFESSIONALS

a. MISUSE OF RESULTS
Rehabilitation counselors will not misuse assessment results, including test results and interpretations, and will take reasonable steps to prevent the misuse of such by others.

b. RELEASE OF RAW DATA
Rehabilitation counselors will ordinarily release data (e. g., protocols, counseling or interview notes, or questionnaires)in which the client is identified only with the consent of the client or the client's legal representative. Such data will be released only to persons recognized by rehabilitation counselors as competent to interpret the data.

F.3. RESEARCH AND TRAINING

a. DATA DISGUISE REQUIRED
Use of data derived from counseling relationships for purposes of training, research, or publication will be confined to content that is disguised to ensure the anonymity of the individuals involved.

b. AGREEMENT FOR IDENTIFICATION
Identification of a client in a presentation or publication will be permissible only when the client has agreed in writing to its presentation or publication.

F.4. PROPER DIAGNOSIS OF MENTAL DISORDERS

a. PROPER DIAGNOSIS
Rehabilitation counselors qualified to provide proper diagnosis of mental disorders will take special care when doing so. Assessment techniques (including personal interview)used to determine client care (e. g.,locus of treatment, type of treatment, or recommended follow-up)will be carefully selected and appropriately used.

b. CULTURAL SENSITIVITY
Disability, socioeconomic, and cultural experience of clients will be considered when diagnosing mental disorders.

F.5. COMPETENCE TO USE AND INTERPRET TESTS

a. LIMITS OF COMPETENCE
Rehabilitation counselors will recognize the limits of their competence and perform only those testing and assessment services for which they have been trained. They will be familiar with reliability, validity, related standardization, error of measurement, and proper application of any technique utilized. Rehabilitation counselors using computer-based test interpretations will be trained in the construct being measured and the specific instrument being used prior to using this type of computer application. Rehabilitation counselors will take reasonable measures to ensure the proper use of psychological assessment techniques by persons under their supervision.

b. APPROPRIATE USE
Rehabilitation counselors will be responsible for the appropriate application, scoring, interpretation, and use of assessment instruments, whether they score and interpret such tests themselves or use computerized or other services.

c. DECISIONS BASED ON RESULTS
Rehabilitation counselors will be responsible for decisions involving individuals or policies that are based on assessment results and will have a thorough understanding of educational and psychological measurement, including validation criteria, test research, and guidelines for test development and use.

d. ACCURATE INFORMATION
Rehabilitation counselors will provide accurate information and avoid false claims or misconceptions when making statements about assessment instruments or techniques. Special efforts will be made to avoid utilizing test results to make inappropriate diagnoses or inferences.

F.6. TEST SELECTION

a. APPROPRIATENESS OF INSTRUMENTS
Rehabilitation counselors will carefully consider the validity, reliability, psychometric limitations, and appropriateness of instruments when selecting tests for use in a given situation or with a particular client.

b. REFERRAL INFORMATION
If a client is referred to a third party provider for testing, the rehabilitation counselor will provide specific referral questions and sufficient objective data about the client so as to ensure that appropriate test instruments are utilized.

c. CULTURALLY DIVERSE POPULATIONS
Rehabilitation counselors will be cautious when selecting tests for disability or culturally diverse populations to avoid inappropriateness of testing that may be outside of socialized behavioral or cognitive patterns or functional abilities.

d. NORM DIVERGENCE
Rehabilitation counselors will be cautious in using assessment techniques, making evaluations, and interpreting the performance of populations not represented in the norm group on which an instrument was standardized and will disclose such information.

F.7. CONDITIONS OF TEST ADMINISTRATION

a. ADMINISTRATION CONDITIONS
Rehabilitation counselors will administer tests under the same conditions that were established in the test standardization. When tests are not administered under standard conditions, as may be necessary to accommodate modifications for clients with disabilities or when unusual behavior or irregularities occur during the testing session, those conditions will be noted in interpretation.

b. COMPUTER ADMINISTRATION
When a computer or other electronic methods are used for test administration, rehabilitation counselors will be responsible for ensuring that programs function properly to provide clients with accurate results.

c. UNSUPERVISED TEST-TAKING.
Rehabilitation counselors will not permit unsupervised or inadequately supervised use of tests or assessments unless the tests or assessments are designed, intended, and validated for self-administration and/or scoring.

F.8. TEST SCORING AND INTERPRETATION

a. REPORTING RESERVATIONS
In reporting assessment results, rehabilitation counselors will indicate any reservations that exist regarding validity or reliability because of the circumstances of the assessment or the inappropriateness of the norms for the person tested.

b. DIVERSITY IN TESTING
Rehabilitation counselors will place test results and their interpretations in proper perspective considering other relevant factors including age, color, culture, disability, ethnic group, gender, race, religion, sexual orientation, marital status, and socioeconomic status.

c. RESEARCH INSTRUMENTS
Rehabilitation counselors will exercise caution when interpreting the results of research instruments possessing insufficient technical data to support respondent results. The specific purposes for the use of such instruments will be stated explicitly to the examinee.

d. TESTING SERVICES
Rehabilitation counselors who provide test scoring and test interpretation services to support the assessment process will confirm the validity of such interpretations. The interpretation of assessment data will be related to the particular goals of evaluation. Rehabilitation counselors will accurately describe the purpose, norms, validity, reliability, and applications of the procedures and any special qualifications applicable to their use.

e. AUTOMATED TESTING SERVICES
The public offering of an automated test interpretation service will be considered a professional-to-professional consultation. The formal responsibility of the consultant will be to the consultee, but the ultimate and overriding responsibility will be to the client.

F.9. TEST SECURITY

Rehabilitation counselors will maintain the integrity and security of tests and other assessment techniques consistent with legal and contractual obligations. Rehabilitation counselors will not appropriate, reproduce, or modify published tests or parts thereof without acknowledgment and permission from the publisher.

F.10. OBSOLETE TESTS AND OUTDATED TEST RESULTS

Rehabilitation counselors will not use data or test results that are obsolete or outdated for the current purpose. Rehabilitation counselors will make every effort to prevent the misuse of obsolete measures and test data by others.

F.11. TEST CONSTRUCTION

Rehabilitation counselors will use established scientific procedures, relevant standards, and current professional knowledge for test design in the development, publication, and utilization of educational and psychological assessment techniques.

F.12. FORENSIC EVALUATION

When providing forensic evaluations, the primary obligation of rehabilitation counselors will be to produce objective findings that can be substantiated based on information and techniques appropriate to the evaluation, which may include examination of the individual with a disability and/or review of records. Rehabilitation counselors will define the limits of their reports or testimony, especially when an examination of the individual with a disability has not been conducted.

SECTION G: TEACHING, TRAINING, AND SUPERVISION

G.1. REHABILITATION COUNSELOR EDUCATORS AND TRAINERS

a. RELATIONSHIP BOUNDARIES WITH STUDENTS AND SUPERVISEES
Rehabilitation counselors will clearly define and maintain ethical, professional, and social relationship boundaries with their students and supervisees. They will be aware of the differential in power that exists and the student or supervisee's possible incomprehension of that power differential. Rehabilitation counselors will explain to students and supervisees the potential for the relationship to become exploitive.

b. SEXUAL RELATIONSHIPS

Rehabilitation counselors will not engage in sexual relationships with students or supervisees and will not subject them to sexual harassment.

c. SUPERVISION PREPARATION

Rehabilitation counselors will supervise only within the boundaries of their competence, based on their education, training, supervised experience, state and national professional credentials, and appropriate professional experience. Rehabilitation counselors who are doctoral students serving as practicum or internship supervisors will be adequately prepared and supervised by the training program.

d. RESPONSIBILITY FOR SERVICES TO CLIENTS

Rehabilitation counselors who supervise the rehabilitation counseling services of others will perform direct supervision sufficient to ensure that rehabilitation counseling services provided to clients are adequate and do not cause harm to the client.

e. ENDORSEMENT

Rehabilitation counselors will not endorse students or supervisees for certification, licensure, employment, or completion of an academic or training program if they believe students or supervisees are not qualified for the endorsement. Rehabilitation counselors will take reasonable steps to assist students or supervisees who are not qualified for endorsement to become qualified.

G.2. REHABILITATION COUNSELOR EDUCATION AND TRAINING PROGRAMS

a. ORIENTATION

Prior to admission, rehabilitation counselor educators will orient prospective students to the counselor education or training program's expectations, including but not limited to the following: (1)the type and level of skill acquisition required for successful completion of the training,(2)subject matter to be covered,(3)basis for evaluation,(4)training components that encourage self-growth or self-disclosure as part of the training process,(5)the type of supervision settings and requirements of the sites for required clinical field experiences,(6)student evaluation and dismissal policies and procedures, and (7)up-to-date employment prospects for graduates.

b. EVALUATION

Rehabilitation counselor educators will clearly state, in advance of training, to students and internship supervisees, the levels of competency expected, appraisal methods, and timing of evaluations for both didactic and experiential components. Rehabilitation counselor educators will provide students and internship supervisees with periodic performance appraisal and evaluation feedback throughout the training program.

c. TEACHING ETHICS

Rehabilitation counselor educators will teach students and internship supervisees the ethical responsibilities and standards of the profession and the students' and supervisees' professional ethical responsibilities.

d. PEER RELATIONSHIPS

When students are assigned to lead counseling groups or provide clinical supervision for their peers, rehabilitation counselor educators will take steps to ensure that students placed in these roles do not have personal or adverse relationships with peers and that they understand they have the same ethical obligations as counselor educators, trainers, and supervisors. Rehabilitation counselor educators will make every effort to ensure that the rights of peers are not compromised when students are assigned to lead counseling groups or provide clinical supervision.

e. VARIED THEORETICAL POSITIONS

Rehabilitation counselor educators will present varied theoretical positions so that students may make comparisons and have opportunities to develop their own positions. Rehabilitation counselor educators will provide information concerning the scientific bases of professional practice.

f. FIELD PLACEMENTS

Rehabilitation counselor educators will develop clear policies within their training program regarding field placement and other clinical experiences. Rehabilitation counselor educators will provide clearly stated roles and responsibilities for the student and the site supervisor. Rehabilitation counselor educators will confirm that site supervisors will be qualified to provide supervision and are informed of their professional and ethical responsibilities in this role. Rehabilitation counselor educators will not accept any form of professional services, fees, commissions, reimbursement, or remuneration from a site for student placement.

g. DIVERSITY IN PROGRAMS

Rehabilitation counselor educators will respond to their institution and program's recruitment and retention needs for training program administrators, faculty, and students with diverse backgrounds and special needs.

G.3. STUDENTS AND SUPERVISEES

a. LIMITATIONS

Rehabilitation counselors, through ongoing evaluation and appraisal, will be aware of the academic and personal limitations of students and supervisees that might impede performance. Rehabilitation counselors will assist students and supervisees in securing remedial assistance when needed, and will dismiss students or supervisees who are unable to provide competent service due to academic or personal limitations. Rehabilitation counselors will seek professional consultation and document their decision to dismiss or to refer students or supervisees for assistance. Rehabilitation counselors will advise students and supervisees of appeals processes as appropriate.

b. SELF-GROWTH EXPERIENCES.
Rehabilitation counselor educators, when designing training groups or other experiences conducted by the rehabilitation counselor educators themselves, will inform students of the potential risks of self-disclosure. Rehabilitation counselor educators will respect the privacy of students by not requiring self-disclosure that could reasonably be expected to be harmful and student evaluation criteria will not include the level of the student's self-disclosure.

c. COUNSELING FOR STUDENTS AND SUPERVISEES
If students or supervisees request counseling, supervisors or rehabilitation counselor educators will provide them with acceptable referrals. Supervisors or rehabilitation counselor educators will not serve as rehabilitation counselors to students or supervisees over whom they hold administrative, teaching, or evaluative roles unless this is a brief role associated with a training experience.

d. CLIENTS OF STUDENTS AND SUPERVISEES
Rehabilitation counselors will make every effort to ensure that clients are aware of the services rendered and the qualifications of the students and supervisees rendering those services. Clients will receive professional disclosure information and will be informed of the limits of confidentiality. Client permission will be obtained in order for the students and supervisees to use any information concerning the counseling relationship in the training process.

e. PROFESSIONAL DEVELOPMENT
Rehabilitation counselors who employ or supervise individuals will provide appropriate working conditions, timely evaluations, constructive consultations, and suitable opportunities for experience and training.

SECTION H: RESEARCH AND PUBLICATION

H.1. RESEARCH RESPONSIBILITIES

a. USE OF HUMAN PARTICIPANTS
Rehabilitation counselors will plan, design, conduct, and report research in a manner that reflects cultural sensitivity, is culturally appropriate, and is consistent with pertinent ethical principles, federal and state/provincial laws, host institutional regulations, and scientific standards governing research with human participants.

b. DEVIATION FROM STANDARD PRACTICES
Rehabilitation counselors will seek consultation and observe stringent safeguards to protect the rights of research participants when a research problem suggests a deviation from standard acceptable practices.

c. PRECAUTIONS TO AVOID INJURY
Rehabilitation counselors who conduct research with human participants will be responsible for the participants' welfare throughout the research and will take reasonable precautions to avoid causing injurious psychological, physical, or social effects to their participants.

d. PRINCIPAL RESEARCHER RESPONSIBILITY
While ultimate responsibility for ethical research practice lies with the principal researcher, rehabilitation counselors involved in the research activities will share ethical obligations and bear full responsibility for their own actions.

e. MINIMAL INTERFERENCE
Rehabilitation counselors will take precautions to avoid causing disruptions in participants ' lives due to participation in research..

f. DIVERSITY
Rehabilitation counselors will be sensitive to diversity and research issues with culturally diverse populations and they will seek consultation when appropriate.

H.2. INFORMED CONSENT

a. TOPICS DISCLOSED
In obtaining informed consent for research, rehabilitation counselors will use language that is understandable to research participants and that (1)accurately explains the purpose and procedures to be followed;(2)identifies any procedures that are experimental or relatively untried;(3)describes the attendant discomforts and risks;(4)describes the benefits or changes in individuals or organizations that might reasonably be expected;(5)discloses appropriate alternative procedures that would be advantageous for participants;(6)offers to answer any inquiries concerning the procedures;(7)describes any limitations of confidentiality; and (8)instructs that participants are free to withdraw their consent and to discontinue participation in the project at any time.

b. DECEPTION
Rehabilitation counselors will not conduct research involving deception unless alternative procedures are not feasible and the prospective value of the research justifies the deception. When the methodological requirements of a study necessitate concealment or deception, the investigator will be required to explain clearly the reasons for this action as soon as possible.

c. VOLUNTARY PARTICIPATION
Participation in research is typically voluntary and without any penalty for refusal to participate. Involuntary participation will be appropriate only when it can be demonstrated that participation will have no harmful effects on participants and is essential to the investigation.

d. CONFIDENTIALITY OF INFORMATION
Information obtained about research participants during the course of an investigation will be confidential. When the possibility exists that others may obtain access to such information, ethical research practice requires that the possibility, together with the plans for protecting confidentiality, will be explained to participants as a part of the procedure for obtaining informed consent.

e. PERSONS INCAPABLE OF GIVING INFORMED CONSENT
When a person is incapable of giving informed consent, rehabilitation counselors will provide an appropriate explanation, obtain agreement for participation, and obtain appropriate consent from a legally authorized person.

f. COMMITMENTS TO PARTICIPANTS
Rehabilitation counselors will take reasonable measures to honor all commitments to research participants.

g. EXPLANATIONS AFTER ATA COLLECTION
After data are collected, rehabilitation counselors will provide participants with full clarification of the nature of the study to remove any misconceptions. Where scientific or human values justify delaying or withholding information, rehabilitation counselors will take reasonable measures to avoid causing harm.

h. AGREEMENTS TO COOPERATE
Rehabilitation counselors who agree to cooperate with another individual in research or publication will incur an obligation to cooperate as agreed.

i. INFORMED CONSENT FOR SPONSORS
In the pursuit of research, rehabilitation counselors will give sponsors, institutions, and publication channels the same opportunity for giving informed consent that they accord to individual research participants. Rehabilitation counselors will be aware of their obligation to future researchers and will ensure that host institutions are given feedback information and proper acknowledgment.

H.3. REPORTING RESULTS

a. INFORMATION AFFECTING OUTCOME
When reporting research results, rehabilitation counselors will explicitly mention all variables and conditions known to the investigator that may have affected the outcome of a study or the interpretation of data.

b. ACCURATE RESULTS
Rehabilitation counselors will plan, conduct, and report research accurately and in a manner that minimizes the possibility that results will be misleading. They will provide thorough discussions of the limitations of their data and alternative hypotheses. Rehabilitation counselors will not engage in fraudulent research, distort data, misrepresent data, or deliberately bias their results.

c. OBLIGATION TO REPORT UNFAVORABLE RESULTS
Rehabilitation counselors will make available the results of any research judged to be of professional value even if the results reflect unfavorably on institutions, programs, services, prevailing opinions, or vested interests.

d. IDENTITY OF PARTICIPANTS
Rehabilitation counselors who supply data, aid in the research of another person, report research results, or make original data available will take due care to disguise the identity of respective participants in the absence of specific authorization from the participants to do otherwise.

e. REPLICATION STUDIES
Rehabilitation counselors will be obligated to make sufficient original research data available to qualified professionals who may wish to replicate the study.

H.4. PUBLICATION

a. RECOGNITION OF OTHERS
When conducting and reporting research, rehabilitation counselors will be familiar with and give recognition to previous work on the topic, observe copyright laws, and give full credit to those to whom credit is due.

b. CONTRIBUTORS
Rehabilitation counselors will give credit through joint authorship, acknowledgment, footnote statements, or other appropriate means to those who have contributed significantly to research or concept development in accordance with such contributions. The principal contributor will be listed first and minor technical or professional contributions are acknowledged in notes or introductory statements.

c. STUDENT RESEARCH
For an article that is substantially based on a student's dissertation or thesis, the student will be listed as the principal author.

d. DUPLICATE SUBMISSION
Rehabilitation counselors will submit manuscripts for consideration to only one journal at a time. Manuscripts that are published in whole or in substantial part in another journal or published work will not be submitted for publication without acknowledgment and permission from the previous publication.

e. PROFESSIONAL REVIEW
Rehabilitation counselors who review material submitted for publication, research, or other scholarly purposes will respect the confidentiality and proprietary rights of those who submitted it.

SECTION I: ELECTRONIC COMMUNICATION AND EMERGING APPLICATIONS

I.1. COMMUNICATION

a. COMMUNICATION TOOLS
Rehabilitation counselors will be held to the same level of expected behavior as defined by the Code of Professional Ethics for Rehabilitation Counselors regardless of the form of communication they choose to use (i. e., cellular phones, electronic mail, facsimile, video, audio-visual).

b. IMPOSTERS
In situations where it is difficult to verify the identity of the rehabilitation counselor, the client, or the client's guardian, rehabilitation counselors will take steps to address imposter concerns, such as using code words, numbers, or graphics.

c. CONFIDENTIALITY
Rehabilitation counselors will ensure that clients are provided sufficient information to adequately address and explain the limits of: (1)computer technology in the counseling process in general; and (2)the difficulties of ensuring complete client confidentiality of information transmitted through electronic communication over the Internet through on-line counseling.

I.2. COUNSELING RELATIONSHIP

a. ETHICAL/LEGAL REVIEW
Rehabilitation counselors will review pertinent legal and ethical codes for possible violations emanating from the practice of distance counseling and supervision. Distance counseling is defined as any counseling that occurs at a distance through electronic means, such as web-counseling, tele-counseling, or video-counseling.

b. SECURITY

Rehabilitation counselors will use encryption methods whenever possible. If encryption is not made available to clients, clients must be informed of the potential hazards of unsecured communication on the Internet. Hazards may include authorized or unauthorized monitoring of transmissions and/or records of sessions.

c. RECORDS PRESERVATION

Rehabilitation counselors will inform clients whether the records are being preserved, how they are being preserved, and how long the records are being maintained.

d. SELF-DESCRIPTION

Rehabilitation counselors will provide information about themselves as would be available if the counseling were to take place face-to-face (e. g.,possibly ethnicity or gender).

e. CONSUMER PROTECTION

Rehabilitation counselors will provide information to the client regarding all appropriate certification bodies and licensure boards to facilitate consumer protection, such as links to websites.

f. CRISIS CONTACT

Rehabilitation counselors will provide the name of at least one agency or counselor-on-call for purposes of crisis intervention within the client's geographical region.

g. UNAVAILABILITY

Rehabilitation counselors will provide clients with instructions for contacting them when they are unavailable through electronic means.

h. INAPPROPRIATE USE

Rehabilitation counselors will mention at their websites or in their initial contacts with potential clients those presenting problems they believe to be inappropriate for distance counseling.

i. TECHNICAL FAILURE

Rehabilitation counselors will explain to clients the possibility of technology failure and will provide an alternative means of communication.

j. POTENTIAL MISUNDERSTANDINGS

Rehabilitation counselors will explain to clients how to prevent and address potential misunderstandings arising from the lack of visual cues and voice intonations from the counselor or client.

SECTION J: BUSINESS PRACTICES

J.1. BILLING

Rehabilitation counselors will establish and maintain billing records that accurately reflect the services provided and the time engaged in the activity, and that clearly identify who provided the service.

J.2. TERMINATION

Rehabilitation counselors in fee for service relationships may terminate services with clients due to nonpayment of fees under the following conditions:

a) the client was informed of payment responsibilities and the effects of nonpayment or the termination of payment by a third party, and

b) the client does not pose an imminent danger to self or others. As appropriate, rehabilitation counselors will refer clients to another qualified professional to address issues unresolved at the time of termination.

J.3. CLIENT RECORDS

a. ACCURATE DOCUMENTATION
Rehabilitation counselors will establish and will maintain documentation that accurately reflects the services provided and that identifies who provided the service. If case notes need to be altered, it will be done so in a manner that preserves the original note and will be accompanied by the date of change, information that identifies who made the change, and the rationale for the change.

b. SUFFICIENT DOCUMENTATION
Rehabilitation counselors will provide sufficient documentation in a timely manner (e. g.,case notes, reports, plans).

c. PRIVACY
Documentation generated by rehabilitation counselors will protect the privacy of clients to the extent that it is possible and appropriate, and will include only relevant information.

d. MAINTENANCE
Rehabilitation counselors will maintain records necessary for rendering professional services to their clients and as required by applicable laws, regulations, or agency/institution procedures. Subsequent to file closure, records will be maintained for the number of years consistent with jurisdictional requirements or for a longer period during which maintenance of such records is necessary or helpful to provide reasonably anticipated future services to the client. After that time, records will be destroyed in a manner assuring preservation of confidentiality.

J.4. FEES AND BARTERING

a. ADVANCE UNDERSTANDING
Rehabilitation counselors will clearly explain to clients, prior to entering the counseling relationship, all financial arrangements related to professional services including the use of collection agencies or legal measures for nonpayment.

b. ESTABLISHING FEES
In establishing fees for professional rehabilitation counseling services, rehabilitation counselors will consider the financial status and locality of clients. In the event that the established fee structure is inappropriate for a client, assistance will be provided in attempting to find comparable services of acceptable cost.

c. BARTERING DISCOURAGED
Rehabilitation counselors will ordinarily refrain from accepting goods or services from clients in return for rehabilitation counseling services because such arrangements create inherent potential for conflicts, exploitation, and distortion of the professional relationship. Rehabilitation counselors will participate in bartering only if the relationship is not exploitative, if the client requests it, if a clear written contract is established, and if such arrangements are an accepted practice in the client's community or culture.

J.5. FEES FOR REFERRAL

a. ACCEPTING FEES FROM AGENCY CLIENTS
Rehabilitation counselors will not accept a private fee or other remuneration for rendering services to persons who are entitled to such services through the rehabilitation counselor's employing agency or institution. However, the policies of a particular agency may make explicit provisions for agency clients to receive rehabilitation counseling services from members of its staff in private practice. In such instances,

the clients will be informed of other options open to them should they seek private rehabilitation counseling services.

b. REFERRAL FEES
Rehabilitation counselors will neither give nor receive commissions, rebates or any other form of remuneration when referring clients for professional services.

SECTION K: RESOLVING ETHICAL ISSUES

K.1. KNOWLEDGE OF STANDARDS

Rehabilitation counselors are responsible for learning the Code and should seek clarification of any standard that is not understood. Lack of knowledge or misunderstanding of an ethical responsibility will not be used as a defense against a charge of unethical conduct.

K.2. SUSPECTED VIOLATIONS

a. CONSULTATION
When uncertain as to whether a particular situation or course of action may be in violation of the Code of Professional Ethics for Rehabilitation Counselors, rehabilitation counselors will consult with other rehabilitation counselors who are knowledgeable about ethics, with colleagues, and/or with appropriate authorities, such as CRCC, state licensure boards, or legal counsel.

b. ORGANIZATION CONFLICTS
If the demands of an organization with which rehabilitation counselors are affiliated pose a conflict with the Code of Professional Ethics for Rehabilitation Counselors, rehabilitation counselors will specify the nature of such conflicts and express to their supervisors or other responsible officials their commitment to the Code of Professional Ethics for Rehabilitation Counselors. When possible, rehabilitation counselors will work toward change within the organization to allow full adherence to the Code of Professional Ethics for Rehabilitation Counselors.

c. INFORMAL RESOLUTION
When rehabilitation counselors have reasonable cause to believe that another rehabilitation counselor is violating an ethical standard, they will attempt to resolve the issue informally with the other rehabilitation counselor if feasible, providing that such action does not violate confidentiality rights that may be involved.

d. REPORTING SUSPECTED VIOLATIONS
When an informal resolution is not appropriate or feasible, rehabilitation counselors, upon reasonable cause, will take action such as reporting the suspected ethical violation to state or national ethics committees or CRCC, unless this action conflicts with confidentiality rights that cannot be resolved.

e. UNWARRANTED COMPLAINTS
Rehabilitation counselors will not initiate, participate in, or encourage the filing of ethics complaints that are unwarranted or intended to harm a rehabilitation counselor rather than to protect clients or the public.

K.3. COOPERATION WITH ETHICS COMMITTEES

Rehabilitation counselors will assist in the process of enforcing the Code of Professional Ethics for Rehabilitation Counselors. Rehabilitation counselors will cooperate with investigations, proceedings, and requirements of the CRCC Ethics Committee or ethics committees of other duly constituted associations or boards having jurisdiction over those charged with a violation.

Acknowledgements

CRCC recognizes the American Counseling Association for permitting the Commission to adopt, in part, the ACA Code of Ethics and Standards of Practice.

A copy of CRCC's Guidelines and Procedures for Processing Complaints along with a Complaint Form may be obtained from CRCC's web site at www.crccertification.com or by contacting CRCC.

Developed and Administered by the Commission on Rehabilitation Counselor Certification

1835 Rohlwing Road, Suite E
Rolling Meadows, Illinois 60008
(847) 394-2104
http://www.crccertification.com

Code of Professional Ethics for Rehabilitation Counselors, Commission on Rehabilitation Counselor Certification (CRCC, 2001.) Reprinted with Permission.

International Association of Marriage and Family Counselors
Ethical Code

Ethical Code of the International Association of Marriage and Family Counselors (IAMFC)
Approved by the Board of IAMFC
2005

Preamble

The International Association of Marriage and Family Counselors (IAMFC) is an organization dedicated to advancing practice, training, and research in couple and family counseling. Members may specialize in areas such as premarital counseling, marriage counseling, family counseling, sex counseling, intergenerational counseling, separation and divorce counseling, relocation counseling, custody evaluation, and parenting training. Marriage and family counselors may work with special populations including stepfamilies, nontraditional couples and family systems, multicultural couples and families, disadvantaged families, and dual career couples. In conducting their professional activities, members commit themselves to protect family relationships and advocate for the healthy growth and development of the family as a whole and each member's unique needs. The IAMFC member recognizes that the relationship between the provider and consumer of services is characterized as professional. However, the IAMFC member should remain informed of social and cultural trends, as well as scientific and technological changes affecting the foundation of the professional counseling relationship.

This code of ethics provides a framework for ethical practices by IAMFC members and other professionals engaged in couple and family counseling. It is divided into eight sections: the counseling relationship and client well-being; confidentiality and privacy; competence and professional responsibilities; collaboration and professional relationships; assessment and evaluation; counselor education and supervision; research and publication; and ethical decision-making and resolution. The observations and recommendations presented within these eight areas are meant to supplement the current ethical standards of the American Counseling Association. Although an ethical code cannot anticipate every possible situation or dilemma, the IAMFC ethical guidelines can assist members in ensuring the welfare and dignity of the couples and families who seek services.

The ethical code of the International Association of Marriage and Family Counselors incorporates the ethics of principles and virtues. The code of ethics articulates some specific principles and guidelines, protecting consumers from potentially harmful practices and encouraging professionals to maintain high standards for effective practice. The ethical code also addresses the character of the professional couple and family counselor. Ethics of character or virtue contribute to professional aspirations and values. Each of the eight sections includes aspirations and principles.

Section A: The Counseling Relationship and Client Well-Being

Marriage and family counselors contribute to the healthy development and evolution of family systems. They are committed to understanding problems and learning needs from multiple contexts. Couple and family counselors, in particular, embrace models of practice based on family dynamics and systems. Professional counselors realize their perspectives influence the conceptualization of problems, identification of clients, and implementation of possible solutions. Couple and family counselors examine personal biases and values. They actively attempt to understand and serve couples and families from diverse cultural backgrounds. Professional marriage and family counselors are willing to remove barriers to the counseling relationship, act as responsible public servants, and become involved in advocacy in the best interests of couples and families.

1. Marriage and family counselors demonstrate caring, empathy, and respect for client well-being. They promote safety, security, and sense of community for couples and families. Due to potential risks involved, couple and family counselors should not use intrusive interventions without sound theoretical rationale, research support, and clinical consultation or supervision.

2.	Marriage and family counselors recognize that each family is unique. Couple and family counselors do not promote bias and stereotyping regarding family roles and functions.

3.	Marriage and family counselors respect the autonomy of the families with whom they work. They do not make decisions that rightfully belong to family members. When indicated and possible, couple and family counselors share with clients clinical impressions and recommendations, decision-making processes, problem-solving strategies, and intervention outcomes.

4.	Marriage and family counselors respect cultural diversity. They do not discriminate on the basis of race, gender, disability, religion, age, sexual orientation, cultural background, national origin, marital status, or political affiliation.

5.	Marriage and family counselors promote open, honest and direct relationships with consumers of professional services. Couple and family counselors inform clients about the goals of counseling, qualifications of the counselor(s), limits of confidentiality, potential risks and benefits associated with specific techniques, duration of treatment, costs of services, appropriate alternatives to marriage and family counseling, and reasonable expectations for outcomes.

6.	Marriage and family counselors promote primary prevention. They advocate for the development of clients' cognitive, moral, social, emotional, spiritual, physical, educational, relational, and vocational skills. Couple and family counselors promote effective marital and family communication and problem solving skills needed to prevent future problems.

7.	Marriage and family counselors have an obligation to determine and inform counseling participants who is identified as the primary client. The marriage and family counselor should make clear when there are obligations to an individual, a couple, a family, a third party, or an institution.

8.	Marriage and family counselors who are IAMFC members have a professional duty to monitor their places of employment to make recommendations so the environment is conducive to the positive growth and development of clients. When there is a conflict of interest between the needs of the client and counselor's employing institution, the IAMFC member works to clarify his or her commitment to all parties. IAMFC members recognize that the acceptance of employment implies agreement with the policies and practices of the agency or institution.

9.	Marriage and family counselors do not harass, exploit, coerce, or manipulate clients for personal gain. Couple and family counselors avoid whenever possible multiple relationships, such as business, social or sexual contacts with any current clients or their family members. Marriage and family counselors should refrain generally from nonprofessional relationships with former clients and their family members because termination of counseling is a complex process. Couple and family counselors are responsible for demonstrating there is no harm from any relationship with a client or family member. The key element in this ethical principle is the avoidance of exploitation of vulnerable clients.

10.	Marriage and family counselors have an obligation to withdraw from a counseling relationship if the continuation of services would not be in the best interest of the client or would result in a violation of ethical standards. If the counseling relationship is no longer helpful or productive, couple and family counselors have an obligation to assist in locating alternative services and making referrals as needed. Marriage and family counselors do not abandon clients. They arrange for appropriate termination of counseling relationships and transfer of services as indicated.

11.	Marriage and family counselors maintain accurate and up-to-date records. They make all file information available to clients unless there is compelling evidence that such access would be harmful to the client. In situations involving multiple clients, couple and family counselors provide individual clients with parts of records related directly to them, protecting confidential information related to other clients who have not authorized release. Marriage and family counselors include sufficient and timely documentation in client records to facilitate delivery of services and referral to other professionals as needed.

12. Marriage and family counselors establish fees that are reasonable and customary depending upon the scope and location of their practices. Couple and family counselors in community agencies, schools, and other public settings do not solicit gifts or charge fees for services that are available in the counselor's employing agency or institution. Culturally sensitive counselors recognize that gifts are tokens of respect and gratitude in some cultures. Marriage and family counselors may receive gifts or participate in family rituals that promote healthy interaction and do not exploit clients.

13. Marriage and family counselors maintain ethical and effective practices as they address the benefits and limitations of technological innovations and cultural changes. Counseling may be conducted or assisted by telephones, computer hardware and software, and other communication technologies. Technology-assisted distance counseling services may expand the scope and influence of marriage and family counseling. However, counselors are responsible for developing competencies in the use of new technologies and safeguarding private and confidential information.

Section B: Confidentiality and Privacy

Marriage and family counselors recognize that trust is the foundation of an effective counseling relationship. Professional counselors maintain appropriate boundaries so that clients reasonably expect that information shared will not be disclosed to others without prior written consent. Due to the nature of couple and family counseling, safeguards must be established in the counseling process to insure privacy of client disclosures without contributing to dysfunctional family secrets. Clients have the right to know the limits of confidentiality, privacy, and privileged communication.

1. Marriage and family counselors may disclose private information to others under specific circumstances known to the individual client or client family members. Ideally, the client consents to disclosure by signing an authorization to release information. Each person receiving counseling who is legally competent to sign a waiver of right to confidentiality should execute an authorization. The authorization should clearly indicate to whom information will be disclosed under which specific circumstances. The authorization should be time-limited, consistent with legal statutes, and limited to the scope agreed by the counselor and client. The client may rescind or withdraw the authorization.

2. Marriage and family counselors inform parents and legal guardians about the confidential nature of the counseling relationship. When working with minor or juvenile clients, as well as adult clients who lack the capacity to authorize release of confidential information, couple and family counselors seek consent from the appropriate custodial parent or guardian to disclose information.

3. Marriage and family counselors inform clients of exceptions to the general principle that information will be kept confidential or released only upon written client authorization. Disclosure of private information may be mandated by state law. For example, states require reporting of suspected abuse of children or other vulnerable populations. Couple and family counselors may have sound legal or ethical justification for disclosing information if someone is in imminent danger. A court may have jurisdiction to order release of confidential information without a client's permission. However, all releases of information not authorized by clients should be minimal or narrow as possible to limit potential harm to the counseling relationship.

4. Marriage and family counselors inform clients who may have access to their counseling records, as well as any information that may be released for third-party payment or insurance reimbursement. State and Federal laws may affect record-keeping and release of information from client records.

5. Marriage and family counselors store records in a way that protects confidentiality. Written records should be kept in a locked file drawer or cabinet and computerized record systems should have appropriate passwords and safeguards to prevent unauthorized entry.

6. Marriage and family counselors inform clients if sessions are to be recorded on tape or digital media and obtain written consent authorizing recording for particular purposes. When more than one person is receiving counseling, all persons who are legally competent must give informed consent in writing for the recording.

7. Marriage and family counselors inform clients that statements made by a family member to the counselor during an individual counseling, consultation, or collateral contact are to be treated as confidential. Such statements are not disclosed to other family members without the individual's permission. However, the marriage and family counselor should clearly identify the client of counseling, which may be the couple or family system. Couple and family counselors do not maintain family secrets, collude with some family members against others, or otherwise contribute to dysfunctional family system dynamics. If a client's refusal to share information from individual contacts interferes with the agreed goals of counseling, the counselor may terminate treatment and refer the clients to another counselor. Some marriage and family counselors choose to not meet with individuals, preferring to serve family systems.

8. Marriage and family counselors provide reasonable access to counseling records when requested by competent clients. In situations involving multiple clients, counselors provide only the records directly related to a particular individual, protecting confidential information related to any other client.

9. Marriage and family counselors provide reasonable access to counseling records of minor children when requested by parents or guardians having legal rights to custody and health decision-making. However, counselors do not become embroiled in custody disputes or parent-child conflicts occasioned by records release. Professional counselors attempt to protect the counseling relationship with children by suggesting limits to disclosure appropriate to the particular situation.

10. Marriage and family counselors maintain privacy and confidentiality in research, publication, case consultation, teaching, supervision, and other professional activities. Ideally, counselors secure informed consent and authorization to release information in all professional activities.

Section C: Competence and Professional Responsibilities

Marriage and family counselors aspire to maintain competency through initial training, ongoing supervision and consultation, and continuing education. They have responsibilities to abide by this ethical code, as well as other professional codes related to professional identity and group membership. In particular, couple and family counselors should become active in professional associations such as the International Association of Marriage and Family Counselors and the American Counseling Association to encourage beneficial changes in professionals and the counseling profession.

1. Marriage and family counselors have the responsibility to develop and maintain basic skills in marriage and family counseling through graduate training, supervision, and consultation. An outline of these skills is provided by the current Council for Accreditation of Counseling and Related Educational Programs (CACREP) *Standards for Marital, Couple, and Family Counseling/Therapy Programs.* The minimal level of training shall be considered a master's degree in a helping profession.

2. Marriage and family counselors recognize the need for familiarizing oneself with new developments in the field of marriage and family counseling. They pursue continuing education afforded by books, journals, courses, workshops, conferences, and conventions.

3. Marriage and family counselors accurately represent their education, expertise, training, and experience. Professional counselors objectively represent their professional qualifications, skills, and specialties to the public. Membership in a professional organization, including IAMFC, is not used to suggest competency.

4. Marriage and family counselors insure that announcements or advertisements of professional services focus on objective information that enables the client to make an informed decision. Providing information, such as highest relevant academic degree, licenses or certifications, office hours, types of services offered, fee structure, and languages spoken, can help clients select marriage and family counselors.

5. Marriage and family counselors do not attempt to diagnose or treat problems beyond the scope of their training and abilities. They do not engage in specialized counseling interventions or techniques unless they have received appropriate training and preparation in the methods.

6. Marriage and family counselors do not undertake any professional activity in which their personal problems might adversely affect their performance. Instead, they focus on obtaining appropriate professional assistance to help them resolve the problem.

7. Marriage and family counselors do not engage in actions that violate the legal standards of their community. They do not encourage clients or others to engage in unlawful activities.

8. Marriage and family counselors have the responsibility to provide public information that enhances marriage and family life. Such statements should be based on sound, scientifically acceptable theories, techniques, and approaches. Due to the inability to complete a comprehensive assessment and provide follow-up, members should not give specific advice to an individual through the media.

9. Marriage and family counselors produce advertisements about workshops or seminars that contain descriptions of the audiences for which the programs are intended. Due to their subjective nature, statements either from clients or from the counselor about the uniqueness, effectiveness, or efficiency of services should be avoided. Announcements and advertisements should never contain false, misleading, or fraudulent statements.

11. Marriage and family counselors promoting tapes, books, or other products for commercial sale make every effort to insure that announcements and advertisements are presented in a professional and factual manner.

Section D: Collaboration and Professional Relationships

Marriage and family counselors work to maintain good relationships with professional peers within and outside the field of counseling. Consultation and collaboration represent means by which couple and family counselors can remove barriers to underserved populations. Interdisciplinary teamwork may be required to best serve clients.

1. Marriage and family counselors are knowledgeable about the roles and functions of other disciplines, especially in the helping professions such as psychiatry, psychology, social work, and mental health counseling. Counselors work to strengthen interdisciplinary relations with colleagues.

2. Marriage and family counselors enter into professional partnerships in which each partner adheres to the ethical standards of their professions. Couple and family counselors should not charge a fee for offering or accepting referrals.

3. Marriage and family counselors do not engage in harmful relationships with individuals over whom they have supervisory, evaluative, or instructional control. They do not engage in harassment or other abuses of power or authority.

4.	Marriage and family counselors work to insure the ethical delivery of effective services in any agency or institution in which they are employed. Couple and family counselors engaging in consultation and collaboration take responsibility for the well-being and ethical treatment of clients. Counselors alert administrators about inappropriate policies and practices in institutions they serve.

5.	Marriage and family counselors working as subcontractors for counseling services for a third party have a duty to inform clients of limitations that the organization may place on the counseling or consulting relationship.

6.	Marriage and family counselors maintain good working relationships with team members and collaborators. They promote healthy boundaries and organizational climate. Couple and family counselors refrain from becoming involved in splitting, triangulation, and indirect forms of communication which could be harmful to colleagues or the organization they share.

7.	Marriage and family counselors do not offer services to clients served by other professionals without securing a referral or release. The counselor should be authorized by the client to contact the other professional to coordinate or transfer care. There may be special considerations regarding transfer of care in the termination of an abusive counseling relationship.

Section E: Assessment and Evaluation

Marriage and family counselors are highly skilled in relational and interpersonal assessment. They recognize the potential values to clients from appropriate educational, psychological, and vocational evaluation. However, marriage and family counselors are sensitive to misuse and abuse of assessment results. Counselors avoid whenever possible evaluation, assessment, or diagnosis that restricts the overall development and freedom of choice of individuals, couples, and families. Recognizing the origins of marriage and family counseling in systems thinking, they avoid whenever possible assigning problems to individuals. Instead, professional counselors aspire to identify solutions that promote the well-being of family systems.

1.	Marriage and family counselors use assessment procedures to promote the best interests and well-being of the client in clarifying concerns, establishing treatment goals, evaluating therapeutic progress, and promoting objective decision making.

2.	Marriage and family counselors recognize that clients have the right to know the results, interpretations, and conclusions drawn from assessment interviews and instruments, as well as how this information will be used. Couple and family counselors safeguard assessment data and maintain the confidentiality of evaluation records and reports.

3.	Marriage and family counselors use assessment methods that are reliable, valid, and relevant to the goals of the client. Couple and family counselors using tests or inventories should have a thorough understanding of measurement concepts, including relevant psychometric and normative data. When using computer-assisted scoring, counselors obtain empirical evidence for the reliability and validity of the methods and procedures.

4.	Marriage and family counselors do not use inventories and tests that have outdated items or normative data. They refrain from using assessment instruments and techniques likely to be biased or prejudiced.

5.	Marriage and family counselors do not use assessment methods that are outside the scope of their qualifications, training, or statutory limitations. They consult with psychologists, mental health counselors, or other professional colleagues in interpreting and understanding particular test results.

6.   Marriage and family counselors conducting custody evaluations recognize the potential impact that their reports can have on family members. They are committed to a thorough assessment of both parents. Therefore, custody recommendations should not be made on the basis of information from only one parent. Couple and family counselors only use instruments that have demonstrated reliability, validity, and utility in custody evaluations. They do not make recommendations based solely on test and inventory scores.

7.   Members strive to follow current guidelines and standards for testing published or disseminated by the American Counseling Association, American Educational Research Association, American Psychological Association, Association for Assessment in Counseling and Education, National Council on Measurement in Evaluation, and other groups dedicated to professional expertise in assessment.

Section F: Counselor Education and Supervision

Marriage and family counselors are likely to engage in some training and supervision activities, including peer consultation and supervision. Couple and family counselors recognize potential power imbalances in teacher-student, supervisor-supervisee, and consultant-consultee relationships. They do not abuse power or influence and work to protect students, supervisees, and consultees from exploitation. Marriage and family counselors maintain appropriate boundaries that promote growth and development for all parties. They recognize and respect cultural differences, adjusting their professional efforts to fit the learning needs of trainees.

1.   Marriage and family counselors who provide supervision acquire and maintain skills pertaining to the supervision process. They are able to demonstrate for supervisees the application of counseling theory and process to client issues. Supervisors are knowledgeable about different methods and conceptual approaches to supervision.

2.   Marriage and family counselors who provide supervision respect the inherent imbalance of power in the supervisory relationship. They do not use their potentially influential positions to exploit students, supervisees, or employees. Supervisors do not ask supervisees to engage in behaviors not directly related to the supervision process, and they clearly separate supervision and evaluation. Supervisors also avoid multiple relationships that might impair their professional judgment or increase the possibility of exploitation. Sexual intimacy with students or supervisees is prohibited.

3.   Marriage and family counselors who provide supervision are responsible for both the promotion of supervisee learning and development and the advancement of marriage and family counseling. Supervisors recruit students into professional organizations, educate students about professional ethics and standards, provide service to professional organizations, strive to educate new professionals, and work to improve professional practices.

4.   Marriage and family counselors who provide supervision have the responsibility to inform students of the specific expectations regarding skill building, knowledge acquisition, and development of competencies. Supervisors also provide ongoing and timely feedback to their supervisees.

5.   Marriage and family counselors who provide supervision are responsible for protecting the rights and well-being of their supervisees' clients. They monitor their supervisees' counseling on an ongoing basis, and maintain policies and procedures to protect the confidentiality of clients whose sessions have been electronically recorded.

6.   Marriage and family counselors who provide supervision maintain ethical standards for counselor supervision. Counselor educators and supervisors may consult publications of the Association for Counselor Education and Supervision to clarify ethical issues in supervisory relationships.

7. Marriage and family counselors who are counselor educators encourage their programs to maintain the current guidelines provided in the CACREP *Standards for Marital, Couple, and Family Counseling/Therapy Programs*. They also encourage training programs to offer coursework and supervision indicated by particular accreditation boards.

8. Marriage and family counselors involved in training and supervision, especially educators and students, should explore ethical principles as well as aspirational goals. Counselor educators should infuse ethical studies throughout the curriculum.

9. Marriage and family counselors refer to the current American Counseling Association *Code of Ethics* as a source document for training and supervision in professional counseling.

Section G: Research and Publication

Marriage and family counselors should engage in research and publication that advances the profession of marriage and family counseling. They act to prevent harm to research participants and produce results that are beneficial to couples and families. Couple and family counselors maintain high ethical standards for informed consent and protection of confidentiality when conducting research projects or producing publications. They solicit input from peers, institutional review boards, and other stakeholders to minimize risks and enhance outcomes.

1. Marriage and family counselors shall be fully responsible for their choice of research topics and the methods used for investigation, analysis, and reporting. They must be particularly careful that findings do not appear misleading, that the research is planned to allow for the inclusion of alternative hypotheses, and that provision is made for discussion of the limitations of the study.

2. Marriage and family counselors safeguard the privacy of their research participants. Data about an individual participant are not released unless the individual is informed about the exact nature of the information to be released and gives written permission for disclosure.

3. Marriage and family counselors protect the safety of their research participants. Researchers follow guidelines of a peer review committee or institutional research board. Prospective participants are informed, in writing about any potential risk associated with a study and are notified that they can withdraw at any time.

4. Marriage and family counselors make their original data available to other researchers. They contribute to the advancement of the field by encouraging the research and publication efforts of colleagues.

5. Marriage and family counselors only take credit for research in which they make a substantial contribution, and give credit to all contributors. Authors are listed from greatest to least amount of contribution.

6. Marriage and family counselors do not plagiarize. Ideas or data that did not originate with the author and are not common knowledge are clearly credited to the original source.

7. Marriage and family counselors are aware of their obligation to be role models for graduate students and other future researchers and act in accordance with the highest standards possible while engaged in research and publication.

8. Marriage and family counselors review materials submitted for research, publication, and other scholarly purposes. They respect the confidentiality and proprietary rights of those who submit their products for review. Counselors engaged in reviews of manuscripts and presentation proposals use valid and defensible standards, act within the limits of their competencies, and refrain from personal biases. In this manner, authors and researchers are supported and the field of marriage and family counseling is advanced.

Section H: Ethical Decision-Making and Resolution

Marriage and family counselors incorporate ethical practices in their daily work. They discuss ethical dilemmas with colleagues and engage in ethical decision-making in all aspects of marriage and family counseling. They hold other counselors to sound ethical principles and encourage professional virtues and aspirations. Couple and family counselors work with other professionals to resolve ethical issues.

1. Marriage and family counselors are responsible for understanding the American Counseling Association *Code of Ethics*, the *Ethical Code of the International Association of Marriage and Family Counselors*, and other applicable ethics codes from professional associations, certification and licensure boards, and other credentialing organizations by which they are regulated.

2. Marriage and family counselors have the responsibility to confront unethical behavior of other counselors or therapists, particularly members of the International Association of Marriage and Family Counselors (IAMFC). The first step should be discussing the violation directly with the caregiver. If the problem continues, the marriage and family counselor may contact the professional organization or licensure board of the counselor or therapist in question. IAMFC members may contact the executive director, president, executive board members, or chair of the ethics committee at any time for consultation on identifying or resolving ethical violations.

3. Marriage and family counselors specify the nature of conflicts between work requirements and other demands of an employing organization and the relevant codes of ethics. Employment and consultation of couple and family counselors should not compromise ethical standards. They work toward beneficial changes in the organizations of which they are members.

4. Marriage and family counselors do not engage in unwarranted or invalid complaints. Ethics violations are reported when informal attempts at resolution have failed or violations are likely to substantially harm an individual or organization. Couple and family counselors should follow the reporting requirements specified by laws and regulations in their jurisdictions.

5. Marriage and family counselors cooperate with ethics committees and other duly constituted organizations having jurisdiction over the professional charged with an ethics violation. Counselors assist professional associations in promoting ethical behavior and professional conduct.

Author Note

The 2005 Ethical Code of the International Association of Marriage and Family Counselors (IAMFC) was written for the Ethics Committee and approved by the Board of IAMFC.
Stephen Southern, Chair of the Ethics Committee, and Marvarene Oliver, Department of Counseling and Educational Psychology, Texas A & M University-Corpus Christi.
Loretta J. Bradley, Department of Counselor Education, Texas Tech University.
Bobbie Birdsall, Counselor Education Department, Boise State University.

National Association of Social Workers
Code of Ethics

Approved by the 1996 NASW Delegate Assembly and revised by the 1999 NASW Delegate Assembly

Preamble

The primary mission of the social work profession is to enhance human well-being and help meet the basic human needs of all people, with particular attention to the needs and empowerment of people who are vulnerable, oppressed, and living in poverty. A historic and defining feature of social work is the profession's focus on individual well-being in a social context and the well-being of society. Fundamental to social work is attention to the environmental forces that create, contribute to, and address problems in living.

Social workers promote social justice and social change with and on behalf of clients. "Clients" is used inclusively to refer to individuals, families, groups, organizations, and communities. Social workers are sensitive to cultural and ethnic diversity and strive to end discrimination, oppression, poverty, and other forms of social injustice. These activities may be in the form of direct practice, community organizing, supervision, consultation, administration, advocacy, social and political action, policy development and implementation, education, and research and evaluation. Social workers seek to enhance the capacity of people to address their own needs. Social workers also seek to promote the responsiveness of organizations, communities, and other social institutions to individuals' needs and social problems.

The mission of the social work profession is rooted in a set of core values. These core values, embraced by social workers throughout the profession's history, are the foundation of social work's unique purpose and perspective:

- service

- social justice

- dignity and worth of the person

- importance of human relationships

- integrity

- competence.

This constellation of core values reflects what is unique to the social work profession. Core values, and the principles that flow from them, must be balanced within the context and complexity of the human experience.

Purpose of the NASW Code of Ethics

Professional ethics are at the core of social work. The profession has an obligation to articulate its basic values, ethical principles, and ethical standards. The *NASW Code of Ethics* sets forth these values, principles, and standards to guide social workers' conduct. The *Code* is relevant to all social workers and social work students, regardless of their professional functions, the settings in which they work, or the populations they serve.

The *NASW Code of Ethics* serves six purposes:

1. The *Code* identifies core values on which social work's mission is based.

2. The *Code* summarizes broad ethical principles that reflect the profession's core values and establishes a set of specific ethical standards that should be used to guide social work practice.

3. The *Code* is designed to help social workers identify relevant considerations when professional obligations conflict or ethical uncertainties arise.

4. The *Code* provides ethical standards to which the general public can hold the social work profession accountable.

5. The *Code* socializes practitioners new to the field to social work's mission, values, ethical principles, and ethical standards.

6. The *Code* articulates standards that the social work profession itself can use to assess whether social workers have engaged in unethical conduct. NASW has formal procedures to adjudicate ethics complaints filed against its members.* In subscribing to this *Code,* social workers are required to cooperate in its implementation, participate in NASW adjudication proceedings, and abide by any NASW disciplinary rulings or sanctions based on it.

*For information on NASW adjudication procedures, see *NASW Procedures for the Adjudication of Grievances.*

The *Code* offers a set of values, principles, and standards to guide decision making and conduct when ethical issues arise. It does not provide a set of rules that prescribe how social workers should act in all situations. Specific applications of the *Code* must take into account the context in which it is being considered and the possibility of conflicts among the *Code*'s values, principles, and standards. Ethical responsibilities flow from all human relationships, from the personal and familial to the social and professional.

Further, the *NASW Code of Ethics* does not specify which values, principles, and standards are most important and ought to outweigh others in instances when they conflict. Reasonable differences of opinion can and do exist among social workers with respect to the ways in which values, ethical principles, and ethical standards should be rank ordered when they conflict. Ethical decision making in a given situation must apply the informed judgment of the individual social worker and should also consider how the issues would be judged in a peer review process where the ethical standards of the profession would be applied.

Ethical decision making is a process. There are many instances in social work where simple answers are not available to resolve complex ethical issues. Social workers should take into consideration all the values, principles, and standards in this *Code* that are relevant to any situation in which ethical judgment is warranted. Social workers' decisions and actions should be consistent with the spirit as well as the letter of this *Code.*

In addition to this *Code,* there are many other sources of information about ethical thinking that may be useful. Social workers should consider ethical theory and principles generally, social work theory and research, laws, regulations, agency policies, and other relevant codes of ethics, recognizing that among codes of ethics social workers should consider the *NASW Code of Ethics* as their primary source. Social workers also should be aware of the impact on ethical decision making of their clients' and their own personal values and cultural and religious beliefs and practices. They should be aware of any conflicts between personal and professional values and deal with them responsibly. For additional guidance social workers should consult the relevant literature on professional ethics and ethical decision making and seek appropriate consultation when faced with ethical dilemmas. This may involve consultation with an agency-based or social work organization's ethics committee, a regulatory body, knowledgeable colleagues, supervisors, or legal counsel.

Instances may arise when social workers' ethical obligations conflict with agency policies or relevant laws or regulations. When such conflicts occur, social workers must make a responsible effort to resolve the conflict in a manner that is consistent with the values, principles, and standards expressed in this *Code*. If a reasonable resolution of the conflict does not appear possible, social workers should seek proper consultation before making a decision.

The *NASW Code of Ethics* is to be used by NASW and by individuals, agencies, organizations, and bodies (such as licensing and regulatory boards, professional liability insurance providers, courts of law, agency boards of directors, government agencies, and other professional groups) that choose to adopt it or use it as a frame of reference. Violation of standards in this *Code* does not automatically imply legal liability or violation of the law. Such determination can only be made in the context of legal and judicial proceedings. Alleged violations of the *Code* would be subject to a peer review process. Such processes are generally separate from legal or administrative procedures and insulated from legal review or proceedings to allow the profession to counsel and discipline its own members.

A code of ethics cannot guarantee ethical behavior. Moreover, a code of ethics cannot resolve all ethical issues or disputes or capture the richness and complexity involved in striving to make responsible choices within a moral community. Rather, a code of ethics sets forth values, ethical principles, and ethical standards to which professionals aspire and by which their actions can be judged. Social workers' ethical behavior should result from their personal commitment to engage in ethical practice. The *NASW Code of Ethics* reflects the commitment of all social workers to uphold the profession's values and to act ethically. Principles and standards must be applied by individuals of good character who discern moral questions and, in good faith, seek to make reliable ethical judgments.

Ethical Principles

The following broad ethical principles are based on social work's core values of service, social justice, dignity and worth of the person, importance of human relationships, integrity, and competence. These principles set forth ideals to which all social workers should aspire.

Value: *Service*

Ethical Principle: Social workers' primary goal is to help people in need and to address social problems.

Social workers elevate service to others above self-interest. Social workers draw on their knowledge, values, and skills to help people in need and to address social problems. Social workers are encouraged to volunteer some portion of their professional skills with no expectation of significant financial return (pro bono service).

Value: Social Justice

Ethical Principle: Social workers challenge social injustice.

Social workers pursue social change, particularly with and on behalf of vulnerable and oppressed individuals and groups of people. Social workers' social change efforts are focused primarily on issues of poverty, unemployment, discrimination, and other forms of social injustice. These activities seek to promote sensitivity to and knowledge about oppression and cultural and ethnic diversity. Social workers strive to ensure access to needed information, services, and resources; equality of opportunity; and meaningful participation in decision making for all people.

Value: Dignity and Worth of the Person

Ethical Principle: Social workers respect the inherent dignity and worth of the person.

Social workers treat each person in a caring and respectful fashion, mindful of individual differences and cultural and ethnic diversity. Social workers promote clients' socially responsible self-determination. Social workers seek to enhance clients' capacity and opportunity to change and to address their own needs. Social workers are cognizant of their dual responsibility to clients and to the broader society. They seek to resolve conflicts between clients' interests and the broader society's interests in a socially responsible manner consistent with the values, ethical principles, and ethical standards of the profession.

Value: Importance of Human Relationships

Ethical Principle: Social workers recognize the central importance of human relationships.

Social workers understand that relationships between and among people are an important vehicle for change. Social workers engage people as partners in the helping process. Social workers seek to strengthen relationships among people in a purposeful effort to promote, restore, maintain, and enhance the well-being of individuals, families, social groups, organizations, and communities.

Value: Integrity

Ethical Principle: Social workers behave in a trustworthy manner.

Social workers are continually aware of the profession's mission, values, ethical principles, and ethical standards and practice in a manner consistent with them. Social workers act honestly and responsibly and promote ethical practices on the part of the organizations with which they are affiliated.

Value: Competence

Ethical Principle: Social workers practice within their areas of competence and develop and enhance their professional expertise.

Social workers continually strive to increase their professional knowledge and skills and to apply them in practice. Social workers should aspire to contribute to the knowledge base of the profession.

Ethical Standards

The following ethical standards are relevant to the professional activities of all social workers. These standards concern (1) social workers' ethical responsibilities to clients, (2) social workers' ethical responsibilities to colleagues, (3) social workers' ethical responsibilities in practice settings, (4) social workers' ethical responsibilities as professionals, (5) social workers' ethical responsibilities to the social work profession, and (6) social workers' ethical responsibilities to the broader society.

Some of the standards that follow are enforceable guidelines for professional conduct, and some are aspirational. The extent to which each standard is enforceable is a matter of professional judgment to be exercised by those responsible for reviewing alleged violations of ethical standards.

1. Social Workers' Ethical Responsibilities to Clients

1.01 Commitment to Clients

Social workers' primary responsibility is to promote the well-being of clients. In general, clients' interests are primary. However, social workers' responsibility to the larger society or specific legal obligations may on limited occasions supersede the loyalty owed clients, and clients should be so advised. (Examples include when a social worker is required by law to report that a client has abused a child or has threatened to harm self or others.)

1.02 Self-Determination

Social workers respect and promote the right of clients to self-determination and assist clients in their efforts to identify and clarify their goals. Social workers may limit clients' right to self-determination when, in the social workers' professional judgment, clients' actions or potential actions pose a serious, foreseeable, and imminent risk to themselves or others.

1.03 Informed Consent

(a) Social workers should provide services to clients only in the context of a professional relationship based, when appropriate, on valid informed consent. Social workers should use clear and understandable language to inform clients of the purpose of the services, risks related to the services, limits to services because of the requirements of a third-party payer, relevant costs, reasonable alternatives, clients' right to refuse or withdraw consent, and the time frame covered by the consent. Social workers should provide clients with an opportunity to ask questions.

(b) In instances when clients are not literate or have difficulty understanding the primary language used in the practice setting, social workers should take steps to ensure clients' comprehension. This may include providing clients with a detailed verbal explanation or arranging for a qualified interpreter or translator whenever possible.

(c) In instances when clients lack the capacity to provide informed consent, social workers should protect clients' interests by seeking permission from an appropriate third party, informing clients consistent with the clients' level of understanding. In such instances social workers should seek to ensure that the third party acts in a manner consistent with clients' wishes and interests. Social workers should take reasonable steps to enhance such clients' ability to give informed consent.

(d) In instances when clients are receiving services involuntarily, social workers should provide information about the nature and extent of services and about the extent of clients' right to refuse service.

(e) Social workers who provide services via electronic media (such as computer, telephone, radio, and television) should inform recipients of the limitations and risks associated with such services.

(f) Social workers should obtain clients' informed consent before audiotaping or videotaping clients or permitting observation of services to clients by a third party.

1.04 Competence

(a) Social workers should provide services and represent themselves as competent only within the boundaries of their education, training, license, certification, consultation received, supervised experience, or other relevant professional experience.

(b) Social workers should provide services in substantive areas or use intervention techniques or approaches that are new to them only after engaging in appropriate study, training, consultation, and supervision from people who are competent in those interventions or techniques.

(c) When generally recognized standards do not exist with respect to an emerging area of practice, social workers should exercise careful judgment and take responsible steps (including appropriate education, research, training, consultation, and supervision) to ensure the competence of their work and to protect clients from harm.

1.05 Cultural Competence and Social Diversity

(a) Social workers should understand culture and its function in human behavior and society, recognizing the strengths that exist in all cultures.

(b) Social workers should have a knowledge base of their clients' cultures and be able to demonstrate competence in the provision of services that are sensitive to clients' cultures and to differences among people and cultural groups.

(c) Social workers should obtain education about and seek to understand the nature of social diversity and oppression with respect to race, ethnicity, national origin, color, sex, sexual orientation, age, marital status, political belief, religion, and mental or physical disability.

1.06 Conflicts of Interest

(a) Social workers should be alert to and avoid conflicts of interest that interfere with the exercise of professional discretion and impartial judgment. Social workers should inform clients when a real or potential conflict of interest arises and take reasonable steps to resolve the issue in a manner that makes the clients' interests primary and protects clients' interests to the greatest extent possible. In some cases, protecting clients' interests may require termination of the professional relationship with proper referral of the client.

(b) Social workers should not take unfair advantage of any professional relationship or exploit others to further their personal, religious, political, or business interests.

(c) Social workers should not engage in dual or multiple relationships with clients or former clients in which there is a risk of exploitation or potential harm to the client. In instances when dual or multiple relationships are unavoidable, social workers should take steps to protect clients and are responsible for setting clear, appropriate, and culturally sensitive boundaries. (Dual or multiple relationships occur when social workers relate to clients in more than one relationship, whether professional, social, or business. Dual or multiple relationships can occur simultaneously or consecutively.)

(d) When social workers provide services to two or more people who have a relationship with each other (for example, couples, family members), social workers should clarify with all parties which individuals will be considered clients and the nature of social workers' professional obligations to the various individuals who are receiving services. Social workers who anticipate a conflict of interest among the individuals receiving services or who anticipate having to perform in potentially conflicting roles (for example, when a social worker is asked to testify in a child custody dispute or divorce proceedings involving clients) should clarify their role with the parties involved and take appropriate action to minimize any conflict of interest.

1.07 Privacy and Confidentiality

(a) Social workers should respect clients' right to privacy. Social workers should not solicit private information from clients unless it is essential to providing services or conducting social work evaluation or research. Once private information is shared, standards of confidentiality apply.

(b) Social workers may disclose confidential information when appropriate with valid consent from a client or a person legally authorized to consent on behalf of a client.

(c) Social workers should protect the confidentiality of all information obtained in the course of professional service, except for compelling professional reasons. The general expectation that social workers will keep information confidential does not apply when disclosure is necessary to prevent serious, foreseeable, and imminent harm to a client or other identifiable person. In all instances, social workers should disclose the least amount of confidential information necessary to achieve the desired purpose; only information that is directly relevant to the purpose for which the disclosure is made should be revealed.

(d) Social workers should inform clients, to the extent possible, about the disclosure of confidential information and the potential consequences, when feasible before the disclosure is made. This applies whether social workers disclose confidential information on the basis of a legal requirement or client consent.

(e) Social workers should discuss with clients and other interested parties the nature of confidentiality and limitations of clients' right to confidentiality. Social workers should review with clients circumstances where confidential information may be requested and where disclosure of confidential information may be legally required. This discussion should occur as soon as possible in the social worker-client relationship and as needed throughout the course of the relationship.

(f) When social workers provide counseling services to families, couples, or groups, social workers should seek agreement among the parties involved concerning each individual's right to confidentiality and obligation to preserve the confidentiality of information shared by others. Social workers should inform participants in family, couples, or group counseling that social workers cannot guarantee that all participants will honor such agreements.

(g) Social workers should inform clients involved in family, couples, marital, or group counseling of the social worker's, employer's, and agency's policy concerning the social worker's disclosure of confidential information among the parties involved in the counseling.

(h) Social workers should not disclose confidential information to third-party payers unless clients have authorized such disclosure.

(i) Social workers should not discuss confidential information in any setting unless privacy can be ensured. Social workers should not discuss confidential information in public or semipublic areas such as hallways, waiting rooms, elevators, and restaurants.

(j) Social workers should protect the confidentiality of clients during legal proceedings to the extent permitted by law. When a court of law or other legally authorized body orders social workers to disclose confidential or privileged information without a client's consent and such disclosure could cause harm to the client, social workers should request that the court withdraw the order or limit the order as narrowly as possible or maintain the records under seal, unavailable for public inspection.

(k) Social workers should protect the confidentiality of clients when responding to requests from members of the media.

(l) Social workers should protect the confidentiality of clients' written and electronic records and other sensitive information. Social workers should take reasonable steps to ensure that clients' records are stored in a secure location and that clients' records are not available to others who are not authorized to have access.

(m) Social workers should take precautions to ensure and maintain the confidentiality of information transmitted to other parties through the use of computers, electronic mail, facsimile machines, telephones and telephone answering machines, and other electronic or computer technology. Disclosure of identifying information should be avoided whenever possible.

(n) Social workers should transfer or dispose of clients' records in a manner that protects clients' confidentiality and is consistent with state statutes governing records and social work licensure.

(o) Social workers should take reasonable precautions to protect client confidentiality in the event of the social worker's termination of practice, incapacitation, or death.

(p) Social workers should not disclose identifying information when discussing clients for teaching or training purposes unless the client has consented to disclosure of confidential information.

(q) Social workers should not disclose identifying information when discussing clients with consultants unless the client has consented to disclosure of confidential information or there is a compelling need for such disclosure.

(r) Social workers should protect the confidentiality of deceased clients consistent with the preceding standards.

1.08 Access to Records

(a) Social workers should provide clients with reasonable access to records concerning the clients. Social workers who are concerned that clients' access to their records could cause serious misunderstanding or harm to the client should provide assistance in interpreting the records and consultation with the client regarding the records. Social workers should limit clients' access to their records, or portions of their records, only in exceptional circumstances when there is compelling evidence that such access would cause serious harm to the client. Both clients' requests and the rationale for withholding some or all of the record should be documented in clients' files.

(b) When providing clients with access to their records, social workers should take steps to protect the confidentiality of other individuals identified or discussed in such records.

1.09 Sexual Relationships

(a) Social workers should under no circumstances engage in sexual activities or sexual contact with current clients, whether such contact is consensual or forced.

(b) Social workers should not engage in sexual activities or sexual contact with clients' relatives or other individuals with whom clients maintain a close personal relationship when there is a risk of exploitation or potential harm to the client. Sexual activity or sexual contact with clients' relatives or other individuals with whom clients maintain a personal relationship has the potential to be harmful to the client and may make it difficult for the social worker and client to maintain appropriate professional boundaries. Social workers--not their clients, their clients' relatives, or other individuals with whom the client maintains a personal relationship--assume the full burden for setting clear, appropriate, and culturally sensitive boundaries.

(c) Social workers should not engage in sexual activities or sexual contact with former clients because of the potential for harm to the client. If social workers engage in conduct contrary to this prohibition or claim that an exception to this prohibition is warranted because of extraordinary circumstances, it is social workers--not their clients--who assume the full burden of demonstrating that the former client has not been exploited, coerced, or manipulated, intentionally or unintentionally.

(d) Social workers should not provide clinical services to individuals with whom they have had a prior sexual relationship. Providing clinical services to a former sexual partner has the potential to be harmful to the individual and is likely to make it difficult for the social worker and individual to maintain appropriate professional boundaries.

1.10 Physical Contact

Social workers should not engage in physical contact with clients when there is a possibility of psychological harm to the client as a result of the contact (such as cradling or caressing clients). Social workers who engage in appropriate physical contact with clients are responsible for setting clear, appropriate, and culturally sensitive boundaries that govern such physical contact.

1.11 Sexual Harassment

Social workers should not sexually harass clients. Sexual harassment includes sexual advances, sexual solicitation, requests for sexual favors, and other verbal or physical conduct of a sexual nature.

1.12 Derogatory Language

Social workers should not use derogatory language in their written or verbal communications to or about clients. Social workers should use accurate and respectful language in all communications to and about clients.

1.13 Payment for Services

(a) When setting fees, social workers should ensure that the fees are fair, reasonable, and commensurate with the services performed. Consideration should be given to clients' ability to pay.

(b) Social workers should avoid accepting goods or services from clients as payment for professional services. Bartering arrangements, particularly involving services, create the potential for conflicts of interest, exploitation, and inappropriate boundaries in social workers' relationships with clients. Social workers should explore and may participate in bartering only in very limited circumstances when it can be demonstrated that such arrangements are an accepted practice among professionals in the local community, considered to be essential for the provision of services, negotiated without coercion, and entered into at the client's initiative and with the client's informed consent. Social workers who accept goods or services from clients as payment for professional services assume the full burden of demonstrating that this arrangement will not be detrimental to the client or the professional relationship.

(c) Social workers should not solicit a private fee or other remuneration for providing services to clients who are entitled to such available services through the social workers' employer or agency.

1.14 Clients Who Lack Decision-Making Capacity

When social workers act on behalf of clients who lack the capacity to make informed decisions, social workers should take reasonable steps to safeguard the interests and rights of those clients.

1.15 Interruption of Services

Social workers should make reasonable efforts to ensure continuity of services in the event that services are interrupted by factors such as unavailability, relocation, illness, disability, or death.

1.16 Termination of Services

(a) Social workers should terminate services to clients and professional relationships with them when such services and relationships are no longer required or no longer serve the clients' needs or interests.

(b) Social workers should take reasonable steps to avoid abandoning clients who are still in need of services. Social workers should withdraw services precipitously only under unusual circumstances, giving careful consideration to all factors in the situation and taking care to minimize possible adverse effects. Social workers should assist in making appropriate arrangements for continuation of services when necessary.

(c) Social workers in fee-for-service settings may terminate services to clients who are not paying an overdue balance if the financial contractual arrangements have been made clear to the client, if the client does not pose an imminent danger to self or others, and if the clinical and other consequences of the current nonpayment have been addressed and discussed with the client.

(d) Social workers should not terminate services to pursue a social, financial, or sexual relationship with a client.

(e) Social workers who anticipate the termination or interruption of services to clients should notify clients promptly and seek the transfer, referral, or continuation of services in relation to the clients' needs and preferences.

(f) Social workers who are leaving an employment setting should inform clients of appropriate options for the continuation of services and of the benefits and risks of the options.

2. Social Workers' Ethical Responsibilities to Colleagues

2.01 Respect

(a) Social workers should treat colleagues with respect and should represent accurately and fairly the qualifications, views, and obligations of colleagues.

(b) Social workers should avoid unwarranted negative criticism of colleagues in communications with clients or with other professionals. Unwarranted negative criticism may include demeaning comments that refer to colleagues' level of competence or to indi-viduals' attributes such as race, ethnicity, national origin, color, sex, sexual orientation, age, marital status, political belief, religion, and mental or physical disability.

(c) Social workers should cooperate with social work colleagues and with colleagues of other professions when such cooperation serves the well-being of clients.

2.02 Confidentiality

Social workers should respect confidential information shared by colleagues in the course of their professional relationships and transactions. Social workers should ensure that such colleagues understand social workers' obligation to respect confidentiality and any exceptions related to it.

2.03 Interdisciplinary Collaboration

(a) Social workers who are members of an interdisciplinary team should participate in and contribute to decisions that affect the well-being of clients by drawing on the perspectives, values, and experiences of the social work profession. Professional and ethical obligations of the interdisciplinary team as a whole and of its individual members should be clearly established.

(b) Social workers for whom a team decision raises ethical concerns should attempt to resolve the disagreement through appropriate channels. If the disagreement cannot be resolved, social workers should pursue other avenues to address their concerns consistent with client well-being.

2.04 Disputes Involving Colleagues

(a) Social workers should not take advantage of a dispute between a colleague and an employer to obtain a position or otherwise advance the social workers' own interests.
(b) Social workers should not exploit clients in disputes with colleagues or engage clients in any inappropriate discussion of conflicts between social workers and their colleagues.

2.05 Consultation

(a) Social workers should seek the advice and counsel of colleagues whenever such consultation is in the best interests of clients.
(b) Social workers should keep themselves informed about colleagues' areas of expertise and competencies. Social workers should seek consultation only from colleagues who have demonstrated knowledge, expertise, and competence related to the subject of the consultation.
(c) When consulting with colleagues about clients, social workers should disclose the least amount of information necessary to achieve the purposes of the consultation.

2.06 Referral for Services

(a) Social workers should refer clients to other professionals when the other professionals' specialized knowledge or expertise is needed to serve clients fully or when social workers believe that they are not being effective or making reasonable progress with clients and that additional service is required.
(b) Social workers who refer clients to other professionals should take appropriate steps to facilitate an orderly transfer of responsibility. Social workers who refer clients to other professionals should disclose, with clients' consent, all pertinent information to the new service providers.
(c) Social workers are prohibited from giving or receiving payment for a referral when no professional service is provided by the referring social worker.

2.07 Sexual Relationships

(a) Social workers who function as supervisors or educators should not engage in sexual activities or contact with supervisees, students, trainees, or other colleagues over whom they exercise professional authority.
(b) Social workers should avoid engaging in sexual relationships with colleagues when there is potential for a conflict of interest. Social workers who become involved in, or anticipate becoming involved in, a sexual relationship with a colleague have a duty to transfer professional responsibilities, when necessary, to avoid a conflict of interest.

2.08 Sexual Harassment

Social workers should not sexually harass supervisees, students, trainees, or colleagues. Sexual harassment includes sexual advances, sexual solicitation, requests for sexual favors, and other verbal or physical conduct of a sexual nature.

2.09 Impairment of Colleagues

(a) Social workers who have direct knowledge of a social work colleague's impairment that is due to personal problems, psychosocial distress, substance abuse, or mental health difficulties and that interferes with practice effectiveness should consult with that colleague when feasible and assist the colleague in taking remedial action.
(b) Social workers who believe that a social work colleague's impairment interferes with practice effectiveness and that the colleague has not taken adequate steps to address the impairment should

take action through appropriate channels established by employers, agencies, NASW, licensing and regulatory bodies, and other professional organizations.

2.10 Incompetence of Colleagues

(a) Social workers who have direct knowledge of a social work colleague's incompetence should consult with that colleague when feasible and assist the colleague in taking remedial action.

(b) Social workers who believe that a social work colleague is incompetent and has not taken adequate steps to address the incompetence should take action through appropriate channels established by employers, agencies, NASW, licensing and regulatory bodies, and other professional organizations.

2.11 Unethical Conduct of Colleagues

(a) Social workers should take adequate measures to discourage, prevent, expose, and correct the unethical conduct of colleagues.

(b) Social workers should be knowledgeable about established policies and procedures for handling concerns about colleagues' unethical behavior. Social workers should be familiar with national, state, and local procedures for handling ethics complaints. These include policies and procedures created by NASW, licensing and regulatory bodies, employers, agencies, and other professional organizations.

(c) Social workers who believe that a colleague has acted unethically should seek resolution by discussing their concerns with the colleague when feasible and when such discussion is likely to be productive.

(d) When necessary, social workers who believe that a colleague has acted unethically should take action through appropriate formal channels (such as contacting a state licensing board or regulatory body, an NASW committee on inquiry, or other professional ethics committees).

(e) Social workers should defend and assist colleagues who are unjustly charged with unethical conduct.

3. Social Workers' Ethical Responsibilities in Practice Settings

3.01 Supervision and Consultation

(a) Social workers who provide supervision or consultation should have the necessary knowledge and skill to supervise or consult appropriately and should do so only within their areas of knowledge and competence.

(b) Social workers who provide supervision or consultation are responsible for setting clear, appropriate, and culturally sensitive boundaries.

(c) Social workers should not engage in any dual or multiple relationships with supervisees in which there is a risk of exploitation of or potential harm to the supervisee.

(d) Social workers who provide supervision should evaluate supervisees' performance in a manner that is fair and respectful.

3.02 Education and Training

(a) Social workers who function as educators, field instructors for students, or trainers should provide instruction only within their areas of knowledge and competence and should provide instruction based on the most current information and knowledge available in the profession.

(b) Social workers who function as educators or field instructors for students should evaluate students' performance in a manner that is fair and respectful.

(c) Social workers who function as educators or field instructors for students should take reasonable steps to ensure that clients are routinely informed when services are being provided by students.

(d) Social workers who function as educators or field instructors for students should not engage in any dual or multiple relationships with students in which there is a risk of exploitation or potential harm to the student. Social work educators and field instructors are responsible for setting clear, appropriate, and culturally sensitive boundaries.

3.03 Performance Evaluation

Social workers who have responsibility for evaluating the performance of others should fulfill such responsibility in a fair and considerate manner and on the basis of clearly stated criteria.

3.04 Client Records

(a) Social workers should take reasonable steps to ensure that documentation in records is accurate and reflects the services provided.

(b) Social workers should include sufficient and timely documentation in records to facilitate the delivery of services and to ensure continuity of services provided to clients in the future.

(c) Social workers' documentation should protect clients' privacy to the extent that is possible and appropriate and should include only information that is directly relevant to the delivery of services.

(d) Social workers should store records following the termination of services to ensure reasonable future access. Records should be maintained for the number of years required by state statutes or relevant contracts.

3.05 Billing

Social workers should establish and maintain billing practices that accurately reflect the nature and extent of services provided and that identify who provided the service in the practice setting.

3.06 Client Transfer

(a) When an individual who is receiving services from another agency or colleague contacts a social worker for services, the social worker should carefully consider the client's needs before agreeing to provide services. To minimize possible confusion and conflict, social workers should discuss with potential clients the nature of the clients' current relationship with other service providers and the implications, including possible benefits or risks, of entering into a relationship with a new service provider.

(b) If a new client has been served by another agency or colleague, social workers should discuss with the client whether consultation with the previous service provider is in the client's best interest.

3.07 Administration

(a) Social work administrators should advocate within and outside their agencies for adequate resources to meet clients' needs.

(b) Social workers should advocate for resource allocation procedures that are open and fair. When not all clients' needs can be met, an allocation procedure should be developed that is nondiscriminatory and based on appropriate and consistently applied principles.

(c) Social workers who are administrators should take reasonable steps to ensure that adequate agency or organizational resources are available to provide appropriate staff supervision.

(d) Social work administrators should take reasonable steps to ensure that the working environment for which they are responsible is consistent with and encourages compliance with the NASW Code of Ethics. Social work administrators should take reasonable steps to eliminate any conditions in their organizations that violate, interfere with, or discourage compliance with the Code.

3.08 Continuing Education and Staff Development

Social work administrators and supervisors should take reasonable steps to provide or arrange for continuing education and staff development for all staff for whom they are responsible. Continuing education and staff development should address current knowledge and emerging developments related to social work practice and ethics.

3.09 Commitments to Employers

(a) Social workers generally should adhere to commitments made to employers and employing organizations.

(b) Social workers should work to improve employing agencies' policies and procedures and the efficiency and effectiveness of their services.

(c) Social workers should take reasonable steps to ensure that employers are aware of social workers' ethical obligations as set forth in the NASW Code of Ethics and of the implications of those obligations for social work practice.

(d) Social workers should not allow an employing organization's policies, procedures, regulations, or administrative orders to interfere with their ethical practice of social work. Social workers should take reasonable steps to ensure that their employing organizations' practices are consistent with the NASW Code of Ethics.

(e) Social workers should act to prevent and eliminate discrimination in the employing organization's work assignments and in its employment policies and practices.

(f) Social workers should accept employment or arrange student field placements only in organizations that exercise fair personnel practices.

(g) Social workers should be diligent stewards of the resources of their employing organizations, wisely conserving funds where appropriate and never misappropriating funds or using them for unintended purposes.

3.10 Labor-Management Disputes

(a) Social workers may engage in organized action, including the formation of and participation in labor unions, to improve services to clients and working conditions.

(b) The actions of social workers who are involved in labor-management disputes, job actions, or labor strikes should be guided by the profession's values, ethical principles, and ethical standards. Reasonable differences of opinion exist among social workers concerning their primary obligation as professionals during an actual or threatened labor strike or job action. Social workers should carefully examine relevant issues and their possible impact on clients before deciding on a course of action.

4. Social Workers' Ethical Responsibilities as Professionals

4.01 Competence

(a) Social workers should accept responsibility or employment only on the basis of existing competence or the intention to acquire the necessary competence.

(b) Social workers should strive to become and remain proficient in professional practice and the performance of professional functions. Social workers should critically examine and keep current with emerging knowledge relevant to social work. Social workers should routinely review the professional literature and participate in continuing education relevant to social work practice and social work ethics.

(c) Social workers should base practice on recognized knowledge, including empirically based knowledge, relevant to social work and social work ethics.

4.02 Discrimination

Social workers should not practice, condone, facilitate, or collaborate with any form of discrimination on the basis of race, ethnicity, national origin, color, sex, sexual orientation, age, marital status, political belief, religion, or mental or physical disability.

4.03 Private Conduct

Social workers should not permit their private conduct to interfere with their ability to fulfill their professional responsibilities.

4.04 Dishonesty, Fraud, and Deception

Social workers should not participate in, condone, or be associated with dishonesty, fraud, or deception.

4.05 Impairment

(a) Social workers should not allow their own personal problems, psychosocial distress, legal problems, substance abuse, or mental health difficulties to interfere with their professional judgment and performance or to jeopardize the best interests of people for whom they have a professional responsibility.

(b) Social workers whose personal problems, psychosocial distress, legal problems, substance abuse, or mental health difficulties interfere with their professional judgment and performance should immediately seek consultation and take appropriate remedial action by seeking professional help, making adjustments in workload, terminating practice, or taking any other steps necessary to protect clients and others.

4.06 Misrepresentation

(a) Social workers should make clear distinctions between statements made and actions engaged in as a private individual and as a representative of the social work profession, a professional social work organization, or the social worker's employing agency.

(b) Social workers who speak on behalf of professional social work organizations should accurately represent the official and authorized positions of the organizations.

(c) Social workers should ensure that their representations to clients, agencies, and the public of professional qualifications, credentials, education, competence, affiliations, services provided, or results to be achieved are accurate. Social workers should claim only those relevant professional credentials they actually possess and take steps to correct any inaccuracies or misrepresentations of their credentials by others.

4.07 Solicitations

(a) Social workers should not engage in uninvited solicitation of potential clients who, because of their circumstances, are vulnerable to undue influence, manipulation, or coercion.

(b) Social workers should not engage in solicitation of testimonial endorsements (including solicitation of consent to use a client's prior statement as a testimonial endorsement) from current clients or from other people who, because of their particular circumstances, are vulnerable to undue influence.

4.08 Acknowledging Credit

(a) Social workers should take responsibility and credit, including authorship credit, only for work they have actually performed and to which they have contributed.

(b) Social workers should honestly acknowledge the work of and the contributions made by others.

5. Social Workers' Ethical Responsibilities to the Social Work Profession

5.01 Integrity of the Profession

(a) Social workers should work toward the maintenance and promotion of high standards of practice.

(b) Social workers should uphold and advance the values, ethics, knowledge, and mission of the profession. Social workers should protect, enhance, and improve the integrity of the profession through appropriate study and research, active discussion, and responsible criticism of the profession.

(c) Social workers should contribute time and professional expertise to activities that promote respect for the value, integrity, and competence of the social work profession. These activities may include teaching, research, consultation, service, legislative testimony, presentations in the community, and participation in their professional organizations.

(d) Social workers should contribute to the knowledge base of social work and share with colleagues their knowledge related to practice, research, and ethics. Social workers should seek to con-tribute to the profession's literature and to share their knowledge at professional meetings and conferences.

(e) Social workers should act to prevent the unauthorized and unqualified practice of social work.

5.02 Evaluation and Research

(a) Social workers should monitor and evaluate policies, the implementation of programs, and practice interventions.

(b) Social workers should promote and facilitate evaluation and research to contribute to the development of knowledge.

(c) Social workers should critically examine and keep current with emerging knowledge relevant to social work and fully use evaluation and research evidence in their professional practice.

(d) Social workers engaged in evaluation or research should carefully consider possible consequences and should follow guidelines developed for the protection of evaluation and research participants. Appropriate institutional review boards should be consulted.

(e) Social workers engaged in evaluation or research should obtain voluntary and written informed consent from participants, when appropriate, without any implied or actual deprivation or penalty for refusal to participate; without undue inducement to participate; and with due regard for participants' well-being, privacy, and dignity. Informed consent should include information about the nature, extent, and duration of the participation requested and disclosure of the risks and benefits of participation in the research.

(f) When evaluation or research participants are incapable of giving informed consent, social workers should provide an appropriate explanation to the participants, obtain the participants' assent to the extent they are able, and obtain written consent from an appropriate proxy.

(g) Social workers should never design or conduct evaluation or research that does not use consent procedures, such as certain forms of naturalistic observation and archival research, unless rigorous and responsible review of the research has found it to be justified because of its prospective scientific, educational, or applied value and unless equally effective alternative procedures that do not involve waiver of consent are not feasible.

(h) Social workers should inform participants of their right to withdraw from evaluation and research at any time without penalty.

(i) Social workers should take appropriate steps to ensure that participants in evaluation and research have access to appropriate supportive services.

(j) Social workers engaged in evaluation or research should protect participants from unwarranted physical or mental distress, harm, danger, or deprivation.

(k) Social workers engaged in the evaluation of services should discuss collected information only for professional purposes and only with people professionally concerned with this information.

(l) Social workers engaged in evaluation or research should ensure the anonymity or confidentiality of participants and of the data obtained from them. Social workers should inform participants of any limits of confidentiality, the measures that will be taken to ensure confidentiality, and when any records containing research data will be destroyed.

(m) Social workers who report evaluation and research results should protect participants' confidentiality by omitting identifying information unless proper consent has been obtained authorizing disclosure.

(n) Social workers should report evaluation and research findings accurately. They should not fabricate or falsify results and should take steps to correct any errors later found in published data using standard publication methods.

(o) Social workers engaged in evaluation or research should be alert to and avoid conflicts of interest and dual relationships with participants, should inform participants when a real or potential conflict of interest arises, and should take steps to resolve the issue in a manner that makes participants' interests primary.

(p) Social workers should educate themselves, their students, and their colleagues about responsible research practices.

6. Social Workers' Ethical Responsibilities to the Broader Society

6.01 Social Welfare

Social workers should promote the general welfare of society, from local to global levels, and the development of people, their communities, and their environments. Social workers should advocate for living conditions conducive to the fulfillment of basic human needs and should promote social, economic, political, and cultural values and institutions that are compatible with the realization of social justice.

6.02 Public Participation

Social workers should facilitate informed participation by the public in shaping social policies and institutions.

6.03 Public Emergencies

Social workers should provide appropriate professional services in public emergencies to the greatest extent possible.

6.04 Social and Political Action

(a) Social workers should engage in social and political action that seeks to ensure that all people have equal access to the resources, employment, services, and opportunities they require to meet their basic human needs and to develop fully. Social workers should be aware of the impact of the political arena on practice and should advocate for changes in policy and legislation to improve social conditions in order to meet basic human needs and promote social justice.

(b) Social workers should act to expand choice and opportunity for all people, with special regard for vulnerable, disadvantaged, oppressed, and exploited people and groups.

(c) Social workers should promote conditions that encourage respect for cultural and social diversity within the United States and globally. Social workers should promote policies and practices that demonstrate respect for difference, support the expansion of cultural knowledge and resources, advocate for programs and institutions that demonstrate cultural competence, and promote policies that safeguard the rights of and confirm equity and social justice for all people.

(d) Social workers should act to prevent and eliminate domination of, exploitation of, and discrimination against any person, group, or class on the basis of race, ethnicity, national origin, color, sex, sexual orientation, age, marital status, political belief, religion, or mental or physical disability.

National Board for Certified Counselors
Code of Ethics

Approved on July 1, 1982. Amended on February 21, 1987, January 6, 1989,
October 31, 1997, June 21, 2002 and February 4, 2005.

Preamble

The National Board for Certified Counselors (NBCC) is a professional certification board which certifies counselors as having met standards for the general and specialty practice of professional counseling established by the Board. The counselors certified by NBCC may identify with different professional associations and are often licensed by jurisdictions which promulgate codes of ethics. The NBCC code of ethics provides a minimal ethical standard for the professional behavior of all NBCC certificants. This code provides an expectation of and assurance for the ethical practice for all who use the professional services of an NBCC certificant. In addition, it serves the purpose of having an enforceable standard for all NBCC certificants and assures those served of some resource in case of a perceived ethical violation. This code is applicable to National Certified Counselors and those who are seeking certification from NBCC.

The NBCC Ethical Code applies to all those certified by NBCC regardless of any other professional affiliation. Persons who receive professional services from certified counselors may elect to use other ethical codes which apply to their counselor. Although NBCC cooperates with professional associations and credentialing organizations, it can bring actions to discipline or sanction NBCC certificants only if the provisions of the NBCC Code are found to have been violated.

The National Board for Certified Counselors, Inc. (NBCC) promotes counseling through certification. In pursuit of this mission, the NBCC:

- Promotes quality assurance in counseling practice
- Promotes the value of counseling
- Promotes public awareness of quality counseling practice
- Promotes professionalism in counseling
- Promotes leadership in credentialing

Section A: General

1. Certified counselors engage in continuous efforts to improve professional practices, services, and research. Certified counselors are guided in their work by evidence of the best professional practices.

2. Certified counselors have a responsibility to the clients they serve and to the institutions within which the services are performed. Certified counselors also strive to assist the respective agency, organization, or institution in providing competent and ethical professional services. The acceptance of employment in an institution implies that the certified counselor is in agreement with the general policies and principles of the institution. Therefore, the professional activities of the certified counselor are in accord with the objectives of the institution. If the certified counselor and the employer do not agree and cannot reach agreement on policies that are consistent with appropriate counselor ethical practice that is conducive to client growth and development, the employment should be terminated. If the situation warrants further action, the certified counselor should work through professional organizations to have the unethical practice changed.

3. Ethical behavior among professional associates (i.e., both certified and non-certified counselors) must be expected at all times. When a certified counselor has doubts as to the ethical behavior of professional colleagues, the certified counselor must take action to attempt to rectify this condition. Such action uses the respective institution's channels first and then uses procedures established by the NBCC or the perceived violator's profession.

4. Certified counselors must refuse remuneration for consultation or counseling with persons who are entitled to these services through the certified counselor's employing institution or agency. Certified counselors must not divert to their private practices, without the mutual consent of the institution and the client, legitimate clients in their primary agencies or the institutions with which they are affiliated.

5. In establishing fees for professional counseling services, certified counselors must consider the financial status of clients. In the event that the established fee status is inappropriate for a client, assistance must be provided in finding comparable services at acceptable cost.

6. Certified counselors offer only professional services for which they are trained or have supervised experience. No diagnosis, assessment, or treatment should be performed without prior training or supervision. Certified counselors are responsible for correcting any misrepresentations of their qualifications by others.

7. Certified counselors recognize their limitations and provide services or use techniques for which they are qualified by training and/or supervision. Certified counselors recognize the need for and seek continuing education to assure competent services.

8. Certified counselors are aware of the intimacy in the counseling relationship and maintain respect for the client. Counselors must not engage in activities that seek to meet their personal or professional needs at the expense of the client.

9. Certified counselors must insure that they do not engage in personal, social, organizational, financial, or political activities which might lead to a misuse of their influence.

10. Sexual intimacy with clients is unethical. Certified counselors will not be sexually, physically, or romantically intimate with clients, and they will not engage in sexual, physical, or romantic intimacy with clients within a minimum of two years after terminating the counseling relationship.

11. Certified counselors do not condone or engage in sexual harassment, which is defined as unwelcome comments, gestures, or physical contact of a sexual nature.

12. Through an awareness of the impact of stereotyping and unwarranted discrimination (e.g., biases based on age, disability, ethnicity, gender, race, religion, or sexual orientation), certified counselors guard the individual rights and personal dignity of the client in the counseling relationship.

13. Certified counselors are accountable at all times for their behavior. They must be aware that all actions and behaviors of the counselor reflect on professional integrity and, when inappropriate, can damage the public trust in the counseling profession. To protect public confidence in the counseling profession, certified counselors avoid behavior that is clearly in violation of accepted moral and legal standards.

14. Products or services provided by certified counselors by means of classroom instruction, public lectures, demonstrations, written articles, radio or television programs or other types of media must meet the criteria cited in this code.

15. Certified counselors have an obligation to withdraw from the practice of counseling if they violate the Code of Ethics, or if the mental or physical condition of the certified counselor renders it unlikely that a professional relationship will be maintained.

Section B: Counseling Relationship

1. The primary obligation of certified counselors is to respect the integrity and promote the welfare of clients, whether they are assisted individually, in family units, or in group counseling. In a group setting, the certified counselor is also responsible for taking reasonable precautions to protect individuals from physical and/or psychological trauma resulting from interaction within the group.

2. Certified counselors know and take into account the traditions and practices of other professional disciplines with whom they work and cooperate fully with such. If a person is receiving similar services from another professional, certified counselors do not offer their own services directly to such a person. If a certified counselor is contacted by a person who is already receiving similar services from another professional, the certified counselor carefully considers that professional relationship as well as the client's welfare and proceeds with caution and sensitivity to the therapeutic issues. When certified counselors learn that their clients are in a professional relationship with another counselor or mental health professional, they request release from the clients to inform the other counselor or mental health professional of their relationship with the client and strive to establish positive and collaborative professional relationships that are in the best interest of the client. Certified counselors discuss these issues with clients and the counselor or professional so as to minimize the risk of confusion and conflict and encourage clients to inform other professionals of the new professional relationship.

3. Certified counselors may choose to consult with any other professionally competent person about a client and must notify clients of this right. Certified counselors avoid placing a consultant in a conflict-of-interest situation that would preclude the consultant serving as a proper party to the efforts of the certified counselor to help the client.

4. When a client's condition indicates that there is a clear and imminent danger to the client or others, the certified counselor must take reasonable action to inform potential victims and/or inform responsible authorities. Consultation with other professionals must be used when possible. The assumption of responsibility for the client's behavior must be taken only after careful deliberation, and the client must be involved in the resumption of responsibility as quickly as possible.

5. Records of the counseling relationship, including interview notes, test data, correspondence, audio or visual tape recordings, electronic data storage, and other documents are to be considered professional information for use in counseling. Records should contain accurate factual data. The physical records are property of the certified counselors or their employers. The information contained in the records belongs to the client and therefore may not be released to others without the consent of the client or when the counselor has exhausted challenges to a court order. The certified counselors are responsible to insure that their employees handle confidential information appropriately. Confidentiality must be maintained during the storage and disposition of records. Records should be maintained for a period of at least five (5) years after the last counselor/client contact, including cases in which the client is deceased. All records must be released to the client upon request.

6. Certified counselors must ensure that data maintained in electronic storage are secure. By using the best computer security methods available, the data must be limited to information that is appropriate and necessary for the services being provided and accessible only to appropriate staff members involved in the provision of services. Certified counselors must also ensure that

the electronically stored data are destroyed when the information is no longer of value in providing services or required as part of clients' records.

7. Any data derived from a client relationship and used in training or research shall be so disguised that the informed client's identity is fully protected. Any data which cannot be so disguised may be used only as expressly authorized by the client's informed and uncoerced consent.

8. When counseling is initiated, and throughout the counseling process as necessary, counselors inform clients of the purposes, goals, techniques, procedures, limitations, potential risks and benefits of services to be performed, and clearly indicate limitations that may affect the relationship as well as any other pertinent information. Counselors take reasonable steps to ensure that clients understand the implications of any diagnosis, the intended use of tests and reports, methods of treatment and safety precautions that must be taken in their use, fees, and billing arrangements.

9. Certified counselors who have an administrative, supervisory and/or evaluative relationship with individuals seeking counseling services must not serve as the counselor and should refer the individuals to other professionals. Exceptions are made only in instances where an individual's situation warrants counseling intervention and another alternative is unavailable. Dual relationships that might impair the certified counselor's objectivity and professional judgment must be avoided and/or the counseling relationship terminated through referral to a competent professional.

10. When certified counselors determine an inability to be of professional assistance to a potential or existing client, they must, respectively, not initiate the counseling relationship or immediately terminate the relationship. In either event, the certified counselor must suggest appropriate alternatives. Certified counselors must be knowledgeable about referral resources so that a satisfactory referral can be initiated. In the event that the client declines a suggested referral, the certified counselor is not obligated to continue the relationship.

11. When certified counselors are engaged in intensive, short-term counseling, they must ensure that professional assistance is available at normal costs to clients during and following the short-term counseling.

12. Counselors using electronic means in which counselor and client are not in immediate proximity must present clients with local sources of care before establishing a continued short or long-term relationship. Counselors who communicate with clients via Internet are governed by NBCC standards for Web Counseling.

13. Counselors must document permission to practice counseling by electronic means in all governmental jurisdictions where such counseling takes place.

14. When electronic data and systems are used as a component of counseling services, certified counselors must ensure that the computer application, and any information it contains, is appropriate for the respective needs of clients and is non-discriminatory. Certified counselors must ensure that they themselves have acquired a facilitation level of knowledge with any system they use including hands-on application, and understanding of the uses of all aspects of the computer-based system. In selecting and/or maintaining computer-based systems that contain career information, counselors must ensure that the system provides current, accurate, and locally relevant information. Certified counselors must also ensure that clients are intellectually, emotionally, and physically compatible with computer applications and understand their purpose and operation. Client use of a computer application must be evaluated to correct possible problems and assess subsequent needs.

15. Certified counselors who develop self-help/stand-alone computer software for use by the general public, must first ensure that it is designed to function in a stand-alone manner that is

appropriate and safe for all clients for which it is intended. A manual is required. The manual must provide the user with intended outcomes, suggestions for using the software, descriptions of inappropriately used applications, and descriptions of when and how other forms of counseling services might be beneficial. Finally, the manual must include the qualifications of the developer, the development process, validation date, and operating procedures.

16. The counseling relationship and information resulting from it remains confidential, consistent with the legal and ethical obligations of certified counselors. In group counseling, counselors clearly define confidentiality and the parameters for the specific group being entered, explain the importance of confidentiality, and discuss the difficulties related to confidentiality involved in group work. The fact that confidentiality cannot be guaranteed is clearly communicated to group members. However, counselors should give assurance about their professional responsibility to keep all group communications confidential.

17. Certified counselors must screen prospective group counseling participants to ensure compatibility with group objectives. This is especially important when the emphasis is on self-understanding and growth through self-disclosure. Certified counselors must maintain an awareness of the welfare of each participant throughout the group process.

Section C: Counselor Supervision

NCCs who offer and/or provide supervision must:

a. Ensure that they have the proper training and supervised experience through contemporary continuing education and/or graduate training
b. Ensure that supervisees are informed of the supervisor's credentials and professional status as well as all conditions of supervision as defined/outlined by the supervisor's practice, agency, group, or organization
c. Ensure that supervisees are aware of the current ethical standards related to their professional practice
d. Ensure that supervisees are informed about the process of supervision, including supervision goals, paradigms of supervision and the supervisor's preferred research based supervision paradigm(s)
e. Provide supervisees with agreed upon scheduled feedback as part of an established evaluation plan (e.g., one (1) hour per week)
f. Ensure that supervisees inform their clients of their professional status (i.e., trainee, intern, licensed, non-licensed, etc)
g. Establish procedures with their supervisees for handling crisis situations
h. Render timely assistance to supervisees who are or may be unable to provide competent counseling services to clients and
i. Intervene in any situation where the supervisee is impaired and the client is at risk

In addition, because supervision may result in a dual relationship between the supervisor and the supervisee, the supervisor is responsible for ensuring that any dual relationship is properly managed.

Section D: Measurement and Evaluation

1. Because many types of assessment techniques exist, certified counselors must recognize the limits of their competence and perform only those assessment functions for which they have received appropriate training or supervision.

2. Certified counselors who utilize assessment instruments to assist them with diagnoses must have appropriate training and skills in educational and psychological measurement, validation criteria, test research, and guidelines for test development and use.

3. Certified counselors must provide instrument specific orientation or information to an examinee prior to and following the administration of assessment instruments or techniques so that the results may be placed in proper perspective with other relevant factors. The purpose of testing and the explicit use of the results must be made known to an examinee prior to testing.

4. In selecting assessment instruments or techniques for use in a given situation or with a particular client, certified counselors must carefully evaluate the specific theoretical bases and characteristics, validity, reliability and appropriateness of the instrument.

5. When making statements to the public about assessment instruments or techniques, certified counselors must provide accurate information and avoid false claims or misconceptions concerning the meaning of the instrument's reliability and validity terms.

6. Counselors must follow all directions and researched procedures for selection, administration and interpretation of all evaluation instruments and use them only within proper contexts.

7. Certified counselors must be cautious when interpreting the results of instruments that possess insufficient technical data, and must explicitly state to examinees the specific limitations and purposes for the use of such instruments.

8. Certified counselors must proceed with caution when attempting to evaluate and interpret performances of any person who cannot be appropriately compared to the norms for the instrument.

9. Because prior coaching or dissemination of test materials can invalidate test results, certified counselors are professionally obligated to maintain test security.

10. Certified counselors must consider psychometric limitations when selecting and using an instrument, and must be cognizant of the limitations when interpreting the results. When tests are used to classify clients, certified counselors must ensure that periodic review and/or retesting are made to prevent client stereotyping.

11. An examinee's welfare, explicit prior understanding, and consent are the factors used when determining who receives the test results. Certified counselors must see that appropriate interpretation accompanies any release of individual or group test data (e.g., limitations of instrument and norms).

12. Certified counselors must ensure that computer-generated test administration and scoring programs function properly thereby providing clients with accurate test results.

13. Certified counselors who develop computer-based test interpretations to support the assessment process must ensure that the validity of the interpretations is established prior to the commercial distribution of the computer application.

14. Certified counselors recognize that test results may become obsolete, and avoid the misuse of obsolete data.

15. Certified counselors must not appropriate, reproduce, or modify published tests or parts thereof without acknowledgment and permission from the publisher, except as permitted by the fair educational use provisions of the U.S. copyright law.

Section E: Research and Publication

1. Certified counselors will adhere to applicable legal and professional guidelines on research with human subjects.

2. In planning research activities involving human subjects, certified counselors must be aware of and responsive to all pertinent ethical principles and ensure that the research problem, design, and execution are in full compliance with any pertinent institutional or governmental regulations.

3. The ultimate responsibility for ethical research lies with the principal researcher, although others involved in the research activities are ethically obligated and responsible for their own actions.

4. Certified counselors who conduct research with human subjects are responsible for the welfare of the subjects throughout the experiment and must take all reasonable precautions to avoid causing injurious psychological, physical, or social effects on their subjects.

5. Certified counselors who conduct research must abide by the basic elements of informed consent:
    a. fair explanation of the procedures to be followed, including an identification of those which are experimental
    b. description of the attendant discomforts and risks
    c. description of the benefits to be expected
    d. disclosure of appropriate alternative procedures that would be advantageous for subjects with an offer to answer any inquiries concerning the procedures
    e. an instruction that subjects are free to withdraw their consent and to discontinue participation in the project or activity at any time

6. When reporting research results, explicit mention must be made of all the variables and conditions known to the investigator that may have affected the outcome of the study or the interpretation of the data.

7. Certified counselors who conduct and report research investigations must do so in a manner that minimizes the possibility that the results will be misleading.

8. Certified counselors are obligated to make available sufficient original research data to qualified others who may wish to replicate the study.

9. Certified counselors who supply data, aid in the research of another person, report research results, or make original data available, must take due care to disguise the identity of respective subjects in the absence of specific authorization from the subjects to do otherwise.

10. When conducting and reporting research, certified counselors must be familiar with and give recognition to previous work on the topic, must observe all copyright laws, and must follow the principles of giving full credit to those to whom credit is due.

11. Certified counselors must give due credit through joint authorship, acknowledgment, footnote statements, or other appropriate means to those who have contributed to the research and/or publication, in accordance with such contributions.

12. Certified counselors should communicate to other counselors the results of any research judged to be of professional value. Results that reflect unfavorably on institutions, programs, services, or vested interests must not be withheld.

13. Certified counselors who agree to cooperate with another individual in research and/or publication incur an obligation to cooperate as promised in terms of punctuality of performance

and with full regard to the completeness and accuracy of the information required.

14. Certified counselors must not submit the same manuscript, or one essentially similar in content, for simultaneous publication consideration by two or more journals. In addition, manuscripts that have been published in whole or substantial part should not be submitted for additional publication without acknowledgment and permission from any previous publisher.

Section F: Consulting

Consultation refers to a voluntary relationship between a professional helper and a help-needing individual, group, or social unit in which the consultant is providing help to the client(s) in defining and solving a work-related problem or potential work-related problem with a client or client system.

1. Certified counselors, acting as consultants, must have a high degree of self awareness of their own values, knowledge, skills, limitations, and needs in entering a helping relationship that involves human and/or organizational change. The focus of the consulting relationship must be on the issues to be resolved and not on the person(s) presenting the problem.

2. In the consulting relationship, the certified counselor and client must understand and agree upon the problem definition, subsequent goals, and predicted consequences of interventions selected.

3. Certified counselors acting as consultants must be reasonably certain that they, or the organization represented, have the necessary competencies and resources for giving the kind of help that is needed or that may develop later, and that appropriate referral resources are available.

4. Certified counselors in a consulting relationship must encourage and cultivate client adaptability and growth toward self-direction. Certified counselors must maintain this role consistently and not become a decision maker for clients or create a future dependency on the consultant.

Section G: Private Practice

1. In advertising services as a private practitioner, certified counselors must advertise in a manner that accurately informs the public of the professional services, expertise, and techniques of counseling available.

2. Certified counselors who assume an executive leadership role in a private practice organization do not permit their names to be used in professional notices during periods of time when they are not actively engaged in the private practice of counseling unless their executive roles are clearly stated.

3. Certified counselors must make available their highest degree (described by discipline), type and level of certification and/or license, address, telephone number, office hours, type and/or description of services, and other relevant information. Listed information must not contain false, inaccurate, misleading, partial, out-of-context, or otherwise deceptive material or statements.

4. Certified counselors who are involved in a partnership/corporation with other certified counselors and/or other professionals, must clearly specify all relevant specialties of each member of the partnership or corporation.

Appendix: Certification Examination

Applicants for the NBCC Certification Examinations must have fulfilled all current eligibility requirements, and are responsible for the accuracy and validity of all information and/or materials provided by themselves or by others for fulfillment of eligibility criteria.

Acknowledgment Reference documents, statements, and sources for development of the NBCC Code of Ethics were as follows:

The Ethical Standards of the American Counseling Association, Responsible Uses for Standardized Testing (AAC), codes of ethics of the American Psychological Association and the National Career Development Association, Handbook of Standards for Computer-Based Career Information Systems (ACSCI) and Guidelines for the Use of Computer Based Information and Guidance Systems (ACSCI).

National Organization for Human Service Education
Ethical Standards of Human Service Professionals

Preamble

Human services is a profession developing in response to and in anticipation of the direction of human needs and human problems in the late twentieth century. Characterized particularly by an appreciation of human beings in all of their diversity, human services offers assistance to its clients within the context of their community and environment. Human service professionals and those who educate them, regardless of whether they are students, faculty or practitioners, promote and encourage the unique values and characteristics of human services. In so doing human service professionals and educators uphold the integrity and ethics of the profession, partake in constructive criticism of the profession, promote client and community well-being, and enhance their own professional growth.

The ethical guidelines presented are a set of standards of conduct which the human service professionals and educators consider in ethical and professional decision making. It is hoped that these guidelines will be of assistance when human service professionals and educators are challenged by difficult ethical dilemmas. Although ethical codes are not legal documents, they may be used to assist in the adjudication of issues related to ethical human service behavior.

SECTION I: STANDARDS FOR HUMAN SERVICE PROFESSIONALS

Human service professionals function in many ways and carry out many roles. They enter into professional-client relationships with individuals, families, groups and communities who are all referred to as "clients" in these standards. Among their roles are caregiver, case manager, broker, teacher/educator, behavior changer, consultant, outreach professional, mobilizer, advocate, community planner, community change organizer, evaluator and administrator.[1.] The following standards are written with these multifaceted roles in mind.

THE HUMAN SERVICE PROFESSIONAL'S RESPONSIBILITY TO CLIENTS

STATEMENT 1

Human service professionals negotiate with clients the purpose, goals, and nature of the helping relationship prior to its onset as well as inform clients of the limitations of the proposed relationship.

STATEMENT 2

Human service professionals respect the integrity and welfare of the client at all times. Each client is treated with respect, acceptance and dignity.

STATEMENT 3

Human service professionals protect the client's right to privacy and confidentiality except when such confidentiality would cause harm to the client or others, when agency guidelines state otherwise, or under other stated conditions (e.g., local, state, or federal laws). Professionals inform clients of the limits of confidentiality prior to the onset of the helping relationship.

STATEMENT 4

If it is suspected that danger or harm may occur to the client or to others as a result of a client's behavior, the human service professional acts in an appropriate and professional manner to protect the safety of those individuals. This may involve seeking consultation, supervision, and/or breaking the confidentiality of the relationship.

STATEMENT 5

Human service professionals protect the integrity, safety, and security of client records. All written client information that is shared with other professionals, except in the course of professional supervision, must have the client's prior written consent.

STATEMENT 6

Human service professionals are aware that in their relationships with clients power and status are unequal. Therefore they recognize that dual or multiple relationships may increase the risk of harm to, or exploitation of, clients, and may impair their professional judgment. However, in some communities and situations it may not be feasible to avoid social or other nonprofessional contact with clients. Human service professionals support the trust implicit in the helping relationship by avoiding dual relationships that may impair professional judgment, increase the risk of harm to clients or lead to exploitation.

STATEMENT 7

Sexual relationships with current clients are not considered to be in the best interest of the client and are prohibited. Sexual relationships with previous clients are considered dual relationships and are addressed in STATEMENT 6 (above).

STATEMENT 8

The client's right to self-determination is protected by human service professionals. They recognize the client's right to receive or refuse services.

STATEMENT 9

Human service professionals recognize and build on client strengths.

THE HUMAN SERVICE PROFESSIONAL'S RESPONSIBILITY TO THE COMMUNITY AND SOCIETY

STATEMENT 10

Human service professionals are aware of local, state, and federal laws. They advocate for change in regulations and statutes when such legislation conflicts with ethical guidelines and/or client rights. Where laws are harmful to individuals, groups or communities, human service professionals consider the conflict between the values of obeying the law and the values of serving people and may decide to initiate social action.

STATEMENT 11

Human service professionals keep informed about current social issues as they affect the client and the community. They share that information with clients, groups and community as part of their work.

STATEMENT 12

Human service professionals understand the complex interaction between individuals, their families, the communities in which they live, and society.

STATEMENT 13

Human service professionals act as advocates in addressing unmet client and community needs. Human service professionals provide a mechanism for identifying unmet client needs, calling attention to these needs, and assisting in planning and mobilizing to advocate for those needs at the local community level.

STATEMENT 14

Human service professionals represent their qualifications to the public accurately.

STATEMENT 15

Human service professionals describe the effectiveness of programs, treatments, and/or techniques accurately.

STATEMENT 16

Human service professionals advocate for the rights of all members of society, particularly those who are members of minorities and groups at which discriminatory practices have historically been directed.

STATEMENT 17

Human service professionals provide services without discrimination or preference based on age, ethnicity, culture, race, disability, gender, religion, sexual orientation or socioeconomic status.

STATEMENT 18

Human service professionals are knowledgeable about the cultures and communities within which they practice. They are aware of multiculturalism in society and its impact on the community as well as individuals within the community. They respect individuals and groups, their cultures and beliefs.

STATEMENT 19

Human service professionals are aware of their own cultural backgrounds, beliefs, and values, recognizing the potential for impact an their relationships with others.

STATEMENT 20

Human service professionals are aware of sociopolitical issues that differentially affect clients from diverse backgrounds.

STATEMENT 21

Human service professionals seek the training, experience, education and supervision necessary to ensure their effectiveness in working with culturally diverse client populations.

THE HUMAN SERVICE PROFESSIONAL'S RESPONSIBILITY TO COLLEAGUES

STATEMENT 22

Human service professionals avoid duplicating another professional's helping relationship with a client They consult with other professionals who are assisting the client in a different type of relationship when it is in the best interest of the client to do so.

STATEMENT 23

When a human service professional has a conflict with a colleague, he or she first seeks out the colleague in an attempt to manage the problem. If necessary, the professional then seeks the assistance of supervisors, consultants or other professionals in efforts to manage the problem.

STATEMENT 24

Human service professionals respond appropriately to unethical behavior of colleagues. Usually this means initially talking directly with the colleague and, if no resolution is forthcoming, reporting the colleague's behavior to supervisory or administrative staff and/or to the Professional organization(s) to which the colleague belongs.

STATEMENT 25

All consultations between human service professionals are kept confidential unless to do so would result in harm to clients or communities.

THE HUMAN SERVICE PROFESSIONAL'S RESPONSIBILITY TO THE PROFESSION

STATEMENT 26

Human service professionals know the limit and scope of their professional knowledge and offer services only within their knowledge and skill base.

STATEMENT 27

Human service professionals seek appropriate consultation and supervision to assist in decision-making when there are legal, ethical or other dilemmas.

STATEMENT 28

Human service professionals act with integrity, honesty, genuineness, and objectivity.

STATEMENT 29

Human service professionals promote cooperation among related disciplines (e.g., psychology, counseling, social work, nursing, family and consumer sciences, medicine, education) to foster professional growth and interests within the various fields.

STATEMENT 30

Human service professionals promote the continuing development of their profession. They encourage membership in professional associations, support research endeavors, foster educational advancement, advocate for appropriate legislative actions, and participate in other related professional activities.

STATEMENT 31

Human service professionals continually seek out new and effective approaches to enhance their professional abilities.

THE HUMAN SERVICE PROFESSIONAL'S RESPONSIBILITY TO EMPLOYERS

STATEMENT 32

Human service professionals adhere to commitments made to their employers.

STATEMENT 33

Human service professionals participate in efforts to establish and maintain employment conditions which are conducive to high quality client services. They assist in evaluating the effectiveness of the agency through reliable and valid assessment measures.

STATEMENT 34

When a conflict arises between fulfilling the responsibility to the employer and the responsibility to the client, human service professionals advise both of the conflict and work conjointly with all involved to manage the conflict.

THE HUMAN SERVICE PROFESSIONAL'S RESPONSIBILITY TO SELF

STATEMENT 35

Human service professionals strive to personify those characteristics typically associated with the profession (e.g., accountability, respect for others, genuineness, empathy, pragmatism).

STATEMENT 36

Human service professionals foster self-awareness and personal growth in themselves. They recognize that when professionals are aware of their own values, attitudes, cultural background, and personal needs, the process of helping others is less likely to be negatively impacted by those factors.

STATEMENT 36

Human service professionals recognize a commitment to lifelong learning and continually upgrade knowledge and skills to serve the populations better.

SECTION II: STANDARDS FOR HUMAN SERVICE EDUCATORS

Human Service educators are familiar with, informed by and accountable to the standards of professional conduct put forth by their institutions of higher learning; their professional disciplines, for example, American Association of University Professors (AAUP), American Counseling Association (ACA), Academy of Criminal Justice (ACJS), American Psychological Association (APA), American Sociological Association (ASA), National Association of Social Workers (NASW), National Board of Certified Counselors (NBCC), National Education Association (NEA); and the National Organization for Human Service Education (NOHSE).

STATEMENT 38

Human service educators uphold the principle of liberal education and embrace the essence of academic freedom, abstaining from inflicting their own personal views/morals on students, and allowing students the freedom to express their views without penalty, censure or ridicule, and to engage in critical thinking.

STATEMENT 39

Human service educators provide students with readily available and explicit program policies and criteria regarding program goals and objectives, recruitment, admission, course requirements, evaluations, retention and dismissal in accordance with due process procedures.

STATEMENT 40

Human service educators demonstrate high standards of scholarship in content areas and of pedagogy by staying current with developments in the field of Human Services and in teaching effectiveness, for example learning styles and teaching styles.

STATEMENT 41

Human service educators monitor students' field experiences to ensure the quality of the placement site, supervisory experience, and learning experience towards the goals of professional identity and skill development.

STATEMENT 42

Human service educators participate actively in the selection of required readings and use them with care, based strictly on the merits of the material's content, and present relevant information accurately, objectively and fully.

STATEMENT 43

Human service educators, at the onset of courses: inform students if sensitive/controversial issues or experiential/affective content or process are part of the course design; ensure that students are offered opportunities to discuss in structured ways their reactions to sensitive or controversial class content; ensure that the presentation of such material is justified on pedagogical grounds directly related to the course; and, differentiate between information based on scientific data, anecdotal data, and personal opinion.

STATEMENT 44

Human service educators develop and demonstrate culturally sensitive knowledge, awareness, and teaching methodology.

STATEMENT 45

Human service educators demonstrate full commitment to their appointed responsibilities, and are enthusiastic about and encouraging of students' learning.

STATEMENT 46

Human service educators model the personal attributes, values and skills of the human service professional, including but not limited to, the willingness to seek and respond to feedback from students.

STATEMENT 47

Human service educators establish and uphold appropriate guidelines concerning self-disclosure or student-disclosure of sensitive/personal information.

STATEMENT 48

Human service educators establish an appropriate and timely process for providing clear and objective feedback to students about their performance on relevant and established course/program academic and personal competence requirements and their suitability for the field.

STATEMENT 49

Human service educators are aware that in their relationships with students, power and status are unequal; therefore, human service educators are responsible to clearly define and maintain ethical and professional relationships with students, and avoid conduct that is demeaning, embarrassing or exploitative of students, and to treat students fairly, equally and without discrimination.

STATEMENT 50

Human service educators recognize and acknowledge the contributions of students to their work, for example in case material, workshops, research, publications.

STATEMENT 51

Human service educators demonstrate professional standards of conduct in managing personal or professional differences with colleagues, for example, not disclosing such differences and/or affirming a student's negative opinion of a faculty/program.

STATEMENT 52

Human service educators ensure that students are familiar with, informed by, and accountable to the ethical standards and policies put forth by their program/department, the course syllabus/instructor, their advisor(s), and the Ethical Standards of Human Service Professionals.

STATEMENT 53

Human service educators are aware of all relevant curriculum standards, including those of the Council for Standards in Human Services Education (CSHSE); the Community Support Skills Standards; and state/local standards, and take them into consideration in designing the curriculum.

STATEMENT 54

Human service educators create a learning context in which students can achieve the knowledge, skills, values and attitudes of the academic program.

Ethical Standards of Human Service Professionals, National Organization for Human Service Education (NOHSE, 1995) Reprinted with Permission.